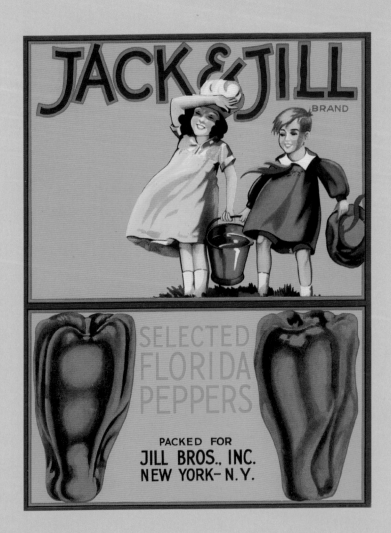

THE COMPLETE
Chile Pepper
BOOK

A Gardener's Guide to Choosing, Growing, Preserving, and Cooking

Dave DeWitt and Paul W. Bosland

TIMBER PRESS
Portland | London

CONTENTS

COOKING WITH CHILE PEPPERS

ACKNOWLEDGMENTS

SPECIAL THANKS TO Harald Zoschke, webmaster of the Fiery Foods and Barbecue SuperSite (www.fiery-foods.com) for many years, who provided significant information for this book and many photographs.

We gratefully acknowledge the support, information, and ideas supplied by the following individuals: Jeff Anderson, Alton Bailey, Jit Baral, Chel Beeson, Chris Biad, Lou Biad, Allen Boatman, Emily Bosland, Judy Bosland, Will Bosland, Mark Bromiley, Marco Budinis, Jeff Campbell, Emma Jean Cervantes, Diane Chamberlain, Danise Coon, Mario Dadomo, LeRoy Daugherty, Beverly Dayton, Cal Dennler, Wang Deyuan, James Ditmore, Jim Duffy, Victor Espinosa, Howard Essl, Jeff Gerlach, Nancy Gerlach, Max Gonzalez, Daphne Gould, John Graham, Wendy Hamilton, Steve Hanson, Cecilia Height, Gene Henderson, Antonio Heras-Duran, Annette Hill, Laurent Hodges, Dick Horst, Sharon Hudgins, Jaime Iglesias, Nick Isaac, David Karp, Pat Kiewicz, Jukka Kilpinen, Sanjeet Kumar, Graham Jacks, Ellen Jacobson, Paul Klinger, Ray Lagoe, Chip Leavitt, Jimmy and Jo Lytle, Sebastiano Marrone, Chris Mathews, Dan McCants, Mark McMullan, Scott Mendel, Ariadna Monroy, Eduardo Moscone, Greg Mullins, Dorothy Noble, Mary O'Connell, Peter Ogura, Jaebok Park, Ken Patterson, Paul Paulson, Mats Peterrsson, Jim Raney, Glenn Rhodes, Richard Rice, Adrian Rodriguez, Carol Shaugnessy, Robert Spiegel, John and Ann Swan, Lauren Swartzmiller, Ousmane Sy, Arnold Talbott, Betty Terrien, Manju Vishwakarma, Eric Votava, Stephanie Walker, Charlie Ward, Perfecta Wiggins, Mary Jane Wilan, F. P. Williamson, Gerry Wood, Henry Yamaoka, Everardo Zamora, Renate Zoschke, and the NMSU Chile Team.

PREFACE

FOR MORE THAN two decades, chile peppers have ruled our lives. While Paul has specialized in the horticultural aspects of the pungent pods and breeding new varieties, Dave has focused on the food history of chiles and their usage in international cooking. During this time, we have witnessed an explosion of interest in chiles, fueled mostly by the media. Chiles have evolved from being viewed as something to avoid ("they're all too hot!") to being considered a necessity in the larder as people have learned about the different varieties of chiles, their varied heat levels and flavor profiles, and their ability to transform ordinary meals into spectacular ones.

While interest in cooking with chiles has exploded, growing them has become a major hobby. We have "chilehead" gardening friends all over the world, from Finland to Australia, and we calculate that between us, we have made chile pepper pilgrimages to nearly thirty countries in our quest to learn more about them. When a nursery in New Jersey raises five hundred varieties of chiles to sell as bedding plants via mail order, you know that they have reached the peak of popularity!

Knowledge about chile peppers, is, of course, multidisciplinary, crossing into the fields of botany, horticulture, history, archaeology, medicine, chemistry, and culinary arts around the world. We could not delve deeply into all of these fields in a book of this length, so we focused on horticulture and culinary arts, two of the most popular avocations internationally. That said, we cover the other disciplines thoroughly at our two Web sites, the Fiery Foods and Barbecue SuperSite (www.fiery-foods.com) and the Chile Pepper Institute site (www.chilepepperinstitute.org).

The past decade has seen many advances in the field of chile peppers, and we cover them all in this volume. The new hottest pepper in the world. The technique for juicing chiles. Hydroponic chiles. Bonsai chiles. New flavor profiles. New chile varieties. We hope that our readers have as much fun using this information as we did in researching and writing it!

PEPE D'INDIA.

Pepe d'India, c. 1577. *Drawing by Pietro Andrea Matthioli, courtesy of Sunbelt Archives.*

About Chiles

CAPSICUM SPECIES ARE MEMBERS of the family Solanaceae, or the nightshade family, a large, economically important family that also includes eggplant, petunia, potato, tobacco, and tomato. They are not related to black pepper, *Piper nigrum,* nor are they related to the Guinea pepper or grains of paradise, *Aframomum melegueta.* All *Capsicum* species originated in the Western Hemisphere and are native to the tropical regions of the Americas. Botanically, chile peppers are perennial subshrubs when grown in their native habitats, but they are grown as annuals in colder climates.

BOTANY

The chile pepper plant varies greatly in habit and size. Although some chile pepper plants grow as tall as 30 feet, the average height of the cultivated plants is less than 3 feet. The leaves of the *Capsicum* species vary between ¼ inch and 5 inches in length. They are usually ovate (shaped like an egg), arise singly, and develop alternately along the stem. The flowers are usually pendant, and their corolla colors are white or purple. Most domesticated chile pepper plants are self-pollinating, meaning they do not need another plant to set fruit. Cross-pollination occurs by insects, and even chile peppers that are self-pollinating can outcross (that is, cross with another unrelated chile pepper) in the garden if there is a lot of insect activity in the area. The plants will set pods if the nighttime temperature is in the

Capsicum, c. 1586. Drawing by Jacques D'Alechamps, courtesy of Sunbelt Archives.

than 17 inches long and are borne either erect or pendant. Most varieties are ready to pick at the green stage after about 70 days and are fully ripened after about 130 days. Botanically speaking, the pods are berries, but horticulturists term them fruits. When harvested at the green stage, the pods are considered a vegetable; when harvested in the dried mature colors, they become a spice.

The true number of species in *Capsicum* is a matter of considerable debate. The first literary references to the classification of chile peppers are found in sixteenth-century botanical books. Before Linnaeus did his seminal work, *Species plantarum* (1753), several authors tried to classify chile peppers. Morison listed thirty-three variants of chile pepper in his 1699 *Plantarum historiae universalis Oxoniensis*. In 1700, de Tourneforte gave the genus its name, *Capsicum*, and listed twenty-seven species. Linnaeus reduced *Capsicum* to two species: *C. annuum* and *C. frutescens*. Later, in 1767, he added two more: *C. baccatum* and *C. grossum*.

Ruiz and Pavon (1790) described the species *Capsicum pubescens*, followed by Willdenow (1798) who named the species *C. pendulum*. In 1852 an attempt was made to clarify questions related to the taxonomy of the genus; Dunal described fifty species in the genus and listed another eleven as possible species. By the end of the nineteenth century, more than ninety species were listed within the genus. However, in 1898, Irish reduced the number of species back to two, *C. annuum* and *C. frutescens*, as initially done by Linnaeus. The two-species concept was widely accepted until 1923,

range between 55 and 80°F, and the daytime temperature does not exceed 95°F.

Capsicum is endowed with a multitude of fruit forms, colors, and sizes. Immature fruits are green, yellow, white, or purple; ripe fruits can be red, orange, brown, yellow, green, or white, with shades in between. Their shapes can be round, conic, elongate, oblate, or bell-like. The pods range in size from ¼ inch to more

when Bailey made the argument that because *C. annuum* (meaning "annual") was a perennial in the tropics or could be grown in a greenhouse as a perennial, there was only one species, *C. frutescens*. To add to the confusion, some authors agreed to the one-species concept but used *C. annuum* as the species name instead of *C. frutescens*. Heiser and Smith (1953) organized the genus into four species—*C. annuum, C. baccatum, C. frutescens,* and *C. pubescens*—and in 1957 they added *C. chinense* as a unique species. This brought the list of domesticated species to its current five species. A lingering question that has been debated is whether *C. chinense* and *C. frutescens* are two species or varieties of one species. In 2004, Baral and Bosland used morphological, hybridization, and molecular markers to show conclusively that they are truly two different species.

Without genetic knowledge, the early taxonomists named *Capsicum* species based mostly on fruit morphology. Scientists define species in two ways, the biological species and the morphological species. Each is based on a different set of criteria. When establishing a morphological species, a taxonomist examines floral traits and looks for similarities and differences in the flower structure. Seeing none, the taxonomist groups two populations of a plant together under one species name. A biological species is defined as a population or series of populations within which genes flow freely under natural conditions. This means that two populations of plants grouped together must be able to produce fertile and healthy progeny in subsequent generations. If a free genetic exchange occurs

Capsicum, c. 1744. *Drawing by Theodorus Zwinger, courtesy of Sunbelt Archives.*

between two populations, they are considered the same species. Within *Capsicum*, morphology has been used to establish species for the most part. As further biological and molecular information on the species listed within *Capsicum* is obtained, the species groupings may change dramatically.

Saccardo and La Gioia (1982) found that when a *Capsicum annuum* accession from Colombia was hybridized to *C. annuum* populations from Mexico and New Mexico, abnormal chromosome pairing occurred. This resulted in reduced fertility and vigor in the progeny and

THE DESCRIBED SPECIES OF *CAPSICUM*

C. annuum
    var. annuum
        (domesticated)
    var. glabriusculum
        (wild)

C. baccatum
    var. baccatum (wild)
    var. pendulum
        (domesticated)

C. buforum

C. campylopodium

C. cardenasii

C. chacoense

C. chinense

C. coccineum

C. cornutum

C. dimorphum

C. dusenii

C. eximium
    var. tomentosum

C. flexuosum

C. friburgense

C. frutescens

C. galapagoense

C. geminifolium

C. hookerianum

C. hunzikerianum

C. lanceolatum

C. leptopodum

C. minutiflorum

C. mirabile

C. parvifolium

C. pereirae

C. praetermissum

C. pubescens

C. recurvatum

C. schottianum

C. scolnikianum

C. tovarii

C. villosum

was caused by several chromosomal translocations that had occurred in the Colombian population as compared to the Mexican and New Mexican chile pepper populations. Geographic isolation of the *C. annuum* populations has begun to differentiate the single *C. annuum* species into two different species.

Today, based on the work of the Argentinian botanists Armando Hunziker and Gloria E. Barboza, thirty-two species of *Capsicum* are recognized, but that number may change as new species are discovered and/or taxonomists change the classification of the genus.

DOMESTICATION AND DISPERSION

When the terms *wild*, *cultivated*, and *domesticated* are used with chile peppers, they actually represent a continuum of human-plant relationships. At one end of this continuum are wild plants that grow outside the human-disturbed habitat and cannot successfully invade human-disturbed areas. This seems to be true of *Capsicum lanceolatum*, a wild species that has been found only in the virgin rainforest of Guatemala. Farther along the continuum are the semi-domesticated cultivars such as *C. annuum* var. *glabriusculum*, the wild chiltepín. Next are the domesticated plants such as bell peppers that have evolved into new forms under continued human manipulation, so that they may have lost the ability to reproduce themselves without human intervention.

From native species in different regions of Mexico, Central America, and South America, humans independently domesticated five species: *Capsicum annuum, C. baccatum, C. chinense, C. frutescens,* and *C. pubescens. Capsicum annuum* (misnamed because these peppers are actually perennial) includes most of the commonest varieties, such as New Mexican, jalapeño, bell, and wax peppers. *Baccatum* means "berrylike," but some varieties of *C. baccatum* have very large fruits. *Chinense* (from China) is also an incorrect designation, because *C. chinense* originated in the Amazon basin of Brazil. *Frutescens* means "shrubby or brushy"; *C. frutescens* includes the famous tabasco. The last domesticated species, and probably the least well known, is *C. pubescens*, with *pubescens* meaning "hairy", a reference to the leaves.

Chile peppers were probably in the human diet long before they were domesticated. Archaeological evidence from Mexico indicates that humans have possibly been using wild chile peppers as a food source for at least 7200 years, not only as occasional condiments but also as components of a complex and sophisticated diet. The oldest evidence of domesticated chile peppers was found in a cave in the Tehuacán Valley of south-central Mexico. Recently, by studying starch grains in southwestern Ecuador at the sites of Loma Alta and Loma Real, scientists have pegged the domestication of chile peppers at 6100 years ago, at least. As reported in *Science* in 2007, the earliest chile pepper starches yet discovered are on the surfaces of milling stones and in cooking vessels as well as in sediment samples, and in conjunction with microfossil evidence of arrowroot, maize, manioc, squash, beans, and palms.

The first varieties of chile peppers grew in

A SIMPLE IDENTIFICATION KEY TO THE FIVE DOMESTICATED SPECIES OF *CAPSICUM*

DESCRIPTION	SPECIES (OR GO TO)
1. Seeds black, corolla purple	*C. pubescens*
1. Seeds tan	2.
2. Corolla with spots	*C. baccatum*
2. Corolla without spots	3.
3. Corolla white	4.
3. Corolla greenish	5.
4. Flowers solitary and filament not purple	*C. annuum*
4. Flowers two or more per node and filament purple	*C. chinense*
5. Flowers solitary	*C. frutescens*
5. Flowers two or more per node	*C. chinense*

the remote geologic past in an area bordered by the mountains of southern Brazil to the east, by Bolivia to the west, and by Paraguay and northern Argentina to the south. This location has the greatest concentration of wild species of chile peppers in the world. In this "nuclear area," and only here, grow representatives of all the major domesticated species within the genus. Over thousands of years, chile peppers migrated from this area and eventually spread over the Americas long before the first human tribes settled the area.

Scientists suspect that birds were primarily responsible for the spread of wild species from the nuclear area. All wild chile peppers share similar pod traits and a common characteristic of being associated with birds. The fruits are small and erect, with a soft pedicel that allows red ripe fruit to be pulled easily from the calyx. This permits easy removal by frugivorous birds and eventual dissemination of the seeds. The red color is attractive to birds, and it seems birds cannot taste or feel the capsaicinoids (the compounds that cause the sensation of heat and ward off pests such as mammals, insects, and fungi). The seeds in the pods must have passed through birds' digestive tracts intact and been deposited on the ground along with a perfect fertilizer. The small pods of the wild species are commonly called bird peppers in languages all over the world because of this association.

A likely scenario for chile peppers is that they were first used as a medicinal plant, then found growing around settlements as a tolerated weed. They were not cultivated, but when the pods were ripe they were collected. The wild forms had erect pods that were deciduous, meaning that they separated easily from the calyx and fell to the ground, spreading the seeds. During the domestication process, humans selected seeds from plants with larger, nondeciduous, and pendant pods.

The larger pods would provide a greater yield, and as the pods became pendant they would be hidden in the foliage and not held above it as a beacon for hungry birds. Even today in commercial fields, birds will peck at large pods, causing economic damage. The selection of varieties with the tendency to be nondeciduous ensured that the pods were resistant to dropping off as a result of wind or physical contact and thus remained on the plant until fully ripe. The domesticated chile peppers gradually lost their natural means of seed dispersal by birds and became dependent upon human assistance. Because chile peppers cross-pollinate easily, hundreds—if not thousands—of new pod types were developed. The five domesticated species have hundreds of pod types, and each pod type has numerous varieties with specific characteristics. These varieties are termed cultivars by horticulturists.

Selection of larger
pods led to the
varieties of today.
*Courtesy of Sunbelt
Archives.*

Top Hundred (or So) Chile Peppers for the Garden

WITH MORE THAN TEN THOUSAND DIFFERENT chile pepper varieties in the world, how do you know what to plant? Choosing the best chile pepper varieties to grow in the garden is important and needs careful thought. Between the two of us, we have spent more than four decades testing, tasting, and growing a lot of chile pepper varieties. After testing literally thousands of chile peppers, we have decided on the top hundred (or so) chile pepper varieties for the garden. We chose the varieties based on their special flavor, unique heat characteristics, or some other distinctive quality. Seed or plants for all these varieties are easy to acquire (see "Resources"). Some of the varieties are actually All-America Selections, which are varieties chosen by gardening experts as the all-around best.

We list the hundred (or so) best chile pepper varieties by species, moving from the smalles number of varieties to the largest number, and within the *Capsicum annuum* by pod type. In addition, we describe the best use of the pods, since some varieties are best suited for pickling, some for drying, some for fresh use, and others for processing and freezing.

CAPSICUM PUBESCENS

Capsicum pubescens was originally described in 1790 by Ruiz and Pavon from plants cultivated in Peru. It is the only domesticated *Capsicum* species with no wild form. This species originated in the

Pod variations, Capsicum pubescens.

highlands of Bolivia and was domesticated about 6000 years ago, making it one of the oldest domesticated plants in the Americas. Botanist Charles Heiser, citing Garcilaso de la Vega (1609), notes that *C. pubescens* was "the most common chile pepper among the Incas, just as it is today in Cuzco, the former capital of the Incan empire." In the Andes, it is often called *locoto* in Quechuan, or *rocoto* in Spanish. Another local name is *canario*, referring to canary, because of the fruit's yellow color. In Guatemala it is called *caballo* (horse) because the heat of the pod kicks like a horse, and *siete caldos* (hot enough to season seven soups). It is grown extensively in courtyards and kitchen gardens in the highlands from Mexico to Peru and is grown on very limited acreage in the rest of the world.

Conspicuous hairiness on the leaves along with black seeds helps to distinguish this chile pepper from any of the other species. It is a large, shrubby herbaceous plant that can grow up to 30 feet tall and can live up to ten years in

frost-free areas. Normally, in small gardens it has a compact to erect habit (sometimes sprawling) and grows up to 4 feet tall, but 2 feet is more usual. The leaves are ovate, light to dark green, and measure up to 3½ inches long and 2 inches wide.

This chile pepper is adapted to cooler temperatures, 40 to 80°F. A myth has been perpetuated that the species is frost tolerant. Although this is not true, when the plant is established (more than one year old) it will reshoot after a frost. Most likely, stored carbohydrates in the roots enable the plant to regrow. Because they are late-maturing and need a long growing season—120 days or more—it has been said that these varieties are unsuitable for cultivation outside of Central and South America. However, our experiments have shown that plants started early can achieve fruiting in one season. *Capsicum pubescens* enthusiast Charlie Ward of Virginia Beach, Virginia, reported that he has the best results when he grows them for twenty-two months. The first year he raises them in pots, and the second year he transplants them into the garden. Despite the fact that his garden is a mere 10 feet above sea level, his plants grow like weeds in the second year and produce many large pods. They also respond well to shading, because the foliage has a tendency to burn in full sun.

Rocotos make good container plants. DeWitt grew two of them in pots, and they lived eleven years, although every year they lost a little vigor and produced fewer fruits. He pruned them back in the spring, and they grew back quite bushy. Note that in the winter greenhouse they are susceptible to aphids.

Instead of white flowers, *C. pubescens* has purple flowers with large nectaries (the part that secretes nectar). The pods measure about 2 to 3 inches long and 2 to 2½ inches wide, but some pods as large as bell peppers are grown in Peru. The pods are green in their immature state, maturing to yellow, orange, or red. A single plant can produce up to thirty pods, depending on the length of the growing season. The pods contain a unique set of capsaicinoids (the chemicals that cause the heat sensation when eaten), causing some people to believe they are hotter than habaneros, but this is not true. The heat level of rocotos is 30,000 to 50,000 Scoville heat units (SHUs), while habaneros usually score well over 100,000 SHUs. Still, in parts of the Americas rocotos are referred to as *el mas picante de los picantes*, the hottest of the hot.

The pods of rocoto combine the suavity and juiciness of the bell pepper with the heat of a habanero. Rocotos are usually consumed in their fresh form because the pods are so thick they are difficult to store or dehydrate. They are commonly used in fresh salsas, and the larger pods can be stuffed with meat or cheese and baked.

'Canario', 'Manzano', 'Peron'

Our three favorite varieties of rocoto are *Capsicum pubescens* 'Canario' (roundish, yellow), 'Manzano' (apple-shaped, red), and 'Peron' (pear-shaped, yellow). There is also a jalapeño-shaped variety, 'Rocoto Longo', that is native to the Canary Islands.

FAR LEFT *Capsicum pubescens* flower.

LEFT *Capsicum pubescens* 'Manzano'.

CAPSICUM FRUTESCENS

'Tabasco' is the best-known cultivar of *Capsicum frutescens*, because the red pod is the main ingredient in Tabasco hot sauce. Malagueta is the common name for *C. frutescens* in Brazil, where it grows wild in the Amazon basin. Some food historians believe that the word *melegueta*—already a Portuguese term for a spicy berry, *Aframomum melegueta*, related to ginger—was transferred to the Brazilian red chile pepper sometime after the Portuguese settlement of Brazil. This scenario follows a pattern that Christopher Columbus began when he misnamed chiles as pepper. The chile peppers, it seems, were given the closest common name when they were "discovered" by Europeans. Interestingly enough, the African melegueta berries were eventually imported into Surinam and Guyana, where they were grown commercially.

Cultivars of *Capsicum frutescens* have a compact habit with an intermediate number of stems and grow between 1 and 4 feet high depending on climate, growing the largest in warmer regions. The leaves are ovate and smooth, and measure 2½ inches long and 2½ inches wide. These varieties are particularly

ABOVE Tabasco plant.

TOP RIGHT Harvested tabascos, Avery Island, Louisiana.

RIGHT Wild Brazilian malagueta.

good for container gardening; one of our specimens lived as a perennial for four years in a pot but gradually lost vigor and produced fewer pods each year.

The flowers have greenish-white corollas with no spots and purple anthers and filaments. The pods are very hot, measuring between 30,000 and 70,000 SHUs. A single plant can produce a hundred or more pods. 'Tabasco' pods are yellow or yellow-green, turning red at maturity. The pods are borne erect and measure 1 to 2 inches long and 3/8 inch wide. Immature pods of the cultivars 'Malagueta' and 'Siling Labuyo', which are smaller than those of 'Tabasco', are green, maturing to bright red.

Capsicum frutescens has fewer pod shapes, sizes, and colors than *C. annuum*, *C. baccatum*, or *C. chinense*. The reason for this is not clear. One must remember that the diversity of pod morphology is human guided—in other words, the differences in pod size, shape, and color result from humans choosing which pods to save for the next growing season. It may be that *C. frutescens* grew wild in the same areas as *C. annuum* and *C. chinense*, and humans made selections from those species instead of *C. frutescens*. In addition, many cultivars listed as *C. frutescens* in seed catalogs are often actually *C. annuum* cultivars. Our four favorite *C. frutescens* cultivars are 'Tabasco', 'Greenleaf Tabasco', 'Malagueta', and 'Siling Labuyo'.

'Tabasco', 'Greenleaf Tabasco'

The mature red fruit of 'Tabasco' is the chile pepper ingredient in Tabasco hot sauce. Other uses include pickling or spicing up cooking oils. The pods can be used fresh in salsas and can be dried to add to stir-fry dishes. 'Greenleaf Tabasco' has all the attributes of the original 'Tabasco' plus virus resistance. 'Greenleaf Tabasco' originated as a hybrid between a tobacco-etch-virus–resistant *Capsicum chinense* and 'Tabasco'.

'Malagueta'

'Malagueta' is a popular cultivar in northeastern Brazil. In this region, it is by far the most common chile pepper found in both the food and the markets. It is commonly used as an ingredient in the cuisine of Bahia and as a condiment in the rest of the area.

'Siling Labuyo'

'Siling Labuyo' is a variety from the Philippines; in Tagalog, one of the major languages of the

Philippines, it literally translates to "wild chile." The leaves of 'Siling Labuyo' are used in the Filipino dish *tinola*, made with chicken and papaya.

ABOVE *Capsicum frutescens* 'Greenleaf Tabasco'.

BELOW *Capsicum frutescens* 'Siling Labuyo'.

CAPSICUM BACCATUM

In South America, *Capsicum baccatum* is the most commonly grown species and is known as ají. The Spanish transferred the phonetic "ah HEE" from the native Arawak peoples of the Caribbean to Peru. In the Quechuan language of the Incas, chile peppers are called *uchu*. The ajís are found from southern Brazil to Bolivia, Ecuador, Peru, and Chile. According to archaeological evidence, the species was probably domesticated in Peru about 2500 years ago. Extensive *C. baccatum* material found at the Huaca Prieta archaeological site shows that the species was gradually improved by pre-Incan civilizations. Fruit size increased, and the fruits gradually became nondeciduous and stayed on the plants through ripening. A wild form (var.

baccatum) and a domesticated form (var. *pendulum*) exist. The domesticated form shows a great diversity of pod shape and size, ranging from short, pointed pods borne erect to long, pendant pods resembling the New Mexican varieties. They are cultivated in Argentina, Colombia, Ecuador, Peru, Brazil, and Bolivia, and the species has been introduced into Costa Rica, India, and the United States.

The plants are tall and treelike, sometimes reaching 5 feet, and have multiple stems and an erect habit, occasionally tending toward sprawling. The stems are square. The large leaves are dark green, measuring up to 7 inches long and 4 inches wide. They tend to stand out in the garden like small trees. Their growing period is 120 days or longer.

The flower corollas are white to cream colored with distinctive dark green, yellow, or brown spots. The anthers are yellow or tan. The pods usually begin erect and become pendant as they mature. They are elongated and measure between 3 and 6 inches long and ¾ to 1½ inches wide. One type of *C. baccatum* called puca-uchu grows on vinelike plants in home gardens.

Our favorites for the garden give a wonderful range of pod shapes, flavors, and colors. The five varieties that make our list of the best are ají amarillo, ají ayucllo, 'Ají Limon', 'Christmas Bell', and 'Omincolor'. All mature to red except ají amarillo, which matures to orange. The plants can produce forty or more pods that score between 30,000 and 50,000 SHUs.

The pods have a distinctive fruity flavor, and ají amarillo pods are used fresh in ceviche (lime-marinated fish) in South America. They are also

Pod variations, *Capsicum baccatum*.

FAR LEFT **Ají amarillo.**
LEFT **Ají ayucllo.**

used in fresh salsas, and the pods are easily dried and ground into colorful powders. The pods vary in heat level from very mild to fiery hot. They embody unique aromatics and flavors.

Ají amarillo

Ají amarillo, also known as ají escabeche, is the commonest variety of *C. baccatum* in Peru. The pods are 4 to 6 inches long and have a deep orange color when mature. The thin-fleshed pods have a fruity flavor with berry overtones and a searing, clear heat. This chile pepper is used almost daily in all kinds of dishes in Peru, either in a sauce or as an ingredient. This is the chile pepper of choice when making ceviche, citrus-marinated seafood. This pod type has been known in Peru since ancient Inca times and is represented in drawings and pottery from that period.

Ají ayucllo

Ají ayucllo is a wild pepper variety found in the Peruvian jungle near the Chanchamayo and Villa Rica valleys. Its name is an original and native name that has no meaning or translation. The beautiful fruits are small, thick fleshed, and oval shaped with a moderate heat level; they begin purple and then ripen to a bright orange-red color. The pod, found only in the local marketplaces in Peru, is not grown commercially but is harvested from backyard plantings or from wild plants. It is eaten fresh with foods or used as an ingredient in all types of dishes.

'Ají Limon'

'Ají Limon' or 'Ají Lemon Drop' gets its name from the bright yellow color of the mature fruit. The fruit starts out green and then turns yellow as it matures. The pod is crinkled and

Capsicum baccatum
'Aji Limon'.

Capsicum baccatum
'Christmas Bell'.

BELOW *Capsicum baccatum* 'Omnicolor'.

cone shaped, about 2½ inches long and ½ inch wide. It has a fabulous *C. baccatum* flavor with lots of fruit overtones and a note of citrus. It is hardy and produces baskets of fruits. The heat is medium high. The plant reaches a height of about 3 feet.

'Christmas Bell'

Originally from Brazil, where it is called *ubatuba cambuc* after the two cities where it is found, this variety produces one of the most unusual pod shapes of any chile pepper. The pods are 1¾ inches long by 2¼ inches wide, but the shape is that of a bell or a bishop's hat. The pods mature from green to red. The plant grows to 2 or 3 feet high, with stems that are green and with green leaves and white flowers that have greenish-yellow spots. The heat level is mild. 'Christmas Bell' is used for pickling, eaten fresh, or strung to make a garland for a Christmas tree.

'Omnicolor'

'Omnicolor' has great flavor and prolific pods, and makes a wonderful color addition to your garden. Small compact plants, great for containers or hanging baskets, grow to 12 to 18 inches tall and 12 inches wide. Upright fruits that grow to about 2 inches long gradually change color from yellow with a violet overtone to light orange to dark orange to red-orange and then finally to a bright red.

CAPSICUM CHINENSE

Capsicum chinense, like all *Capsicum* species, originated in the Western Hemisphere. However, the Dutch physician Kikolaus von Jacquinomist, who named this species in 1776, believed its homeland was China, though why he thought China was its place of origin is still a mystery. Because of the taxonomic convention that the first name given to a species is used seemingly forever, the misnomer *chinense* is still attached to this Western Hemisphere native.

Capsicum chinense is popular in all tropical regions and is the most common chile pepper species grown in the Caribbean. Fruit shapes are diverse, as are those found in *C. annuum*. Pods can be extremely hot and aromatic, with a persistent heat that can last for hours after the pods are eaten. 'Bhut Jolokia' has the distinction of being the hottest chile pepper in the world, rated at more that 1,000,000 SHUs.

The plants range between 1 and 4½ feet tall, depending on environmental conditions. Some perennial varieties have grown as tall as 8 feet in tropical climates, but the average height in the U.S. garden is about 2 feet. *Capsicum chinense* has multiple stems and an erect habit. The leaves are pale to medium green, large, and wrinkled, reaching 6 inches long and 4 inches wide.

The flowers have white corollas and purple anthers and filaments. The plant sets two to six fruits per node. The pods are pendant and campanulate (having a flattened bell shape), and some are elongate and pointed at the end. Others are flattened at the end and resemble a tam, or bonnet. They are usually about 2½

Pod variations, *Capsicum chinense.*

Capsicum chinense 'Aji Limo'.

inches long and 1 to 2 inches wide, green at immaturity, and red, orange, yellow, or white when mature. Although the varieties of *C. chinense* range in heat from none to the hottest ever measured, they average between 80,000 and 150,000 SHUs. A unique feature of *C. chinense* is the presence of a constriction between the calyx and the pedicel.

The seeds tend to take a long time to germinate. Being tropical plants, the varieties of *C. chinense* do best in areas with high humidity and warm nights. They are slow growers, especially in the Southwest, and the growing period is 80 to 120 days or more.

There are a myriad of pod types within *C. chinense*, with the Amazon basin having some of the greatest diversity. In the Caribbean, where several of the pod types have been named, the two most familiar pod types are the habanero and Scotch bonnet. These names are sometimes wrongly used interchangeably. Also, if the native language is Spanish, "habanero" is preferred, and when English is the native language, "Scotch bonnet" is commonly used. There are many pod types that lack any description. There are also names such as "country pepper" that apply to more than one pod type.

All the varieties of *C. chinense* are termed "full season," meaning that they need at least 200 days to produce ripe pods. The fourteen we think are the best to grow are 'Ají Limo', 'Ají Panca', 'Bhut Jolokia', 'Cajamarca', 'Charapita' (wild), 'Chocolate Habanero', 'Datil', 'Fatalii', 'NuMex Suave Orange', 'NuMex Suave Red', 'Orange Habanero', 'Red Carribean', 'Rocotillo', and 'Scotch Bonnet'.

'Ají Limo'

Although this pepper is referred to as 'Ají Limo', the word *limo* has no real meaning or translation and is a regional identification name given by local people. Do not confuse this pepper with *Capsicum baccatum* 'Ají Limon'. The pod is small and measures 1½ to 3 inches long by 1 to 1¼ inches wide. It ripens to a deep red, yellow, or orange. When dried, the pod becomes tapered and wrinkled. It is mostly grown and used on the northern coast of Peru, where it is very popular. It is highly pungent and used mostly fresh with seafood, especially in ceviche, a marinated seafood dish. However, in the Andes, 'Ají Limo' finds great acceptance as whole dried pods because it stores very well.

FAR LEFT *Capsicum chinense* 'Aji Panca'.

LEFT *Capsicum chinense* 'Bhut Jolokia', fresh (left) and dry (right).

'Ají Panca'

Even though most ají chile peppers belong to *Capsicum baccatum*, this pod type is truly a member of *C. chinense*. It is the second most common chile pepper variety in Peru, after ají amarillo. 'Ají Panca' is grown mainly near the coast. The pod measures 3½ to 5 inches in length and 1 inch to 1¼ inches across. The pod has a medium thick flesh, and when mature is burgundy-brown and mild in heat intensity. It provides a fruity, berrylike flavor that goes well in stews, sauces, and fish dishes. It is sun-dried at farms and sold as dry whole pods in the marketplace, where fresh 'Ají Panca' is not found. It is used for making sauces, to flavor most fish dishes, and is popular as powder to sprinkle over pizza.

'Bhut Jolokia'

The world's hottest pepper is 'Bhut Jolokia'. Every gardener needs this one, if not for eating at least to give to that annoying neighbor. Even though this chile pepper originates in an area that is warm and humid, it will grow in most areas of the United States. With a little tender care and effort it can be grown in cooler climates. 'Bhut Jolokia' seeds germinate best when the soil temperature is at 85 to 90°F. The plants grow to be about 4 feet tall and produce a profusion of flowers, sometimes as many as three per node.

Bhut Jolokia' has a unique ancestry. DNA analysis leads to the conclusion that it is a *C. chinense* cultivar, but in its pedigree it has a bit of *Capsicum frutescens*. This origin as an interspecific hybrid causes pollen abortion and

ABOVE *Capsicum chinense* 'Cajamarca'.

RIGHT *Capsicum chinense* 'Charapita'.

reduces the number of flowers that get pollinated, so flower drop is very common. But the great thing about 'Bhut Jolokia' is that it is so extremely hot that a few pods go a long way!

'Cajamarca'

'Cajamarca' has a tantalizing pod color transition. Named after the region in northern Peru where it originates, part of the Amazon rain forest, it is as appealing to the eye as it is to eat. Its beautiful fruit begins a vibrant violet unique to *C. chinense* and then changes to a rich red. The wonderfully fragrant aroma of 'Cajamarca' captures attention with an intense, spicy-citrus fragrance and the classic habanero fruity undertone. It has the delayed heat characteristic of *C. chinense*; the heat level is in the medium range for a *C. chinense* cultivar.

The plants have semiglossy foliage and grow into a tall, upright bush generously loaded with fruits that will provide a bountiful harvest all summer. The fruit shape and size are much like the regular orange habanero: wrinkled, 1 inch to 1½ inches long, resembling a Chinese lantern with a tapered end.

'Charapita'

'Charapita' is a small-fruited pod type from Brazil, also called *pimenta do cheiro*. The word *cheiro* in Portuguese translates as "odorous." A feature of all *C. chinense* fruits is the strong aromatic scent from the pods. 'Charapita' is a wild variety found in the Peruvian jungle close to the city of Iquitos, where the people are called charapas; thus the name of the chile pepper. The spherical pod is very small (less than ¼ inch in diameter) and very hot. The thin-fleshed pods, which resemble chiltepíns, start as a very light yellow or ivory and mature into rich yellow. Unlike the chiltepíns, these pods stay attached to the plant when ripe. They are eaten fresh with foods or used as an ingredient in preparing all types of dishes.

'Chocolate Habanero'

This chile pepper is named "chocolate" not because of its flavor but because the pod matures to a chocolate brown. It originated in the Carribean but is sometimes called 'Congo Black'. One of hottest and most productive of the habanero types, 'Chocolate Habanero' has pods that reach 2 inches long and 1½ inches wide. The plants grow to 3 to 4 feet tall by 2 to 3 feet wide. 'Chocolate Habanero' is used in the Caribbean to make barbecue sauces and marinades.

'Datil'

'Datil' is cultivated in the area of St. Augustine, Florida, where much mythology surrounds it. It is said that a group of indentured workers originally from the island of Minorca brought it to St. Augustine in 1777 from an abandoned settlement in New Smyrna, Florida. Some say they carried the seeds all the way from Spain, but experts believe that is unlikely. David Nolan of St. Augustine says that "it was brought to St. Augustine about 1880 from Chile, in South America, by a jelly manufacturer named S. B. Valls." He has never seen any reference to 'Datil' being in St. Augustine before that time. He believes it was adopted by the local Minorcan

ABOVE *Capsicum chinense* 'Chocolate Habanero'.
LEFT *Capsicum chinense* 'Datil'.

residents as part of their cuisine rather than being brought with them or picked up along the way. Furthermore, he says that *datil* is not only a Spanish word for date, it is also a word in the Quechua language of the Inca Empire.

In fact, the pod is not shaped like a date. The pod is elongated, 3½ inches long and ¾ inch wide at the shoulders, and green turning to a yellowish-orange at maturity. 'Datil' is unique in that it is extremely hot but also has a sweet and fruity overtone. It is most commonly used to make a sweet but intense hot sauce. It is also used to make relishes and other condiments.

'Fatalii'

The ominously named 'Fatalii' originates in Central Africa, developed from chile peppers that returning slaves brought back home. It is one of the few *C. chinense* pod types found in Africa. Plants grow to 2 or 3 feet in height, producing good yields. The pendant pods are pointed at the tips and get to be 2½ to 3½ inches long and about ¾ inch to 1½ inches wide. The pods are fairly thin-fleshed and change from a pale green to a bright yellow as they mature. The plants love full sun and really thrive in a greenhouse. The plants are also suitable for containers—which is great, because you can pick the sunniest place in the house and get them indoors before the first frost.

The fruits are very hot, and because they are high in dihydrocapsaicin, they cause not only an instant heat sensation but also a delayed heat sensation that sneaks up, giving a double whammy. Add an intense, fruity flavor, and you have a very special chile pepper. The pods freeze quite well, but their fruity fragrance is best enjoyed when the pods are fresh.

'NuMex Suave Orange', 'NuMex Suave Red'

The word *suave* is Spanish for mellow, smooth, or mild, and these pods go down smoothly, as

FAR LEFT *C apsicum chinense* 'NuMex Suave Red'.

LEFT *Capsicum chinense* 'Orange Habanero'.

they are some of the mildest habaneros around, bred for those who want to enjoy the fantastic flavor and aroma of a habanero but not the heat. The plants grow to 3 to 4 feet high in full sun or partial shade. The pods look like standard habanero pods, and each plant produces up to a hundred of them. The pods have the same flavor and aroma as the more powerful habanero peppers, but they have a heat rating of only 800 SHUs. The pods have a citruslike flavor with an orangey-lemony overtone and an apricot aroma. The heat is in the back of the mouth and throat and not on the lips and tongue.

'Orange Habanero'

'Orange Habanero' could be considered the gold standard for habaneros. Its pod is lantern-shaped, the standard shape of habaneros. The habanero is grown on the Yucatán Peninsula of Mexico and in Belize, and commercial production has expanded to Costa Rica and the United States. It is probably the first "exotic" chile pepper to gain fame and acceptance among the chile pepper–appreciating public in the United States. The pods, which are 2½ inches long and 1 inch wide at the shoulders, begin green and then mature into a shiny, waxy orange. The fruits are used fresh in salsas, cooked directly in dishes, or fermented to make a hot sauce.

'Red Caribbean'

'Red Caribbean' is twice as hot as 'Orange Habanero', with a heat rating of greater than 400,000 SHUs, making it more than eighty times hotter than a jalapeño! Plants produce heavy yields of slightly wrinkled pods, 1¾ inches long by 2 inches wide. The pods turn from light green to bright glossy red when mature and have the same distinctive flavor as the habanero. The plant reaches about 3 feet tall and can be grown indoors. The pods can used in salsas, marinades, and, of course, in hot sauce.

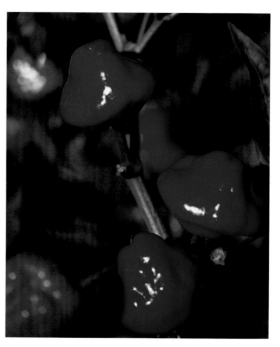

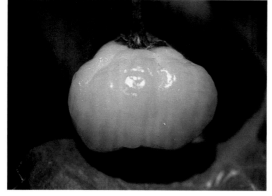

TOP LEFT *Capsicum chinense* 'Red Caribbean'.

TOP RIGHT *Capsicum chinense* 'Scotch Bonnet'.

RIGHT *Capsicum chinense* 'Rocotillo'.

'Rocotillo'

On the island of Puerto Rico and in the West Indies, the most common chile pepper is 'Rocotillo', not to be confused with the variety of *Capsicum baccatum* that goes by the common name of rocotillo. The 'Rocotillo' pod is similar in shape to the Scotch bonnet but has a very long pedicel. Its heat is considerably less than that of the standard Scotch bonnet, around 1000 SHUs. The pods change from green to red over a period of 150 days, making this a full-season variety. 'Rocotillo' plants grow to 3 to 4 feet tall, a little taller than other chile peppers, and develop into a thick canopy. Plants produce good yields of pendant pods, measuring 1 inch to 1½ inches long by 1 inch to 1¼ inches wide, that mature from green to red. The pods are perfect for seasoning authentic Puerto Rican dishes.

'Scotch Bonnet'

'Scotch Bonnet' bears a resemblance to the tam-o'-shanter, thus the name "bonnet." It can go by other names such as 'Bahamian', 'Bahama

Mama', Martinique pepper, and goat pepper in the Bahamas. It is grown extensively on the island of Jamaica. The heat level is in the range of 150,000 to 325,000 SHUs. 'Scotch Bonnet' pods usually change from green to yellow, orange, or red. A chocolate color is rare. Pods are about the same size as a habanero, 1 inch to 1½ inches long, 1 inch to 1½ inches wide.

Scotch bonnets are especially important in Caymanian and Jamaican cooking but are used in other Caribbean recipes, too. The Scotch bonnet has a flavor distinct from its habanero cousin. This is what gives Jamaican "jerk" dishes and other Caribbean dishes their unique flavor. Jerk is a style of cooking native to Jamaica in which meats are dry-rubbed with a very hot spice mixture called Jamaican jerk spice. Jerk seasoning principally relies upon two items: allspice (Jamaican pimento) and 'Scotch Bonnet' chile peppers.

CAPSICUM ANNUUM

The most likely ancestor of the common *Capsicum annuum* varieties grown in the garden today is the wild chiltepín (*C. annuum*

Pod variations, five *Capsicum* species.

var. *glabriusculum*). It has a wide distribution, from South America to southern Arizona and Texas, but the domesticated pod types were concentrated in Mexico, South America, and Central America.

By the time the Spanish arrived in Mexico, indigenous farmers had already selected for dozens of varieties. According to Bernardino de Sahagún, a Franciscan missionary who lived in Mexico, "hot green peppers, smoked peppers, water peppers, tree peppers, beetle peppers, and sharp-pointed red peppers" existed there in 1529. Undoubtedly, these chile peppers were the precursors to the large number of varieties found in Mexico today. Christopher Columbus took seeds back to the Old World, and they were planted extensively in the Portuguese and Spanish colonies, resulting in even more diversification of the species. Within one hundred years, chiles had circumnavigated the world and were growing everywhere in temperate and tropical climates.

Capsicum annuum is the most extensively cultivated species in the world, both commercially and in home gardens. It is the principal species grown in Hungary, India, Mexico, China, Korea, and the East Indies. Because the varieties cross-pollinate so easily, thousands of different varieties exist around the world. Each has a common name, making identification difficult. In Mexico, for example, more than two hundred common names are used for about forty pod types.

Plant growth is highly variable. The young stems are angular, becoming circular in cross section as they mature. The stem may have anthocyanin (the pigments responsible for the colors purple, violet, blue, lilac, and black) along its length, and anthocyanin may or may not be present at the nodes. The stem can be smooth and glossy (glabrous), hairy (pubescent), or a gradation between the two extremes. There are indeterminate (not terminating in a flower) types that grow like vines and semi-indeterminate types, plants that slow their growth as fruit sets. Some types—such as mirasol, 'Poinsettia', and 'Santaka'—have a fasiculated habit, meaning they have branches that end in a fruit cluster.

Most *C. annuum* cultivars develop eight to fifteen leaves before the appearance of the first flower. The number of leaves that appear before the first flower seems to be controlled by temperature and cultivar genotype. With the development of the first flower bud, the plant branches at the apex into two or more shoots. Each shoot bears one or two leaves, terminates in a flower, and then divides into two second-order branches.

The leaves vary in size, shape, and color. Most are simple, entire, and symmetrical. They can be flat and smooth or wrinkled, and glossy or semiglossy. Some are hairy, as in the serrano types. The leaf blade may be ovate, elliptic, or lanceolate. The leaves are usually green, but types with purple, variegated, or yellowish leaves are known. The leaf petiole can be short or long depending on the cultivar.

The flower corolla is usually white, with a small number of varieties having purple corollas. Forming of flowers on chile pepper plants does not appear to be affected by day length.

The most important factor determining flower differentiation is air temperature, especially nighttime temperature. The flower opens within the first two hours after sunrise and is open less than one day. The anthers may open from one to ten hours after the flower opens, but frequently they fail entirely to open to discharge (dehisce) pollen.

Nectar is produced and accumulates in the nectary at the base of the ovary. The quantity of nectar depends on many factors, but the genotype of the cultivar seems to be the most important. The flowers are visited by bees for both nectar and pollen. Older cultivars and wild species have conspicuous nectar drops. The nectar drops are in the middle of the lower section of the flower petals associated with a pore that is visible with a hand lens. Many new cultivars do not produce significant amounts of nectar, so bee visitation can be low. Bee visitation is also dependent on the relative attractiveness of competing flowering plants in the locale.

Flowers are self-compatible, meaning they can be fertilized by their own pollen. Erwin, in 1937, measured the effect of pollination on set of fruit in *C. annuum*. He found that only 46 percent of self-pollinated flowers set, compared to 71 percent of those left to open pollinate by bee activity. The degree of cross-pollination is not as rare as textbooks lead one to believe. In many locales, cross-pollination is predominant. The amount of cross-pollination depends on several factors but can range from 2 to 90 percent.

Capsicum annuum starts flowering with a single flower at the first branching node, but there can be exceptions: two flowers can be found at some nodes. Then a flower forms at each additional node, a geometric progression. Generally, more than a hundred flowers develop on one plant. The rate of fruit set is negatively correlated to the number of fruits developing on the plants. When the plant has set several fruits, the rate of flower production decreases. Fruits from early flowers are usually larger and have more red color and a greater heat level at maturity. Fruit set may be stalled if temperatures become too high, causing a split in the fruit-setting continuum; this is called a split set. Early yield is determined by the first flowers that set fruits. A delay in fruit set can reduce yields and may cause fruit to set high on the plant, which makes plants more prone to wind damage as they mature. Fruit normally reaches the mature green stage 35 to 50 days after the flower is pollinated.

Capsicum annuum varieties are usually classified by pod characteristics, such as heat level, color, shape, flavor, size, and use. Because this is the most popular *Capsicum* species, most of our favorite chile peppers are in this group.

ANCHO OR MULATO

Ancho means "wide," an allusion to the broad, flat, heart-shaped pods in the dried form. Ancho fruit is mildly hot and thin-walled, with an indented stem attachment. The immature fruit is dark green. If the fruit matures to red, ancho types retain the name "ancho," but if it matures to dark brown, the fruit is called mulato. The produce industry uses the name "poblano" for

RIGHT **Variations in the ancho pod type.**

FAR RIGHT *Capsicum annuum* 'Ancho 101'.

any green ancho fruit, but technically, poblano is a specific ancho grown in Puebla, Mexico. In the United States, any green ancho or mulato is a poblano.

This variety is one of the most popular peppers grown in Mexico, where about 37,000 acres are under cultivation. Plant height, along with leaf size, form, and color, varies among ancho cultivars. The plants are multiple-stemmed and compact to semi-erect, semi-woody, and about 2 feet high. The leaves are dark green and shiny, approximately 4 inches long and 2¼ inches wide. Flowering begins 50 days after sowing and continues until the first frost. The pods are pendant, vary between 3 and 6 inches long, and are 2 to 3 inches wide. They are conical or truncated and have indented shoulders. They are fairly mild, ranging from 1000 to 1500 SHUs. The usual growing period is 100 to 120 days and the yield is about fifteen pods per plant, although up to thirty pods per plant is possible.

Fresh poblanos are roasted and peeled, then preserved by canning or freezing. Poblanos are the chile peppers of choice for making chile rellenos (stuffed peppers) in Mexico. The dried pods can be stored in airtight containers for months, or they can be ground into a powder. Anchos are commonly used in sauces called moles.

An excellent variety to grow is 'Ancho 101'.

'Ancho 101'

'Ancho 101' is a mild ancho with a heat level of approximately 3000 SHUs. The pods, which can be up to 6 inches long, begin as deep, dark green and mature to bright red. This pepper has been reported to have a note of apple flavor.

ASIAN

Chile peppers were introduced to Asia in the sixteenth century by Portuguese and Spanish explorers via trade routes from South America and were quickly incorporated into the regional

cuisines. Many kinds of chile peppers are cultivated throughout Asia to fit the various Asian
tastes. We have selected Asian chiles to illus-
trate the various types grown in that region. If
cooking authentic Asian is your goal, these chile
peppers are the ones to use.

'Pusa Jwala'

From India, 'Pusa Jwala' is the most popular
chile pepper grown and used in various spicy
foods there. This variety is also often called
finger hot Indian pepper. The umbrella-type
plant habit produces lots of green fruits in the

Capsicum annuum
'Pusa Jwala'.

Thai chiles in the
Bangkok wholesale
market.

RIGHT *Capsicum annuum* 'Takanotsume'.

FAR RIGHT *Capsicum annuum* 'Shishito'.

early stage, later turning ripe red. The pod has high heat and can be used fresh or dried. The fruit is about 4 inches long, with wrinkled skin. This variety has wide adaptability and is easy to grow in containers or the garden.

'Takanotsume'

From Japan we have chosen three varieties; two are hot, the other not. The first is 'Takanotsume', which is Japanese for "hawk claw" because of its talon shape and its sharp heat. The pods, set in clusters on the plant, are 1½ to 2½ inches long. The fruits are considered hot, but the heat dissipates rapidly. They are dried in the red ripe stage and used as a seasoning.

'Shishito'

The second chile pepper from Japan is 'Shishito.' The 3-to-4-inch-long pods are mildly hot and thin-walled, with a wrinkled skin. They are popular for use in tempura, yakitori, and stir-fries.

'Santaka'

A popular chile used mostly in its dry form in soups and stir-fries, 'Santaka' has pods that are 2½ inches long and ½ inch wide and that stand erect on the plant. Also called 'Asian Hot', this chile has pods that are quite hot, between 30,000 and 50,000 SHUs. A similar cultivar is 'Hontaka'.

'Prik Kee Nu'

Many types of chile peppers in Thailand could be called Thai chiles. Three of the best known are 'Prik Kee Nu', 'Prik Chee Fa', and the ubiquitous 'Thai Chile'. 'Prik Kee Nu', which translates to "mouse-dropping chile pepper," is a very short, small green to red pepper. It is very hot.

FAR LEFT *Capsicum annuum* 'Santaka'.

LEFT *Capsicum annuum* 'Prik Kee Nu' in the Bangkok wholesale market.

Capsicum annuum 'Prik Chee Fa'.

'Prik Chee Fa'

'Prik Chee Fa' is a milder, larger chile than 'Prik Kee Nu'.

'Thai Chile'

The last variety is commonly called 'Thai Chile'. This chile pepper is a compact plant that does well in a container. The pods are small and very hot. The green (immature) and red (ripe) pods are harvested together and mixed when preparing dishes. The red pods can be dried and ground.

BELL

The bell group may be the most economically important pepper type, with 100,000 acres under cultivation in the United States and Mexico. It also has the largest number of culti-vars of any *Capsicum* group. Bell peppers are fruits that are blocky and about 4 inches long

Capsicum annuum 'Thai Chile'.

and wide. A square shape with a flat bottom is preferred. A single plant produces ten to twenty pods. More than two hundred cultivars of bell peppers have been bred, and we have made our selections on the basis of color, heat, disease resistance, and availability to the home grower.

Jack & Jill fruit crate label.

´California Wonder´

'California Wonder' is an heirloom cultivar typical of the pod type. The pod is thick-walled and blocky, about 4 inches tall and wide, with a crisp, mild flavor and terrific sweetness. This is one of the best-tasting sweet bell peppers. The pods mature from green to red on the plant. It takes about 70 days from sowing to green fruit harvest. If kept picked, the 2½-foot-high plants will continue producing throughout the growing season. A very good pod for stuffing, fresh eating, and adding to salads, salsa, and pickles.

´Dove´

'Dove' has a pod that is not green like most bell peppers but is white maturing to red. It is one of our favorite bell peppers for color. In the United States, the consumption of high-quality colored bell peppers has increased dramatically during the past decade. These peppers bring three to five times the price of green fruits. 'Dove' has a pod 3½ inches long and 3 inches wide. Like most bell peppers, it takes 70 days to harvest for the best white fruits.

´Golden Bell´

'Golden Bell' continues to be among our favorites in the colored bells, having high yields of medium-sized pods with a sweet, fruity flavor. It is ready for harvest 10 days earlier than most bell peppers. The pods have four lobes, shiny medium-green in color, turning yellow when ripe. Plants are 3 to 5 feet high.

FAR LEFT *Capsicum annuum* 'California Wonder'.

LEFT *Capsicum annuum* 'Dove'.

'Valencia'

'Valencia', like 'California Wonder' and 'Golden Bell', has pods that start green; however, with 'Valencia' the final color is an attractive orange. The pods are 3¾ inches long and 3 inches wide. This cultivar has always been a clear standout among the orange-fruited peppers in our garden. The pod has a blocky shape and superior eating qualities.

'Lilac Belle'

The last to round out the colored bell peppers is 'Lilac Belle'. We like this one because the pods mature from ivory to lavender to crimson and stay at the lavender (lilac) stage longer than most other purple peppers. The plants, which attain a height of 2 feet and a width of 1 foot, are hardy producers of large, blocky, four-lobed pods. The sweet pods are 3½ inches long and 2½ inches wide. This cultivar has resistance to tobacco mosaic virus.

Capsicum annuum 'Golden Bell'.

RIGHT *Capsicum annuum* 'Valencia'.

FAR RIGHT *Capsicum annuum* 'Lilac Belle'.

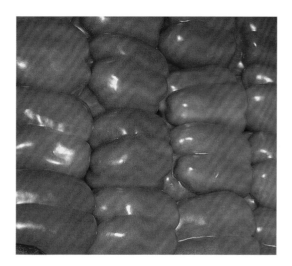

'Mexi-Bell'

'Mexi-Bell' is an All-America Selections winner. This F$_1$ hybrid (meaning a plant that grows from the first-generation seed resulting from the hybridization of different parents) was the first commercially sold bell pepper that had heat, albeit mild heat. Plants reach a height of 2 feet or more and bear plenty of three-to-four-lobed pods that are 2¾ inches long and 2¾ inches wide. The pod ripens from green to red.-

CASCABEL

Cascabel means "rattle" in Spanish, referring to the fact that in the dry form in which the pods are most often used, the seeds of this pepper rattle. The pods begin green and turn to red, and then when they are dried, their skin turns a translucent red-brown color. The pods are spherical and shiny, similar in shape to a cherry, with a thinner wall. They are moderately hot.

The cascabel should not be confused with the cultivar 'Cascabella', which is in the wax group. Each year as chile peppers grow in popularity, one sees more and more cultivars in the different pod types, so someday there will probably be a cultivar of cascabel. But at present, the seed is just sold as cascabel seed.

CAYENNE

No one seems to know the origin of the cayenne pepper. Although it was named after the Cayenne River in French Guiana, it is not grown in South America. Some speculate that the Portuguese may have transferred it to Europe, then into Africa and India, where it appears today in many forms. The plants are almost treelike, with multiple stems and an

FAR LEFT *Capsicum annuum* 'Mexi-Bell'.

LEFT Cascabel.

erect habit, growing up to 3 feet tall and 2 feet wide. The leaves are ovate, smooth, and medium green, about 3½ inches wide and 2 inches long. For most cayennes, the pods are pendant, long, and slender, measuring up to 10 inches long and 1 inch wide. They are often wrinkled and irregular in shape. A mature plant can easily produce forty pods. The cayenne is very hot, measuring between 30,000 and 50,000 SHUs. These peppers are grown commercially in New Mexico, Louisiana, Africa, India, Japan, and Mexico.

'Large Red Thick'

'Large Red Thick' cayenne can almost be considered an heirloom. It sets a standard for the large-pod cayennes with the traditional flavor associated with cayenne. The plant produces a concentrated set of as many as twenty pods

measuring 6 inches long by ¾ inch wide. The pods often grow curled, twisted, or wrinkled. They are very hot, with an SHU rating of more than 30,000. This cayenne is commonly used in Cajun foods and is mashed to make the famous Louisiana-style hot sauces. It can be dried, pickled, or used in salsas. The pods dry easily for colorful winter wreaths.

ABOVE *Capsicum annuum* 'Large Red Thick'.

'NuMex Nematador'

'NuMex Nematador' is a New Mexico State University (NMSU) chile pepper release. Any chile pepper with the moniker "NuMex" was developed at NMSU. This cayenne is unique in that it is resistant to the devastating root-knot nematode, a microscopic worm that attacks the plant's roots. Root-knot nematodes attack between two thousand and three thousand different species of plants. The parasitic worms, which live in the soil, attack the chile pepper's roots, grow into them, and eventually form a knot or gall on the root itself. Damage is especially severe in sandy soils, the prime nematode breeding ground. 'NuMex Nematador' is a standard big-fruited type that makes harvesting easier. The pods can be used fresh in their immature green form in salsa, but the most common use is to grind the dried red pods into powder.

'NuMex Las Cruces'

'NuMex Las Cruces' is a large-fruited cayenne like 'Large Red Thick' and matures in the same amount of time. Like all cayennes, it is very hot. Its greatest attribute is its resistance to curly top virus.

CHERRY

The resemblance of the pods to giant cherries is the reason this type is called cherry. The cherry type is familiar because the pods are commonly pickled and served as an accompaniment to sandwiches. The plant has single to multiple stems and an erect habit, and grows about 2 feet tall. The leaves are smooth, dark green, and about 3 inches long and 1½ inches wide. The pods are erect and spherical, measuring about 1¾ inches wide. At maturity, they are normally red and are fairly mild to moderately hot, measuring from zero to about 3500 SHUs. Some gardeners grow the cherry type as an ornamental, and it does well in the home garden. About 1600 acres are under commercial cultivation in

FAR LEFT Cherry type pods.

LEFT Chilhuacles in the market, Oaxaca.

the United States. The pods can be used fresh in salads but are most commonly pickled.

An ornamental potted plant called Jerusalem cherry is not a pepper but *Solanum pseudocapsicum*. It is important to correctly identify Jerusalem cherry because the fruits are poisonous. The best way to identify them is to look at the anthers, which are orange in Jerusalem cherry but bluish in *Capsicum*.

Good open-pollinated cultivars are 'Besler's Cherry', an heirloom sweet variety, and 'Hot Cherry Pepper'. There are also F_1 hybrids available that give greater uniformity with very prolific yields. A good sweet cherry hybrid is 'Cherry Pick'. For a hot one, try 'Cherry Bomb'.

CHILHUACLE

Chilhuacle is a rare pod type grown only in southern Mexico around Oaxaca. The name suggests a pre-Colombian domestication. Chilhuacle pods are thin-walled, measuring 2 inches to 3 inches across. They range in appearance from that of a miniature bell pepper to pods that are broad shouldered and taper to a point. Immature fruit are green, ripening to yellow, red, or even a black color, hence the cultivar names 'Chilhuacle Amarillo', 'Chilhuacle Rojo', and 'Chilhuacle Negro'. They provide a deep, intense flavor to the unique mole sauces for which the Mexican state of Oaxaca is famous.

CHILTEPÍN OR CHILE PIQUIN

Every chile pepper garden needs a chiltepín plant, if for no other reason than that it is a great conversation piece. This is the "mother of all chile peppers." The pods are small and round, only ¼ inch in diameter, and mature from green to red. The little pods are very hot. The chiltepíns and the chile piquins can have a seed dormancy that makes germination difficult. Treatment to aid in seed germination is discussed later in "Capsicum Cultivation." A good tip is that germination is

RIGHT Chiltepín harvest, La Aurora, Sonora.

BELOW *Capsicum annuum* 'NuMex Bailey Piquin'.

fruits can be crushed into soups, stews, and bean dishes. The green fruit is chopped and used in salsas or to produce a chile pepper vinegar. Second, you can watch the birds come and pick fruit off the plant. Studies have shown that seeds of wild chile peppers are in fact dispersed almost exclusively by birds.

'NuMex Bailey Piquin'

'NuMex Bailey Piquin' is a piquin type, meaning that the pods are elongated instead of being round like chiltepín pods. 'NuMex Bailey Piquin' has pods ¾ inch long and ¼ inch wide at the base. In the wild, piquin plants can grow 6 feet high or more, and in the greenhouse they have grown 15 feet high in one season. Some varieties have a prostrate habit, spreading across the ground like a ground cover. The pods are extremely hot, measuring between 50,000 and 100,000 SHUs. 'NuMex Bailey Piquin' was the first domesticated form of the chile piquin, developed for machine harvesting. It has been successfully grown in the Mesilla Valley of New Mexico. The dried pods can be ground into powders or made into extremely hot sauces, but they are most commonly crushed into soups, stews, and bean dishes.

CHIPOTLE

Chipotle is not really a pod type, but we would be remiss if we did not mention it here. The chipotle is a smoked red ripe jalapeño. These peppers lend a wonderful smoky flavor to sauces. They're usually canned in adobo sauce or sold dry.

faster and rates are higher when the planting medium is warm, between 70 and 80°F.

Growing chiltepíns in the garden can be a double pleasure. First, they provide a wonderful heat source to season any dish. The red dried

COSTEÑO

Costeños are good in salsas, sauces, and soups.

'Costeño', 'Costeño Amarillo'

'Costeño' and 'Costeño Amarillo' are from the regions of Oaxaca and Guerrero in Mexico. Both have pods that begin green; 'Costeño' matures to a red-orange color, while 'Costeño Amarillo' matures to yellow. 'Costeño' pods taper to a point and measure about 2 to 3 inches long and ½ to ¾ inch across at the shoulders. The pod has thin to medium-fleshed walls and an apricot fruit tone with a fiery, intense, lingering heat. 'Costeño Amarillo' is shiny, amber in color, tapering to a point, and measuring about 2 to 3 inches long and ¾ to 1 inch across at the shoulders. The pods have very thin flesh with a light, crisp lemon-citrus flavor and green tomato and grassy tones. The heat is lower as compared to 'Costeño', with a subtleness to it. The dried pods are used to prepare yellow mole sauces, and they are also good in soups and stews.

DE ÁRBOL

The name of this Mexican pod type means "treelike," an allusion to the appearance of the mature plant. The plant has multiple stems and an erect habit. It grows up to 3 feet tall, often resembling a small tree. The leaves vary from smooth to hairy, are light green in color, and are small—about 1¼ inches long and ½ inch wide. The pods are pendant, occasionally erect, and elongate, and are about 3 inches long and ⅜ inch wide. They are green, often maturing to red, and

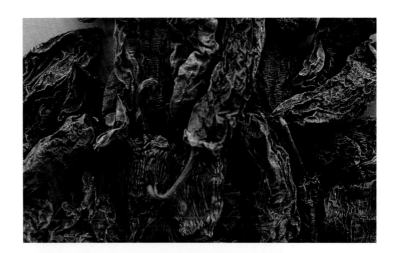

ABOVE Chipotle.
LEFT *Capsicum annuum* 'Costeño Amarillo'

RIGHT De árbol pods.

FAR RIGHT Left to right, *Capsicum annuum* 'NuMex Sunglo', 'NuMex Sunburst', 'NuMex Sunflare'.

they are hot, measuring between 15,000 and 30,000 SHUs.

'NuMex Sunburst', 'NuMex Sunflare', 'NuMex Sunglo'

The three cultivars 'NuMex Sunburst', 'NuMex Sunflare', and 'NuMex Sunglo' were developed to provide a source for making mini-ristras (from pods smaller than the usual New Mexican type) and chile pepper wreaths. The immature fruit is green, maturing to yellow, red, and orange for 'NuMex Sunglo', 'NuMex Sunflare', and 'NuMex Sunburst', respectively. The pods are about 3 inches long and ½ inch wide. For the kitchen, the pods are often either ground into a powder to be added to cooked sauces or combined with water and vinegar to make table sauces.

JALAPEÑO

The jalapeño pepper was named for the town of Jalapa, Mexico, were it was originally marketed. However, it was not originally grown there, but was imported from the surrounding regions. The pods are thick-walled, conical in shape, dark green when immature with most turning red at maturity, and very hot. The fruit skin may show a brown netting pattern called corkiness. The corkiness does not affect the flavor. Because the thick fruit walls keep the pod from drying naturally on the plant, the mature red jalapeños are dried by smoking them over mesquite or another hardwood, and the product is called chipotle.

Because jalapeños have been selected and bred for thousands of years, they have developed unique flavors. The majority of commercial jalapeños are preserved by canning or pickling, while some are dehydrated in either the green or red stage. Most jalapeños from the home garden are used fresh in salsas, sliced into rings

for use with nachos, or pickled for later use.

Jalapeños usually grow from 2½ to 3 feet tall. The plants have a compact single stem or an upright, multibranched, spreading habit. The leaves are light to dark green and measure about 3 inches long and 2 inches wide. It takes about 70 to 80 days from sowing to beginning to harvest green pods, and a plant produces twenty-five to thirty-five pods. Our five favorites are 'Early Jalapeno', 'NuMex Jalmundo', 'NuMex Piñata', 'NuMex Primavera', and 'NuMex Vaquero'.

'Early Jalapeno'

'Early Jalapeno', as the name implies, matures earlier than other cultivars. It is usually ready to pick about a week or two before other

jalapeños. The plant attains a height of 2 feet, which is the common height for most jalapeños.

'NuMex Jalmundo'

'NuMex Jalmundo' produces large fruits with little corkiness. It has high yields and a sweetness not found in other jalapeños.

ABOVE *Capsicum annuum* 'NuMex Piñata'.

RIGHT *Capsicum annuum* 'NuMex Primavera'.

'NuMex Piñata'

'NuMex Piñata' originated spontaneously in the cultivar 'Early Jalapeno'. 'NuMex Piñata' is unique in the transition of colors the pods undergo as they mature. Immature fruits are light green, maturing to yellow, orange, and finally red. The foliage of 'Early Jalapeno' and other jalapeño cultivars is dark green, while

'NuMex Piñata' has golden-yellow foliage. 'NuMex Piñata' plants are smaller and tend to decline earlier in the season due to the lack of chlorophyll production by the foliage. While its yield and pod width are not significantly different from 'Early Jalapeno', 'NuMex Piñata' has pods that are longer than those of 'Early Jalapeno'. 'NuMex Piñata' is a unique jalapeño for making colorful salsas. It has kept the natural flavors and aromas of traditional jalapeños and is considered hot with a heat level of 50,000 SHUs.

'NuMex Primavera'

'NuMex Primavera' has pods with rounded shoulders, little to no corkiness, and a semi-pointed tip that is characteristic of the standard jalapeño shape. The pods are dark green and have no anthocyanin, so they do not change to red as they mature. 'NuMex Primavera' displays a uniformly mild heat level at 8000 SHUs, much milder than industry standard jalapeños. 'NuMex Primavera' fruits are 2 inches long and 1 inch wide, and have thick walls. 'NuMex Primavera' is a favorite of home gardeners because of its mild heat and presence of traditional flavors and aromas.

'NuMex Vaquero'

'NuMex Vaquero' is an open-pollinated jalapeño that produces yields at the same level as F_1 hybrids (12 tons an acre for commercial growers) and has tolerance to the root rot disease *Phytophthora capsici*. The pod has a green color, smooth skin (no corkiness), a blunted tip, rounded shoulders, multiple cavities (called

FAR LEFT *Capsicum annuum* 'NuMex Vaquero'.

LEFT *Capsicum annuum* 'NuMex Mirasol'.

Capsicum annuum 'Guajillo'.

locules), and uniform heat. Pods are 2½ inches long and almost 1 inch wide. The heat level of 'NuMex Vaquero' is 25,000 to 30,000 SHUs, similar to 'Early Jalapeno'.

MIRASOL

Mirasol (meaning "looking at the sun") pod types are known for their translucent fruit and fruity flavor.

'NuMex Mirasol'

'NuMex Mirasol' is a multistemmed bush, 2 feet tall and 1 foot wide, with erect fruit. The pods, which start out green when immature and turn red at maturity, are thin walled and dry to a beautiful translucent red. Each plant produces an average of sixteen fruit clusters per plant, with five fruits per cluster. The conical fruits are 2 inches long and ¾ inch wide, with two cavities (locules). 'NuMex Mirasol' is used as both an ornamental on wreaths and a ground powder in cooking.

Capsicum annuum
'Pulla'.

'Guajíllo'

'Guajíllo' dries to a rich burgundy red color. It has the shape of a small New Mexican type. The pods are 4½ inches long and 1 inch wide. The plants can yield up to fifty pods per plant. The pods are dried and mostly used to make sauces.

'Pulla'

'Pulla' plants have an intermediate number of stems and an erect habit tending toward compact; they grow 2 to 3 feet high. The leaves are smooth and medium green, 2 inches long and 1¼ inches wide. 'Pulla' pods are smaller than those of 'Guajíllo', about 3 to 4 inches long and ¾ inch wide at the widest point. The pod is elongated with a curved and tapered tip. The pepper is a deep, translucent dark red with a shiny, thin skin. The flavor is tinged with hints of licorice. These varieties measure between 2500 and 5000 SHUs. The pods are usually dried and can be ground into powders. They are used in sauces, soups, stews, and meat dishes.

NEW MEXICAN

The New Mexican pod type is sometimes mistakenly called long green chile, Anaheim, or Hatch chile. Actually, the pod type is New Mexican, and 'Anaheim' is a cultivar within this pod type. 'Anaheim' seed originated in New Mexico and was brought to Anaheim, California, where it was widely cultivated. There is no 'Hatch' chile cultivar—Hatch is merely one of many locations where New Mexican chile peppers are grown. A mythology has evolved about Hatch chiles being superior to other varieties, but it's just not true, and there's simply not enough acreage around Hatch to grow all the chiles labeled as Hatch in the southwestern states. During one session a few years ago at the New Mexico Chile Conference, two Arizona chile growers confessed to us that they shipped their chiles to Hatch, where they were labeled "Hatch chiles" and sold at roadside stands. Numerous landraces have evolved in New Mexico. Most are in northern New Mexico and are named for the growing area, such as 'Chimayó', 'Dixon', and 'Velarde'.

The modern New Mexican pod type was developed beginning in 1894 when Fabian Garcia at New Mexico State University started improving, through selection and cross-breeding, the local chile peppers grown by the Hispanic gardeners around Las Cruces. His goal was to produce a chile pepper cultivar that was a "larger, smoother, fleshier, more tapering and shoulderless pod for canning purposes." He selected fourteen chile lines from pasilla (dark brown), colorado (red), and negro (black) chile peppers that were growing in the Las Cruces area. In 1913, after nine years of growing and selecting, Dr. Garcia released the first New Mexico State University chile cultivar, 'New Mexico No. 9', which introduced the world to the new pod type. All New Mexican type chile peppers grown today gained their genetic base from cultivars first developed at New Mexico State University.

The New Mexican plant has a mostly compact habit with an intermediate number of stems and grows between 2 and 3 feet high. The leaves are ovate, medium green, fairly smooth, and about 3 inches long and 2 inches wide. The pods are pendant, elongate, and bluntly pointed, and they measure between 4 and 12 inches long. They are dark green, maturing to various shades of red. Their heat ranges from zero ('NuMex Garnet') to hot ('Sandia')—2500 SHUs. Each plant produces between ten and twenty pods, depending on variety and cultural techniques.

New Mexican pods are the basis for the green chile, the red chile, and much of the paprika production in the world. Green and red

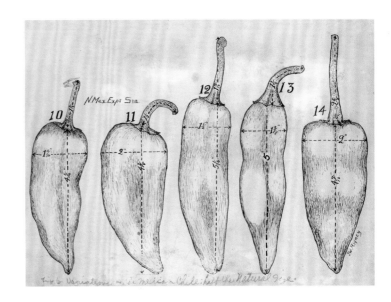

pods represent two developmental states of the same fruit. Green pods are roasted and peeled, then either used fresh for stuffed chile peppers (chile rellenos) or sauces, or canned, frozen, or dried (chile pasado). The skins must be removed before using. Red chiles are usually kept on the bush until they dessicate and become leathery. Then they are tied into strings (ristras) that are dried in the sun and hung near the entrance of homes as symbols of hospitality. They can also be dried in a food dehydrator. After drying, they can be ground into powders of varying fineness for use in sauces. Today, the long green pods that turn red are the pod of choice for Mexican-style cooked sauces in the United States.

With such a versatile chile pepper, the choice of varieties is large.

Chile drawings from the files of Fabian Garcia, c. 1914. *Courtesy of the Rio Grande Historical Collection at New Mexico State University, #00710228.*

Capsicum annuum 'Chimayó'.

Capsicum annuum 'Española Improved'.

Capsicum annuum 'NuMex Heritage 6-4'.

'Chimayó'

'Chimayó' is a landrace from northern New Mexico with thin-walled, 6-inch pods. The heat level is medium.

'Española Improved'

'Española Improved' is similar to 'Chimayó' in that it matures early and has the same fruit characteristics. On the other hand, it is more uniform and better yielding than 'Chimayó'. This variety is great for producing early pods in the garden.

'New Mexico No. 6-4', 'NuMex Heritage 6-4'

'New Mexico No. 6-4', the standard and most popular New Mexican pod type, was released in 1957 as an improvement over 'New Mexico No. 6.' 'New Mexico No. 6-4' produces a high proportion of large, smooth, thick-fleshed pods that range from 6 to 8 inches in length and average 2 inches in width; it produces a higher proportion of well-shaped pods than 'Anaheim'. The pods are a uniform medium green in color. The heat level is from 700 to 900 SHUs.

In 1997, Paul Bosland was approached by chile growers who told him that the 'New Mexico No. 6-4' variety was losing its flavor. Bosland located two hundred original 'New Mexico No. 6-4' seeds that had been stored cryogenically for forty years. Over the next ten years, he did seed increases and selected the best pods for the next year's grow-out. Seed of the new variety, called 'NuMex Heritage 6-4', was available to growers for the 2009 season.

'NuMex Big Jim' and 'NuMex Heritage Big Jim'

'NuMex Big Jim' is listed in *Guinness World Records* as the world's largest pepper (13½ inches long). The 2-foot-high plant produces long, thick, smooth, fleshy fruits. Mature light green pods are moderately flattened, with round shoulders tapering to a distinctive hook at the tip; they average 7¾ inches in length and 2 inches in width. On average, 'NuMex Big Jim' is slightly hotter than 'New Mexico 6-4'; however, the heat level varies from plant to plant, with some plants producing mild pods and others producing hot pods. Because of the large pods, the cultivar is a favorite of home gardeners and chefs for making chiles rellenos. Paul Bosland has developed an improved variety, 'NuMex Heritage Big Jim'.

'NuMex Conquistador'

'NuMex Conquistador', along with 'NuMex R Naky', 'NuMex Garnet', and 'NuMex Sweet', is a low- or no-heat paprika-type cultivar. 'NuMex Conquistador' pods have round shoulders, pointed tips, a smooth surface, thick flesh, and two cavities (locules). The pods average 6 inches in length. Plants, which grow to just under 3 feet, have a single, strong main stem with sturdy branches. Pods can be harvested in the green stage, where they are stuffed with jalapeño-flavored cheese to produce chiles rellenos with uniform heat levels.

'NuMex R Naky'

'NuMex R Naky' was the first New Mexican pod released as a paprika. Dr. Roy Nakayama released this cultivar in 1985 and named it after

Capsicum annuum 'NuMex Big Jim'.

Capsicum annuum 'NuMex Conquistador'.

his wife, Rose. It sets fruit under high temperature and low humidity, and yields better than 'New Mexico No. 6-4'. The pods are 5 to 7 inches long and very mild, with a heat level between 260 and 760 SHUs. This is a good starter cultivar for those who do not want much heat.

Capsicum annuum 'NuMex R Naky'.

Capsicum annuum 'NuMex Sweet'.

BELOW *Capsicum annuum* 'NuMex Sunset', 'NuMex Eclipse', and 'NuMex Sunrise'.

'NuMex Sweet'

'NuMex Sweet', released in 1990, has smooth pods of low heat that have round shoulders, a pointed tip, and two locules. The plant has a single, strong main stem and sturdy branches that provide foliage cover for sun scald protection and support for an excellent pod set. Plant height is 2 feet and width is just under 3 feet. The heat level of the pods is 300 SHUs.

'NuMex Sunrise', 'NuMex Eclipse', and 'NuMex Sunset'

'NuMex Sunrise', 'NuMex Eclipse', and 'NuMex Sunset' are considered to be ornamentals but are also edible and delicious. They are unique in providing alternative mature pod color in the New Mexican pod type. The pods begin green and then turn bright yellow, chocolate brown, and orange, respectively. These varieties make attractive ristras and as a food are similar in pod characteristics and heat level to 'New Mexico No. 6-4'.

'NuMex Joe E. Parker'

'NuMex Joe E. Parker' is the premier cultivar for a green New Mexican pod. Released in 1990 and exhibiting less variability for horticultural traits than 'New Mexico No. 6-4', it has become the number one green chile grown in Mexico and the United States. The plants have single, strong main stems and are uniformly branched, providing foliage cover for sunscald protection and support for an excellent fruit set. Plant height and width are similar to 'New Mexico No. 6-4'; the two cultivars are also similar in heat level, fruit width, green fruit color, and days to maturity (149 days). The best features of this cultivar are its pod wall thickness and yield. A high percentage (88 percent) of the pods have only two locules (cavities), making for easy freezing. The heat level is mild, at 800 SHUs.

'Sandia'

'Sandia' was released by New Mexico State University in 1956. 'Sandia' produces long, medium-wide pods with medium-thick walls. Pods are straight with a slightly roughened surface but devoid of the severe folds that were commonly present on 'Anaheim'. Its shoulders are rounded, and the pods taper gradually to the blossom end. Mature 'Sandia' pods average 6½ inches in length and 1½ inches at their widest dimension. 'Sandia' plants set pods well on the lower nodes during high-temperature periods. Plants are upright in growth habit and average 2 feet in height. 'Sandia' is considered a hot cultivar in the New Mexican group, with a rating of 1500 to 2000 SHUs. This is a popular cultivar with home gardeners.

ONZA

'Onza Roja' and 'Onza Amarillo'

'Onza Roja' and 'Onza Amarillo' are varieties from the Oaxaca region of Mexico. Both pods are green when immature, with 'Onza Roja' changing to a bright red and 'Onza Amarillo' maturing to yellow. The pendant pods are slim and tapered, to a length of 2½ to 3 inches. The pods are thin fleshed with a back-of-the-mouth heat, similar to a habanero. The plant has hairy green stems and leaves, and grows to a height of

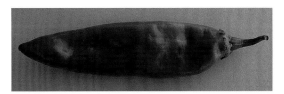

Capsicum annuum 'NuMex Joe E. Parker'.

Capsicum annuum 'Sandia'.

3 feet. It is used in the dry form to season sauces and soups.

ABOVE *Capsicum annuum* 'Onza Roja' in the market in Oaxaca.

ORNAMENTAL

Ornamentals are a unique class of chile peppers—not really a pod type, but a distinct group of *Capsicum annuum* cultivars. Ornamental peppers are very popular as potted plants in Europe and are gaining in popularity in the United States. Seed propagation is easy, cropping time is relatively short, the plants are heat and drought tolerant, and the peppers have excellent keeping quality. Although they are edible, ornamentals are not particularly flavorful and are grown primarily for their unusual pod shapes, colorful fruits, or for their dense and sometimes variegated foliage. Ornamental chile peppers sport all the colors of the rainbow, often displaying pods in four or five colors on the same plant at the same time. Originally, they were known as Christmas peppers and given at Christmastime as a gift because the green and red fruits were the colors of Christmas. They also work well in the landscape as a border plant. Our favorites include novel foliage, a range of colors, and one unusual pod shape.

'Black Cuban'

'Black Cuban' has very dark purple pods, looking black in the garden. The pods measure ¾ inch long by ½ inch wide and turn red at maturity. Plants have purple-green stems, purple leaves with tint of green, and violet flowers.

Ornamentals in the Chile Pepper Institute garden.

'Chilly Chili'

'Chilly Chili', an ornamental that has no heat, is an All-America Selections winner. The plant, suitable for indoor pots, produces 2-inch-long pods that grow upright above the foliage. The pods transition from yellow to orange to red as they mature.

'Jigsaw'

'Jigsaw' has beautiful green and white variegated foliage on plants 1½ to 2 feet tall. Pendant fruits are between 2 and 3 inches long, ripening from cream with green stripes to orange with brown stripes to all red. The ripening pods can also be variegated. Grown more for the foliage than the pods, 'Jigsaw' makes an attractive plant in the garden.

TOP LEFT *Capsicum annuum* 'Black Cuban'.

TOP RIGHT *Capsicum annuum* 'Chilly Chili'.

LEFT *Capsicum annuum* 'Jigsaw'.

TOP *Capsicum annuum* 'NuMex Centennial'.

ABOVE *Capsicum annuum* 'NuMex Twilight'.

'NuMex Centennial'

'NuMex Centennial' was the first ornamental chile pepper released by New Mexico State University, to celebrate NMSU's centennial in 1988. The plant grows well in a container but is suitable for cultivation in a formal garden bed. 'NuMex Centennial' has purple flowers and green and purple foliage. The erect pods are purple, then ripen to yellow, orange, and finally red.

'NuMex Twilight'

'NuMex Twilight' has a white flower and green leaves. The plants grow erect and have smooth stems. The erect pods are similar in color to those of 'NuMex Centennial', but the yellow stage is more pronounced. 'NuMex Twilight' has become important to plant breeders as a source of resistance to cucumber mosaic virus.

'NuMex Christmas'

The latest series of ornamentals from New Mexico State University is the holiday series. These ornamentals, bred to grow in a container, are dwarf plants that grow less than 1 foot tall. Each ornamental has holiday-specific colors. 'NuMex Christmas' has pods that are green and red, while 'NuMex Halloween' pods turn from black to orange. 'NuMex Memorial Day' has pods that are white and yellow, and 'NuMex St. Patrick's Day' pods are green and orange, the colors of Ireland. Others include 'NuMex Thanksgiving', with yellow and orange pods, and 'NuMex Valentine's Day', with red and white pods. The plants can be used in the same manner as traditional indoor holiday plants, either placed around the house or as a table centerpiece. After

FAR LEFT *Capsicum annuum* 'NuMex Christmas'.

LEFT *Capsicum annuum* 'Peter Pepper'.

the holiday season, they can be planted outdoors in the spring. The pods are edible and hot, but not lethally hot, and can be plucked off and used for spice.

'Peter Pepper'

'Peter Pepper' is grown for the unusual shape of the pod, which resembles a human penis. It tends to stimulate conversation at a garden party!

'Poinsettia'

'Poinsettia' produces clusters of slender upright pods, 2½ to 3½ inches long with pointed tips. The pods mature from green to bright red and are very hot. The plants attain a height of 2 feet. 'Poinsettia' makes a dramatic display in the garden.

Capsicum annuum 'Poinsettia'.

RIGHT Pasilla pods.
FAR RIGHT Piment d´
Espelette pod.

PASILLA

Pasilla means "little raisin" in Spanish, an allusion to the dark brown color and raisinlike aroma of the dried pod. The produce industry in California confusingly calls dried anchos pasilla peppers. The plant, which grows up to 3 feet tall and is not common in home gardens in the United States, has an intermediate number of stems and an erect habit. The leaves are ovate, smooth, and medium green, about 3 inches long and 1½ inches wide. The pods are elongate, cylindrical, and furrowed, measuring 6 to 12 inches long and 1 inch wide. They start out very dark green and mature to dark brown. Pasilla peppers are medium hot, at 1000 to 1500 SHUs. Each plant can produce twenty or more pods. The green pods, called chilaca, can be used in the same manner as the New Mexican varieties. The dried pods are one of the main chiles used in mole sauces.

We recommend the cultivars 'Apaseo', with pods up to 12 inches long and mildly hot, and 'Salvatierra', also mildly hot with 6- to 8-inch-long pods. There is even a hybrid pasilla available, 'Holy Mole'.

PIMENT D' ESPELETTE

Piment d' Espelette is an heirloom chile pepper from Espelette in southwestern France. Chile peppers were introduced in France along with corn in 1523 but were established as a tradition in just one region: the Nive Valley in the southwest, and especially in the village of Espelette. The name "piment d' Espelette" is a controlled name, granted *Appellation d'Origine Controlee* (AOC) status by France's National Institute for Trade Name Origins in 1999, giving it the same protection as more famous names, such as Champagne sparkling wine. The plant grows to a height of 2 feet, and each plant produces about twenty deep red pods with a smoky flavor and mild heat. Piment d' Espelette is dried and used whole or ground into a powder. It is a favorite to season Basque dishes.

PIMIENTO

Pimiento, sometimes spelled *pimento*, is characterized by a heart-shaped, thick-walled fruit that is green when immature and red at maturity. The fruits have no heat, and the pod flesh is sweeter than that of bell peppers. Pimiento is used in processed foods, such as pimiento cheese and stuffed olives, but can be eaten fresh. Allspice, *Pimenta dioica*, usually known as pimento or Jamaican pepper outside the United States, is not related to this variety of *C. annuum*. The word *pimiento* seems to have been acquired in connection with the canned product exported from Spain and applied particularly to thick-meated pods of conical shape. The spelling

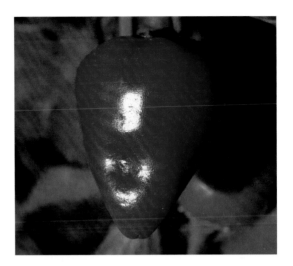

Pimiento pod.

of *pimiento* is muddled in the literature because the Spanish word for pepper is *pimiento* and the anglicized form of the same word is *pimento*. Today, the word *pimiento* is the choice in both English and Spanish writings.

'Perfection Pimiento' is one of the most recognizable pimiento cultivars. It was first listed in a seed catalog in 1914 and cited as a sport of a cultivar received from Valencia, Spain. The introduction of 'Perfection Pimiento' and the invention of canning machinery for roasting to remove the skin began the pimiento canning industry in the United States. The plant is multistemmed with a subcompact habit tending toward prostrate, growing between 1 foot and 2½ feet tall. The leaves are medium green, ovate to lanceolate, and smooth, and measure about 3 inches long and 1½ inches wide. The pods are pendant, heart-shaped, and thick-fleshed, measuring between 2 and 4½ inches long and 2 to 3½ inches wide. Each plant

Serrano pepper.

BELOW *Capsicum annuum* 'Floral Gem'.

yields about ten dark green pods, maturing to bright red. Pimientos are often canned and are the familiar stuffing of olives. They are also used fresh in salads and are pickled.

Recommended cultivars, all with no heat, include 'Pimiento Select', with heart-shaped, deep red pods, and 'Pimiento Sweet', with bright red pods. 'Pimiento L' has resistance to tobacco mosaic virus.

SERRANO

This pod type probably originated in the mountains of northern Puebla and Hildago, Mexico; serrano means "from the highland or mountain." The plant varies in habit from compact to erect, with an intermediate number of stems, and grows from 1½ to 5 feet high. The hairy leaves vary from light to dark green and measure 3½ to 5 inches long and 1½ to 2 inches wide. The pods are cylindrical, pendant, and bluntly pointed, and measure between 1 and 4 inches long and ½ inch wide, with up to fifty pods growing on a single plant. The immature pod color ranges from light to dark green, with pods becoming red at maturity. The heat level is higher than jalapeño, with serrano measuring between 10,000 and 20,000 SHUs. Serrano is the pepper of choice for making pico de gallo, a salsa-type relish.

Recommended cultivars are the bullet-shaped 'Balin' and 'TAM Hidalgo', which is mildly pungent. Another popular cultivar is 'Serrano Tampiqueño', which is hot.

WAX

Wax pepper pods are yellow when immature, with a waxy appearance, and turn orange, orange-red, or red at maturity. In Spanish, they are referred to as *güero*, meaning light-skinned or blond. Our three favorites are 'Floral Gem', 'Mississippi Sport', and 'Santa Fe Grande'. The plants have a strong single stem and a compact growth habit, growing up to 2½ feet high. The leaves are ovate, medium green, and up to 5 inches long and 3 inches wide. Each plant can produce twenty-five or more pods.

'Floral Gem'

The pods of 'Floral Gem' are pointed, measuring 1 inch long and ¾ inch wide.

'Mississippi Sport'

'Mississippi Sport' is the chile pepper served with Chicago-style hot dogs. This pepper can be served as a condiment to accompany hot dogs and sandwiches or added chopped to pasta, pizza, omelettes, and garden salads. 'Mississippi Sport' has smooth green foliage. The pod color begins as green and matures into a rich red. The pod is slim, pointed, and erect, and measures 2 inches long and ½ inch wide. It has a medium heat like 'Floral Gem' and 'Santa Fe Grande'.

'Santa Fe Grande'

'Santa Fe Grande' can be considered a large-sized 'Floral Gem', with pod lengths in the range of 2 inches. 'Santa Fe Grande' has resistance to tobacco mosaic virus. Both have a medium heat in the range of 2500 to 5000 SHUs.

ABOVE *Capsicum annuum* 'Santa Fe Grande'.

LEFT *Capsicum annuum* 'Mississippi Sport'.

Capsicum Cultivation

PEPPER GARDENERS SHOULD ALWAYS PLAN before they plant. The planning involves many elements: choosing the varieties of peppers to grow, deciding which other vegetables and herbs to plant in the garden, settling on the type of garden, and allowing for preparation of the garden before planting.

PLANNING THE CROP

Selecting the right varieties for your garden

As we have seen, many pepper varieties are available to the home gardener. Choosing the best pepper varieties to grow is important. Seed companies and state college experiment stations devote tremendous effort to the development of disease-resistant, highly productive varieties that are tailor-made for different climatic conditions. Some of these new varieties may be better than the ones gardeners have grown in the past.

In the winter, when planning the garden, study our recommendations and examine the Web sites of the providers of seeds and plants listed in "Resources." These companies offer a far wider choice of varieties than do local nurseries and retail shops. Web sites and seed catalogs are also the most dependable sources of new varieties, and many of the seed companies offer what they call proprietary cultivars, varieties that are sold exclusively by one company. Often,

Chile field, Mesilla Valley, New Mexico.

A selection of seed packets.

these proprietary cultivars are hybrids, first-generation crosses that must be hand-pollinated each year. Web sites and seed catalogs also offer better access to the All-America Selections, which are varieties chosen by experts as the all-around best.

Gardeners often purchase pepper seed without knowing if the variety is adapted to their local climatic conditions. For example, the New Mexican varieties grow well in the Southwest but not that well in the Northwest and Northeast. Conversely, bells and habaneros do not grow as well in the Southwest as they do in other regions. According to the seed companies, all the varieties grow well everywhere. This is simply not true.

To decide which varieties to plant, consult your neighbors who garden, local garden clubs, or the county agricultural or extension agent;

or simply learn from experience. When reading the variety description on the seed packet, in the catalog, or on the Web site, look for the qualities that are most important, such as growing period, yield, disease resistance, and recommendations for climatic zones. Some varieties are best suited for pickling, some for drying, some for fresh use, and some for processing and freezing.

A variety that performs well in one region may be unsuitable in another location because of disease susceptibility or maturity date. However, it is difficult to persuade dedicated pepper growers not to grow a specific variety. Even if the soil conditions and climate are wrong, following some of the tips later in this chapter can help. Also, pepper gardeners can modify the microclimate in their gardens. For example, shading habaneros in the Southwest generally improves their performance and yield, and creating a scree in the garden to improve drainage can save peppers that are susceptible to root rot.

In many climates, the variety makes the difference between a bumper harvest and outright failure. In the Southeast and Midwest, where summer rains are common, peppers with resistance to bacterial leaf spot should be grown. This disease, caused by a bacterium, cannot be controlled by chemicals, so planting resistant varieties is the best and most effective way to ensure a bountiful harvest. The catalogs, Web sites, and seed packets often describe the resistance factors of the varieties.

The early or late maturity of a variety is also a very important consideration. At high altitudes or in cool climates, both with short growing seasons, the pepper variety must be able to mature and set fruit rapidly. Early-maturing varieties are valuable to the cool-climate gardener who might not be able to mature the late cultivars at all because of their heat requirements, and to the hot-climate gardener who wants an early harvest.

The growing period—the number of days from sowing the seed to maturity, which is usually listed in catalogs, on Web sites, and on seed packets, is an important clue for the gardener. Be aware, however, that the number of days in the stated growing period is based upon ideal conditions. In some cases, the growing period is the number of days from transplanting to pod picking. A bell pepper listed to mature in 60 days, which may be the approximate number of days for Davis, California, located in the warm Sacramento Valley, may require 80 days to mature in Corvallis, Oregon, or 100 days in Seattle, Washington.

Knowing even the approximate growing period can be useful to gardeners in hot climates, who can plant early varieties at the beginning of the season so that they can be harvested before the really hot weather arrives. An early, sixty-day pepper, planted under plastic tunnels in California or Florida in December or January, will mature in March. However, if this same variety is planted in late spring, it might mature in 50 days or less but with an underdeveloped plant and small, sunburned pods.

Many new varieties of peppers are hybrids that are superior to the older variety of the same or similar name. Hybrid varieties often have resistance to one or more diseases, grow rapidly, and produce more uniform pods than the older variety. Hybrids usually cost more, but for most gardeners, the disease resistance alone is worth the additional cost. This is especially true for organic gardeners, who eschew pesticides. Hybrids do not reproduce true to type because they are first-generation crosses, so saving the seed produced by hybrid plants is not worthwhile.

Here are some hints about how to choose the varieties to grow. First, know your own needs. Pepper enthusiasts John and Ann Swan of West Chester, Pennsylvania, put it this way: "Before we order seeds, we decide how many fruits of each variety we will need to grow for our own kitchen and for the Pennsylvania Horticultural Society's Harvest Show. Then we project how many plants we will need to produce that number. Finally, we add a few varieties that we've never grown before."

Keep records about the pepper garden, especially a list of varieties planted and which ones performed well. Use a loose-leaf or bound notebook rather than individual notes, to prevent losing important information. Record when the seeds or transplants were planted, how many pods were produced, and when they matured. Also record any disease problems, unusual weather, insect infestations, or any other observations that are significant. At the end of the growing season, you can review these records and determine the best-performing varieties. Then you can eliminate the poor ones and replace them with others the following year.

Cooked beans: black (left), pinto (middle), and kidney (right).

Other plants in the garden

Another important factor in planning the crop is the selection of accompanying plants in the garden. Because most people grow peppers for their culinary use, it makes sense to select other vegetables and herbs that blend harmoniously with peppers in meals, especially if peppers are a primary crop in the garden. Peppers are, of course, consumed by themselves in fresh or pickled form. But their most common use is in combination with other foods. We conducted an informal survey of books with collections of hot and spicy recipes to determine which vegetables and herbs are most commonly combined with peppers. Based on the results of that survey, gardeners should use the following list, along with their own tastes, to select the vegetables to accompany favorite peppers in the garden.

BASIL. This herb adds flavor to hot and spicy Italian sauces, and can be combined with fresh green chile peppers such as New Mexican, serranos, and jalapeños to make powerful pestos. It also flavors stuffed bell or pimiento peppers. Purple basil is a dramatic garden plant, so choose a variety like 'Dark Opal' or 'Purple Ruffles'.

BEANS. The combination of beans and peppers is traditional. Green beans are often seasoned, but the most common blend is pinto beans and the red pods or powders of anchos, pasillas, chipotles, or New Mexican varieties.

CARROTS. This root crop is pickled with peppers, cooked with small hot peppers and dill, and used as a base for habanero pepper sauces.

CAULIFLOWER. Used raw, cauliflower often accompanies peppers in pickled or marinated vegetable combinations.

CILANTRO. Also called coriander leaf, this herb is the principal seasoning in fresh Mexican and southwestern salsas. It combines well with serranos, jalapeños, habaneros, and piquins. Be sure to buy a slow-bolt variety such as 'Santo'.

CORN. When processed into meal and then tortillas, corn with chile peppers is a traditional combination, appearing as tacos and enchiladas. However, fresh corn is often cooked with New Mexican green varieties and is also used in fresh salsas. That said, corn takes up a lot of room in the home garden and uses a lot of water, so think twice about planting much of it.

CUMIN. The seeds of this herb are commonly used to spice Mexican and southwestern cooked chile pepper sauces.

EGGPLANTS. Fellow members of the family Solanaceae, eggplants and peppers are often combined in casseroles. Our advice is to experiment with heirloom varieties and their entertaining fruit shapes.

GARLIC. The bulbs of this pungent herb are commonly combined with peppers in salsas, sauces, pickles, chutneys, salads, soups, and curries. Hundreds of varieties of garlic are available, and you can select garlic by its flavor profile.

JICAMA. A favorite salad ingredient in the Southwest and Mexico, jicama is often sprinkled first with lime juice and then with red chile powder.

LETTUCE. Gardeners have fun growing various types of exotic lettuce and combining them in salads with bell peppers, pimientos, and sometimes hotter peppers.

ONIONS. Onions are probably the vegetable most commonly combined with peppers. They are used in sauces, salsas, salads, pickles, and casseroles. Gardeners must decide whether they really want to grow onions, because they are so commonly available and take up room in the garden that might be used for more pepper varieties.

OREGANO. Mexican oregano (*Lippia graveolens* and *L. palmeri*) is commonly combined with Mexican peppers in salsas, sauces, stews, soups, and combination dishes.

POTATOES. Another ancient combination, this time from South America, is potatoes and peppers.

Cilantro.

Cooked potatoes are commonly topped with chile powders and sauces. However, like corn and onions, they take up a lot of room in the home garden.

SPINACH. Like lettuce, spinach combines with peppers in salads. However, it is also cooked with New Mexican varieties in dishes such as *quelites*.

Jicama.

Tomatillo.

with fresh hot peppers such as serranos and jalapeños in salsas and sauces.

TOMATOES. Many different varieties of tomatoes blend with peppers in salads, salsas, sauces, casseroles, and numerous combination dishes. We recommend heirloom varieties because we believe their fruits not only taste better than the usual commercial varieties but also are more interesting and colorful.

GARDEN DESIGN

After choosing the varieties of peppers to plant, along with accompanying plants, the gardener must next plan the garden. Many considerations affect garden design, including site, soil type, rainfall, method of irrigation, mature height of various plants, need for structural support for plants like pole beans and tomatoes, and access to the garden for weeding and

SQUASH. Varieties of squash, such as zucchini and crookneck, are often cooked with fresh hot peppers. Winter squash and pumpkins are baked with chile powders.

TOMATILLOS. These small husk tomatoes are popular in the Southwest and Mexico. They combine

Chile field, Deming, New Mexico.

FAR LEFT **Rows and furrows.**

LEFT **Flat bed.**

harvesting. Following are descriptions of the most commonly used pepper garden designs, along with their benefits and drawbacks.

Ridges and furrows

Perhaps the most familiar of all garden designs, this type has alternating ridges (or hills) and furrows (or trenches). The plants grow along the ridges and are irrigated from the furrows. This method works well for commercial growers, who must use farm equipment to plow, till, weed, and apply fertilizers, herbicides, and insecticides. The furrows are very handy for quick irrigating, too. Ridges and furrows are also useful in regions with heavy rainfall because the moisture tends to drain off the ridges and into the furrows.

For the home gardener, however, the ridges-and-furrows design has some drawbacks. It wastes space, and plants cannot be packed efficiently into smaller gardens. In desert regions, the ridges tend to draw salts to their peaks that injure the plants. Also, unless proper mulch is used, the ridges tend to dry out quickly.

Flat beds

This garden design is perhaps the simplest to construct. After soil preparation, the site is surrounded by a berm (raised soil) that will hold water during flood irrigating or after rainfall. The interior part of the flat bed is carefully leveled to avoid high spots, which will dry out too quickly. The flat beds should be only about four feet wide to allow easy access for weeding and harvesting.

The advantages of flat beds are that they tend to hold water better than ridges and furrows, and the beds use space more efficiently. Yields of peppers tend to be larger because more plants can fit into the available space. A disadvantage is the relative difficulty of accessing the plants; without furrows, there are no walkways to them. Another disadvantage is that the necessity of level beds precludes their use on sloping sites.

Raised beds

Used primarily for good drainage, this

ABOVE DeWitt's raised bed with black plastic mulch.

BELOW A multi-tiered raised bed before filling with soil.

aboveground system uses bricks, cinder blocks, logs, or wood planks to contain the garden above the usual soil level. A well-drained soil mixture is filled into the huge container. This design is often used in damp climates or in places where the soil contains a lot of clay.

There are a couple of drawbacks to this system: it can dry out quickly, and the material retaining the beds must be maintained. However, raised beds can be irrigated easily with drip hoses, a simple solution.

Sunken beds

This design, used by the ancient Egyptians as well as the Zunis in New Mexico, is the opposite of ridges and furrows. The plants are placed in the furrows, where they are protected from high winds until they are well established. The disadvantage to this system is that the plants are placed where the most water accumulates, so the garden must be well drained.

Modified irrigated beds

After years of growing peppers in small plots in the Southwest, we have developed a system that works well because it allows us to grow peppers with most of the other vegetables and herbs mentioned earlier. It also maximizes space in a narrow garden, provides excellent access, and allows quick and efficient irrigation. Essentially, it combines elements of both ridges and furrows and flat beds, and can be used in gardens with a slight slope.

A brick, stone, or concrete walkway down the center of the garden allows easy access. In the plot on each side of the walkway, a shallow center furrow is cut to provide irrigation. From these center furrows, side furrows are cut so that the plants have their own slightly raised beds that are not as tall as conventional ridges. During irrigation, these small beds will usually be surrounded by water on three sides.

Irrigation is easy because the hose is placed at one end of each bed, and the furrows quickly fill. The gardener can control the spread of water in sloping gardens with small dams made from soil or sections of two-by-fours.

This design will also work in wetter regions if the soil is well drained. In extremely wet regions, a flat bed without furrows is better. One drawback is that the walkway takes up a lot of space; however, it is relatively weed-free and can be utilized during irrigation.

After choosing the design of the pepper garden, the gardener should prepare a scale drawing and choose locations for the peppers and accompanying plants. The next steps involve improving the garden site.

COMPOSTING

The key to a great pepper garden is the addition of compost, which improves workability, water-holding capability, drainage, and fertility of the soil. Many gardeners have no choice about composting because many landfills across the country do not accept organic yard refuse such as grass clippings. Thus, composting is a necessity.

Composting is the process whereby organic material decomposes into humus, with the help of microorganisms, insects, earthworms, and water. Also necessary is oxygen, for anaerobic decomposition is a slow process that causes foul odors.

Several books have been written on composting, which seems to indicate that the process is enormously complicated. In reality, composting is quite simple, and a compost

ABOVE "Waffle gardens," sunken beds used by the Zunis, Zuni Pueblo, 1925.

LEFT Modified irrigated bed with newspaper mulch.

Redwood compost bins with removable front slats.

pile should always be a part of pepper gardening. Following are the procedures for easy composting.

Site selection

Several criteria are important for selecting a good site for the compost pile: ample available water, an inconspicuous location convenient to the garden, and at least six hours of sunlight a day.

Compost containers

A compost pile can be just that—a pile of organic material. However, such piles are sloppy and difficult to control, so most gardeners prefer to use containers or bins for composting. The simplest containers are holes in the ground, or trenches, but the compost in them is difficult to turn and to remove.

Containers can be constructed from a wide variety of materials, but in all cases they should be enclosed on three sides, leaving the front and top open. Some suggested container materials include wire screening, wooden slats or pallets, cinder blocks or bricks without mortar, and snow fencing. Some sources suggest that piles can be as large as ten feet long and five feet high, but such large piles are difficult to maintain. The ideal pile in a bin or container is three feet high by three feet wide. Anything larger is difficult to turn and tends to compact too much, preventing oxygen from reaching all parts of the pile. If you have too much organic material, start another pile.

Materials to compost

These materials make good compost: coffee grounds, corn stalks and leaves, egg shells, garden plants killed by frost, grass clippings, kitchen scraps (fruits and vegetables), leaves, manure from herbivores, pine needles, sawdust, shredded newspaper (no color pages), straw, and weeds (unseeded).

These materials are *unacceptable* for compost: bones, branches from trees and shrubs, colored newsprint, diseased garden plants, fats and grease, grass clippings treated with herbicides, kitty litter, magazine pages, manure from carnivores like pets, meat, plastics, synthetic products, and wood ashes.

It is important that dissimilar materials be added in layers. For example, the pile should not consist solely of grass clippings, which tend to pack together and prevent air circulation. Rather, the clippings should be interspersed with layers of other materials.

Most sources on composting insist that garden soil must be added to the pile to introduce microorganisms. But Dr. Clarence Goluke, an engineer who researched composting at the University of California at Berkeley, discovered that bacteria and fungal spores occur naturally in the air and on just about any organic material, so adding soil to the pile to "inoculate" it is superfluous. It does not hurt the pile to add soil, but soil does not speed up composting at all and will make the pile bulkier.

Dr. Gouleke also discovered that the process of shredding all materials into tiny particles is overrated. Yes, shredding makes the pile smaller, but it is not necessary for large, soft materials such as weed stems or heads of cabbage. Shredding should only be used for large, hard materials such as tree branches, which can be used as mulch in the garden.

Many sources state that the compost pile needs manure in order to add sufficient nitrogen and make the pile heat up. Actually, green matter such as grass clippings will do a good job when applied in a ratio of one part green material to three parts brown (dried) material.

The question of whether or not compost provides enough natural fertilizer to the garden is much debated. Some sources insist that compost is actually a soil dressing, not a fertilizer, and that a pint of high-nitrogen fertilizer such as a 12-12-12 (N-P-K) or 10-6-4 should be included each time a layer is added to the pile.

They state that the fertilizer not only adds nitrogen, which speeds decomposition, but also adds valuable nutrients missing from the compost.

Organic gardeners disagree and avoid using chemical fertilizers, preferring to add aged manure to the compost pile or directly in the garden. While organic gardeners concede the point that most compost is low in soluble nitrogen, potassium, and phosphorous, gardening writer Jack Ruttle observes: "I have grown many fine vegetable gardens with no other fertilizer than an inch or two of pure compost applied once a year, and I have known plenty of other gardeners who do the same." Since peppers do not need high amounts of nitrogen, compost and manure generally provide enough nutrition for the plants.

The composting process

Microorganisms decompose the plant material (which is mostly carbon), producing carbon dioxide and heat. As the pile rots, the temperature of the pile may reach 160°F. This heat tends to kill weed seeds and disease organisms. Still, some parts of the pile may remain cooler, so the pile should be turned to ensure that all parts heat up. Another reason for turning the compost is to speed up the decomposition process. Each turning cuts the rotting time approximately in half, but unturned piles will be ready in about a year, and the compost will be just as good. The determination of how often to turn the pile depends upon how quickly the compost is needed in the garden.

Keep the pile covered and protected from rainwater, for the water will leach out

COMPOST TROUBLESHOOTING

Here are common composting problems and their solutions:

The pile has a strong odor. The pile is too wet or has insufficient oxygen, so add dry materials or turn the pile.

The pile is damp but produces heat. There is insufficient nitrogen, so add grass clippings or other green matter.

The pile is too acidic. Add lime.

The pile is dry and not composting. Add water.

The pile is too hot and starts burning. Turn the pile more often.

The pile has an ammonia smell. There is too much nitrogen, so add sawdust, dry leaves, or other high-carbon materials, and turn the pile.

potassium and nitrogen. Water the pile with a hose until there is runoff. It should be moist and springy to the touch—like a damp sponge. Then cover the pile with plastic sheeting.

Applying the compost

Some gardeners sift the compost from their bins through a half-inch mesh screen and return larger particles to the pile for further decomposition. Compost should be applied at the rate of one to four bushels per 100 square feet of garden and then rototilled into the soil. During the growing season a layer 2 or 3 inches thick can be used as a mulch if desired.

SOIL AND GARDEN PREPARATION

Before adding compost, the pepper gardener should determine what type of soil exists at the site and what steps, other than adding compost, might be necessary to achieve pepper-growing perfection.

The ideal pepper soil

It is unlikely that the perfect soil for growing peppers exists in the natural state anywhere, so some soil treatment will undoubtedly be necessary. Generally speaking, the best pepper-growing plot has several characteristics:
- a warm, full-sun location
- well-drained loam or sandy loam high in organic material but with moderate fertility
- an herbicide-free environment
- little or no alkali
- a pH registering from 6.0 to 8.0 (ideally 6.7 to 7.3)

Soil testing

Home gardeners commonly apply fertilizers, lime, sulfur, or other materials indiscriminately to their garden plots and believe in the old adage that if one pound is good, two must be better. Usually, such applications do more harm than good. Gardeners who have any doubts about their soil should have it tested to determine which soil enhancers to apply. Such tests will determine whether a problem in growing healthy plants is due to nutrition or to a physical defect in the soil, such as poor texture or chemicals.

The first step is to contact county extension

agents and request their information, procedures, and forms for soil testing. In some states, it will be necessary to contact the soil- and water-testing laboratories or agronomy departments of state agricultural universities. Generally speaking, home soil-testing kits are designed for eastern soils and are not accurate for western soils.

Taking soil samples from the garden is a simple procedure. The best method is to take six samples from various parts of the garden and combine them into a composite sample. First, remove any surface litter such as leaves and old stalks. To collect the samples, use either a soil auger or a small shovel and dig down about six to eight inches. Ideally, each sample should measure six to eight inches long and about one-half to one inch wide. Combine the samples in a clean pail or box and mix them together thoroughly. Break up any lumps and allow the composite sample to dry at room temperature. Remove stones and debris and crush the soil so that there are uniform small grains but do not pulverize completely. Label the sample, fill out the appropriate form received from the county agent, and mail it.

The soil sample report will typically give information about soil type or texture, pH, salinity (expressed as electroconductivity), percentage of organic matter, and fertility status as indicated by the levels of nitrogen, potassium, and phosphorous. Some reports do not give nitrogen content because it is assumed that yearly additions of nitrogen to the garden are necessary. The report will usually make recommendations about what to add to the soil to

Home soil-testing kit.

improve its condition. It will probably *not* report about drainage, the amount of irrigation needed, or the presence of pesticides or herbicides. In some states, specialized tests also report on zinc, manganese, copper, boron, sulfates, and silt.

Solarizing the soil

Solarization uses the sun's energy to pasteurize the soil. Temperatures in excess of 125°F will kill soilborne pests, including pathogens, nematodes, insects, and weed seeds up to 4 inches below the soil surface, but it takes 4 to 6 weeks of very sunny weather to eliminate disease-causing organisms at greater depths. The soil solarization method has been demonstrated to be very effective for small garden areas, and the technique is commonly used in integrated pest management systems. The only drawback to solarization is that it should be done in the summer, when air temperatures are high and solar radiation is intense, so it is usually applied to fallow plots. In the Southwest, the method will work during the late spring, summer, and early fall.

The soil to be treated should be cleared of plant material, loosened, watered, and covered with a thin, clear polyethylene film. Use clear film rather than black film, because the clear plastic will transmit more solar radiation and increase the temperature of the soil. The thinnest film available (4 mill, or 4/1000 of an inch) is the most effective and least expensive to use. The edges of the plastic film should be sealed with a layer of soil to prevent heat loss and to retain moisture.

The soil should be kept damp for the duration of the solarization, because moist soil has improved heat conduction and hot, damp soil

kills more resting fungal spores than dry soil. A single deep irrigation may be sufficient, but additional moisture will enhance the treatment. A soaker hose can be left under the film if additional watering is needed.

The longer the solarization period, the greater the kill of organisms will be, especially at greater depths. Solarizing for several weeks is recommended. Remember that solarized soil can become re-infested if contaminated soil is brought into the plot by dirty shoes or tools, so clean all garden shoes and disinfect rototiller blades, shovels, and hoes with flames from a propane torch before using them.

Solarization also works well for preparing small amounts of garden soil that will be used for potted plants. Fill a large zip bag with garden soil and place it in direct sun for several weeks, and the soil will become pasteurized.

Correcting problem soils

Based on the soil sample report and your own experience, you can take some steps to improve the soil for growing peppers and other vegetables.

ACIDIC SOILS. Soils with a low pH can be treated with lime or dolomite to neutralize them. After the pH of the soil is determined, follow the manufacturer's directions for the application of lime.

ALKALINE SOILS. These soils have heavy accumulations of calcium carbonate (lime), which raises the pH to unacceptably high levels. The addition of peat moss, which is slightly acidic, can help neutralize alkaline soils. The application of

Solarizing the soil with clear plastic sheeting.

organic material also helps improve the workability of alkaline soils.

SALINE SOILS. This condition is caused by shallow irrigating and overfertilization, which causes salts such as sodium bicarbonate, sodium chloride, and magnesium sulfate (which are all present in the irrigation water) to accumulate as a crust on the soil that burns foliage and kills plants. Usually, saline soils are a problem in climates in which rainfall is insufficient to leach the salts out of the soil. The only solution to saline soils is good drainage and heavy irrigation to dissolve and remove the salts.

SANDY SOILS. These soils drain quickly and dry out too fast. Adding compost or other organic material such as aged manure will bind sand particles together, decreasing erosion and assisting in water retention.

CLAY SOILS. The small particles of clay tend to compact and prevent drainage and aeration. The addition of compost, or other organic material such as aged manure, clusters the small clay particles into lumps that will improve drainage and aeration and will make the soil easier to work and more friable (easily crumbled). Also, adding about 2 inches of coarse sand to clay soil will increase drainage. *Never* add sand without also adding organic material, or a low-grade cement may form in the garden!

LOW-NUTRIENT SOILS. The most commonly applied organic nutrients, besides compost, are manures from herbivores such as horses, cattle, goats, poultry, hogs, rabbits, and sheep. Green manure is high in ammonia and can burn young plants, so it should not be used. Aged or composted steer manure provides low to moderate applications of nitrogen, potassium, and phosphorous, and can be applied at the rate of 500 to 1000 pounds per 1000 square feet of garden. Poultry, rabbit, sheep, and goat manures are higher in nutrient content and should be applied at the rate of 200 to 400 pounds per 1000 square feet of garden.

POORLY DRAINED SOILS. Since one of the most common causes of disease in peppers is fungal infection of the roots caused by poor drainage, it makes sense to have optimum drainage in the garden. Some gardeners, those with soils high in clay or who live in locations with a high water table, actually go to the trouble of creating a scree for drainage. Screes are thick layers of crushed rock (or gravel) and sand that are constructed beneath the garden to drain water from the plant roots. They are used to build rock or cactus gardens in wet areas and for growing alpine plants, which also need good drainage. However, screes are extremely labor-intensive to build, and raised beds are probably a better solution.

Under extreme conditions, no amount of drainage can prevent disaster. In the summer of 1992, Rick DeWitt's pepper garden in Sarasota, Florida, which was planted in sandy, well-drained soil, was destroyed by 17 inches of rain that fell in just 2 days. Entire fields of New Mexican chiles in southern New Mexico are wiped out by *Phytophthora* wilt when summer storms dump too much water on already irrigated fields. In these cases, no amount of drainage is adequate to deal with the moisture.

When care is taken to improve the soil and provide the best drainage possible, great pepper plants are usually the result. Since you have now selected the varieties, planned the garden, started composting, and improved the soil, it is time to germinate the seeds and get the planting started.

SEEDS AND SEEDLINGS

A pepper garden can only be as good as the original genetic material used to start it—the seed. Bad seed produces unsatisfactory results, no matter how skilled the gardener is. At least good seed stands a chance of producing excellent plants and pods.

One of the biggest disappointments for the pepper gardener is discovering that the seed planted does not produce the pods it is supposed to produce. Instead of jalapeños, say,

the gardener finds an unrecognizable hybrid and realizes that time and energy has been wasted by growing this plant. Therefore, the first step toward a great pepper garden is to select good seed.

Selecting seed
Pepper growers can start with seeds that are either homegrown or obtained from a seed company.

HOMEGROWN SEEDS. Home gardeners often produce unwanted hybrids (outcrosses) because peppers are notorious cross-pollinators. When different varieties are planted close together in the garden, bees and other insects will carry pollen from flower to flower, cross-pollinating them. The pods of the current year's plants will be true, but the seed in those pods will produce hybrids thereafter.

For seed that is true to type, individual varieties must be pollinated only by their own pollen. Commercial seed producers avoid cross-pollination by isolating varieties and planting them at least a mile from each other, which is farther than the average bee flies. Home gardeners can produce true seed by isolating peppers from insects and growing them in greenhouses or under netting. These techniques are described later under "Breeding and Hybridization."

Many pepper gardeners exchange seed with other growers, but this seed may also not grow true to type. Home growers can either ask the sender how the seed was grown, or plant it and see what happens. Gardeners and seed

Capsicum pubescens seedlings.

collectors from all over the world send us seed, and the more unusual the variety is, the greater our temptation is to grow it regardless of origin.

COMMERCIAL SEED. Seed produced by seed companies is generally more reliable than homegrown seed, because the companies try to safeguard the genetic purity of the cultivar. They use a systematic seed-growing process, which begins with crop improvement associations in each state. In the association, a plant breeder responsible for developing a specific variety of pepper or other crop produces small quantities of breeder seed. This is multiplied into foundation seed, which is controlled by the crop improvement association. The association grows the foundation seed to produce registered seed, which is sold to seed companies to produce certified seed for farmers and the general public.

Large seed companies have their own internal process, which mirrors the one used by crop improvement associations. Company plant breeders develop breeder seed and foundation seed for specific varieties. It is then passed on to company seed production managers, who oversee the growing of registered and certified seed. In some cases, the production of certified seed is farmed out to independent growers on farms distant from each other to avoid cross-pollination.

Unfortunately, some small seed companies and cottage seed industries either do not practice proper isolation techniques or buy their seed from growers who do not. Thus, their seed is undependable and often yields hybrids. Home gardeners should either question small seed

Seeds in zip bags from home growers.

companies about their isolation techniques or confine seed purchases to the major companies. Always buy seed from a reliable seedsman, one who consistently provides varieties true to type,

ANATOMY OF A SEED.

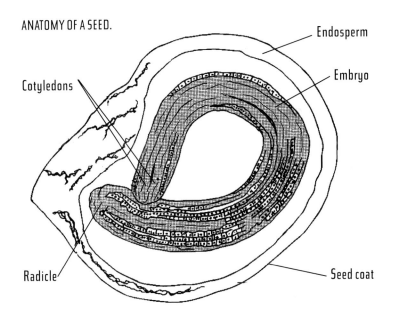

Endosperm

Embryo

Cotyledons

Radicle

Seed coat

Courtesy of the Chile Pepper Institute.

Emerging seedling.

free from disease, and with a high germination percentage. High-quality, fresh seed is dependable; cheap seed is neither dependable nor inexpensive.

Growers should check the seed packet for a germination percentage when buying commercial seed. The federal pepper regulations are as follows: seeds with a germination percentage below 55 cannot be sold; seeds with a percentage between 55 and 85 must have the percentage listed on the packet; and seeds with a germination percentage above 85 percent need not have the percentage listed.

Inspecting and testing seed

Once the seeds of the selected varieties are in hand, there are several easy culling techniques to increase germination percentage and potential seedling vigor. First, place the seeds in a jar of water and discard any that float. These are damaged, partial seeds and those lacking embryos. Next, inspect the seeds, preferably under a magnifying glass, and remove any that are undersized, shriveled, discolored, cracked, or otherwise damaged.

Some pepper growers, especially those who use direct seeding methods, like to know the expected germination percentage for each variety, so they conduct a germination test in the late winter. To conduct this test, place the seed between damp (not sopping wet) layers of paper towels, with no two seeds touching. Transfer the layers of towels to a plastic zip bag and then set it on something warm, such as heating cables, or on top of the hot water heater or refrigerator. After 2 weeks have passed, enough time for the average pepper seed to sprout, open the bag and count the sprouted seeds. Divide the number of sprouted seeds by the total number of seeds used, to arrive at the approximate germination percentage. There are seed-testing laboratories in every state that will conduct this test for a fee, but allow the agency at least two months to run the test.

Factors affecting seed germination

Pepper seed germination even under optimum conditions is often slow and irregular. Although some studies have shown that pepper seeds germinate very quickly and have very high germination percentages under high temperatures, some exotic varieties we've grown have taken more than 5 weeks to germinate at ideal temperatures.

Basically, pepper seeds need warmth, oxygen, and moisture to germinate. However, home gardeners should consider other factors that influence germination before planting seed.

POD MATURITY, SEED DORMANCY, AND AFTER RIPENING.
The maturity of the pods at the time seed
is extracted greatly influences germination.
Immature pods usually produce infertile seed,
which will not germinate. In a 1986 study
conducted at the Louisiana Agricultural
Experiment Station, R. L. Edwards and F.
J. Sundstrom extracted seed from red and
orange pods of tabasco peppers harvested 150,
195, and 240 days after transplanting. They
tested the seed for germination percentage and
found, as expected, that seed from the red pods
outperformed seed from the orange pods in all
cases. However, they also discovered that the
germination performance of seed from the red
pods decreased as the season progressed; the 81
percent germination at 150 days dropped to 63
percent at 240 days. This study indicates that
seeds from the earliest-picked red pods will have
the highest germination percentage, at least for
tabasco peppers.

Some peppers, like other perennials,
produce seed that does not immediately germinate when extracted from the fresh pods and
planted, even though all environmental factors
favor germination. This survival mechanism,
called dormancy, helps prevent germination in
the fall, just before cold weather would kill the
seedlings. However, because peppers are perennials that are grown as annuals in temperate
climates, the degree of dormancy varies from
variety to variety. The strongest dormancy
appears in wild varieties, such as chiltepíns,
which overwinter well. Hybrids, grown as annuals, have the weakest degree of dormancy.

In the same 1986 study, Edwards and

Extreme
germination.

Sundstrom also tested the process called after-
ripening, which is the gradual drying of seed
so that its moisture content drops from about
34 percent to 7 percent during a 3-week period.
In one test, the germination percentage of seed
from red pods increased from 58 percent to
94 percent after 3 weeks of after-ripening. No
significant effect of after-ripening on seed from
immature pods occurred.

This study, combined with our observations over the years, indicates that the highest
germination percentage occurs in pepper seed
harvested from early red pods that are dried for
one to four months. Some varieties have other
colors at maturity, such as orange or yellow, so
growers should pick these pods for seeds when
that color reaches its deepest hue.

TEMPERATURE AND IRRIGATION. During the winter
of 1934–35, H. L. Cochran of the Georgia
Experiment Station conducted a classic study
of the effects of temperature and irrigation on
the germination of bell pepper seed. Two flats

of seeds were placed in each of five greenhouses that were kept at the following temperature ranges (°F): 40–50, 50–60, 60–70, 70–80, and 90–100. In each greenhouse, one of the flats was surface irrigated by a simple watering can, and the other was sub-irrigated by placing it in an inch of water in a large tank until the soil had taken up enough water to dampen the surface.

Both the percentage and speed of germination increased dramatically as the temperature increased. No seeds germinated at 40–50°, and the percentage increased from 59 percent at 50–60° to 74 percent at 90–100°. The rate of seedling emergence also dropped from 30 to 6 days at those same temperature ranges. Also interesting was the fact that seeds that did not germinate after 45 days at 40–50° sprouted in 6 days when transferred to the 90–100° greenhouse.

The highest germination percentage occurred at 70–80° (79.5 percent), and the quickest germination occurred at 90–100° (6 days, 73 percent). Watering by sub-irrigation reduced the germination percentage at all temperatures, probably because that procedure reduced the soil temperature more than did surface irrigation.

The inescapable conclusion from Cochran's experiment, and many subsequent ones, is that for optimum germination, pepper seed should be grown at 70°F or more and should be watered with warm water from the top.

PREPLANTING TREATMENTS. Cochran also experimented with soaking some of the seeds in water before planting, but he soaked them for only 6 hours.

Soaking the seeds for 2 or 3 days can sometimes aid the germination rate and percentage, but probably not a significant amount.

Germination problems often occur in pepper seeds with a particularly tough seed coat, such as wild varieties like the chiltepín. Growers should soak the seeds for 5 minutes in a 10 percent bleach solution, rinse well, and then plant. This procedure will soften the seed coat so the seed will germinate more quickly. If the seed has not germinated in 14 days, the bleach treatment can be repeated.

Another treatment that increases the germination rate and percentage in peppers is soaking seed in gibberellin, a plant hormone. Seed should be soaked for 1 to 2 hours in a 100-parts-per-million (ppm) solution. Gibberellin is available from Internet garden shops—do a search for it.

Peppers are susceptible to plant pathogens on the seed coat such as bacterial leaf spot and tobacco mosaic virus. Fortunately, a relatively simple procedure will remove these pathogens. First, soak the seeds for a half hour in a 10 percent (weight to volume) trisodium phosphate (TSP) solution. (TSP is available at most hardware stores as a wall cleaner.) After soaking, rinse the seeds thoroughly in cold running water. Second, soak the seeds in a 10 percent bleach solution for 5 minutes, then rise thoroughly in cold running water until all the bleach odor is gone. Dry the seed and sow within a month of treatment. Harald Zoschke, a German chile expert, has good luck soaking his seeds in chamomile tea.

One of the most ingenious preplanting

treatments we've come across is the technique developed by Charlie Ward of Virginia Beach, Virginia. Charlie was bothered by the low germination rates of chiltepín seeds and then read an article about the spread of chiltepíns by birds. He decided to prepare a treatment that simulated the alimentary canal of birds. He gathered seagull excrement, which is plentiful in Virginia Beach, then made a slurry out of the excrement and water, added the seeds, and let the mixture sit in the sun for a few days. After extracting the seeds with forceps and planting them, Charlie discovered that his germination rate increased to 95 percent!

Such a technique can be used by pepper gardeners who also raise birds such as parrots, finches, and canaries. These birds will readily eat small red pods, because they contain pigments which improve the coloration of the birds' plumage. The droppings can be collected on newspaper and the seeds can be removed and planted.

Seedling growing environments

An ideal pepper-growing environment is one that provides optimum levels of light, heat, moisture, and oxygen. The home gardener has a number of options to choose from, but not all of the environments (cold frames, for example) will keep the seeds warm enough for quick, high-percentage germination. We advise growers to use heating cables under their growing containers in all environments. The plastic-covered cables will keep the soil temperature stable, usually between 70 and 80°F, and are equipped with a thermostat that shuts off the heat when

the preset temperature is reached. Master gardener Carolyn Esparsen suggests that if cables are not available, you can simply place the growing containers on top of a refrigerator. Suppliers now offer propagation mats that keep the temperature at 75°F, but they are more expensive than cables.

GREENHOUSES AND WINDOW GREENHOUSES. Heated greenhouses are probably best for starting seeds indoors. Gardeners fortunate enough to have a greenhouse enjoy plenty of diffused sunlight, heat from both solar gain and heaters, humidity from the proximity of other plants, and air circulation from fans. However, greenhouses also have a few drawbacks. Some greenhouses, especially those attached to the north side of a house, have low light duration and levels, causing the pepper seedlings to become leggy and topple over. In this case, the newest growth of the seedlings may need to

Seedlings in the greenhouse.

be pinched back to cause lateral growth and produce a bushier plant.

Some greenhouses, especially south-facing ones, may overheat during the spring and may need shading. Greenhouse supply stores and some nurseries sell shading cloth of various densities. Greenhouses also need adequate ventilation to avoid problems with damping off and stem rot.

Many gardening books suggest that windows are good places to germinate pepper seed and to grow seedlings, but this is simply not true. The amount of available light decreases through the windows as the sun rises higher in the sky and the days approach the summer solstice, resulting in spindly plants. Cats are another problem with windowsill cultivation, because they are notorious seedling

South-facing cold frame protected by house.

grazers and can quickly ruin the freshly-sprouted crop. Cold drafts at night and inadequate air circulation during the day also cause problems.

Window greenhouses, which extend outside the house, are much better than windowsills because they provide more light. They also cool down at night, so heating cables should be used under the containers. Unfortunately, window greenhouses lack the space to grow large numbers of seedlings and they tend to trap hot air, so they must be well ventilated. However, if used carefully, they are fine for the gardener raising only a few favorite peppers.

COLD FRAMES AND HOTBEDS. Cold frames are the second most efficient environment for growing seedlings and probably the least expensive to construct and operate. There are two types of cold frame: permanent ones and temporary ones that are dismantled after the seedlings are transplanted.

A cold frame is a wooden or brick box with a glass, plastic, or fiberglass top. Permanent cold frames can be constructed in various sizes, but about 3 feet wide and 6 feet long is average. However, gardeners should take into consideration that the average tray for six-pack cells measures 11 by 21 inches, so the cold frame should be constructed to accommodate multiples of these measurements or other dimensions of the growing containers.

The top of the cold frame can be made of old window sashes, or it can be a wooden frame covered with fiberglass or plastic film. Some greenhouse supply stores sell portable cold frames or premade sashes for cold frames. The top should be hinged so that it can be propped open during the day for ventilation. The cold frame should face south so that the top is angled to best catch the rays of the sun. It should be equipped with a thermometer and heating cables and should be sealed with weather stripping or caulking. Permanent cold frames should have good drainage and installed heating cables covered with wire screening and sand to insure even heating.

Temporary cold frames can be constructed of cinderblocks sealed with plastic film or from old lumber that can be knocked apart and stored after use. Both permanent and temporary cold frames can be insulated by mounding a berm of soil or sawdust around the frame. Electric light-bulbs can also be installed in cold frames for additional heating.

Hotbeds are simply cold frames with heating cables installed. They are doubly useful because they can quickly germinate seeds and grow seedlings, and then their heat can be turned off so that the seedlings can harden off. During a typical spring day, the cold frame should be opened when the sun's first rays strike it in the morning and closed in the late afternoon to retain the heat that has been absorbed inside the cold frame.

Some growers have their cold frames perform double duty in the winter as composting sites. Commonly composted materials such as kitchen vegetable scraps, rabbit manure, and other organic material is placed in the cold frame. Despite the cold outside temperatures, the solar gain in the cold frame causes the material to compost over the winter months so that it is ready for spring planting.

CONTAINERS UNDER ARTIFICIAL LIGHT. Some indoor gardeners do not even have an outdoor garden but rather raise their peppers from seedlings to fruiting plants in containers under artificial light. (See "Container Cultivation" for a complete discussion of this technique.) Outdoor gardeners without greenhouse or cold frame can successfully germinate seeds and grow seedlings under fluorescent lights.

All that is needed are one or two 4-foot-long fluorescent fixtures mounted on a stand or hung from the rod in a spare closet. Mail-order companies and retail shops sell a number of models of light stands on wheels. Any cool-white fluorescent bulb will work. The containers are placed beneath the lights so that when the seedlings germinate, they are only a few inches from the bulbs. The fluorescent bulbs will warm the containers but will not burn the tender foliage. The inverse square law applies here; doubling the distance between the bulbs and the plants results in only one-quarter of the amount of light reaching the foliage. Placing the seedlings too far from the bulbs will cause spindly plants.

Seedlings should grow well under artificial light, but they may become leggy and then need to be pinched back. Also, they are tempting targets for cats or pet birds to munch on. These seedlings will be more tender than those grown in a greenhouse or cold frame and may need a more careful process of hardening off, as they will be more susceptible to sunburn and wind damage.

Labeled seedlings in plastic six packs.

Seedling containers and growing media

Every pepper gardener has his or her own preference for the soil mixture and containers for raising seedlings. Soil mixtures range from commercial potting mixtures to garden soil to various blends of organic and inorganic materials. Containers vary from plastic six-pack cells to peat pots to clay pots. Some companies sell propagation systems that combine the elements of a cover, an insulated growing tray, capillary matting, and a water reservoir.

The key is to find the best mixture and containers for the environment in which the seedlings will sprout. For example, the combination of a peat pot and a loose mix might work well in humid areas but could dry out too quickly in arid environments.

CONTAINERS. Factors to consider when choosing containers include the number of seedlings that will be sprouted for each pepper variety, the size of seedlings when they are transplanted, and whether a one-step or two-step method will be used. In a one-step method, seedlings are usually raised in a peat pot or a cube of biodegradable materials that will disintegrate in the garden. In a two-step method, seedlings grow in six-pack cells until they have reached the four-to-five-leaf stage, then are transplanted into larger pots and from there set into the garden.

Home gardeners who grow only about two plants each of about five varieties will not have space problems, so they might as well plant seeds in 6-inch or larger plastic pots or peat pots and thin them to one plant per pot. Six-pack cells in plastic trays are by far the easiest and most space-effective containers to use when growing large quantities of many varieties of peppers.

One drawback of the six-pack cells is that the roots of the seedlings sometimes become cramped and start circling the inside of the cell. Root cramping sets back the seedling if the roots are not gently untangled. A root continues to grow in the direction it is set in the ground, so one that is not pointed outward will not grow out. Two more drawbacks should be noted. Root-bound plants tend to dry out and need water more often, and sometimes vigorously growing seedlings compete for sunlight as they bush out. The obvious solution here is to transplant cramped seedlings into larger containers.

Commercial nurseries use a slightly different two-step process: the seeds are germinated in open flats and the tender, two-leafed seedlings are transplanted into the six-pack cells after a couple of days. This method insures maximum utilization of the cells and avoids empty cells from nongerminating seeds.

GROWING MEDIA. The perfect germination and seedling growing medium has good drainage and aeration but also some moisture retention. The medium should promote rapid root expansion, which produces vigorous seedling foliage growth. The particles of the medium should be fairly large so that the medium does not pack together and allows the roots easy penetration. Dense or clay soils are the worst possible seedling growing media because the roots are drowned in water and receive no oxygen.

Although some growers believe that peppers should be germinated in the soil in which they will eventually live, we do not recommend using garden soil. It is usually too dense for the tender plants and may contain disease-bearing organisms. Gardeners who insist on using garden soil should sterilize it by baking it for at least an hour in the oven at 350°F. Then it should be mixed half and half with soil expanders such as as perlite or vermiculite.

A number of commercial media are on the market, notably Jiffy Mix and Pro-Mix, which are usually combinations of milled peat moss or sphagnum moss, fine vermiculite, and fertilizer. These pasteurized mixtures work well in most situations but sometimes are unavailable to the home gardener. In that case, the grower can prepare a custom seedling medium by mixing together readily available materials that meet the criteria of drainage, moisture retention, and aeration. For our medium, we

Simple seedling container in the Tobago Botanic Station.

use commercial, sterile potting soil, perlite, and vermiculite mixed in equal proportions. Coarse sand can be substituted for the perlite, but never use builders' sand (too fine) or ocean beach sand (too salty). Peat moss is difficult to wet, is too acid, and compacts badly, so use it sparingly. Potting soil and vermiculite hold moisture and nutrients, and the perlite prevents compaction, aids in drainage and aeration, and promotes root growth.

A suggested seedling propagation technique

We get excellent results from the technique described in the following paragraphs to grow seedlings for transplanting. Although we use it in semi-arid New Mexico, it should work equally well in other parts of the country. We use greenhouses for our growing environment.

About 6 to 8 weeks before transplanting, prepare six-pack cells by filling them with the suggested growing medium and place the cells in plastic trays. Place the trays on heating cables and plug in the cables. Water the cells with a diluted solution of Peters 20-20-20 fertilizer (½ teaspoon in 1 gallon of water) or a slow-release fertilizer like 10-10-10, because the medium has virtually no nutrients.

Select the seeds according to the criteria suggested earlier and use a preplanting treatment if you wish. With a stick or the eraser end of a pencil, punch a hole in each cell ¼ inch deep. Drop two or three seeds in each hole, then cover them with the planting medium. In each six pack, insert a plastic tag with the variety name and the date marked on it in permanent ink or pencil. Some growers keep a journal in which they record the variety name, date, number of seeds planted, and later, the germination percentage and other notes on the progress of each variety.

When the seeds sprout, cull all but the most vigorous seedlings from each cell by clipping them at the base with scissors. Gently water the cells from the top and make certain the cells are kept moist, but do not allow water to sit in the trays and keep the mixture soggy. If the seedlings are stressed at all by drying out or wilting, it will be difficult if not impossible to revive their normal growth. Make certain there is adequate ventilation and air circulation in the growing environment. Fertilize the six-packs once a week with the same mixture described earlier.

In a heated greenhouse, the heating cables can be turned off after the seeds have sprouted. But in a cold frame where the only heat is from the cables, the cables should be kept on until the nighttime temperatures warm above freezing.

Cigarette smokers should wash their hands with a strong soap or with rubbing alcohol before touching the seeds or seedlings. The tobacco in cigarettes may contain tobacco mosaic virus that can infect the pepper seeds or plants.

Avoiding pests and damping-off

The same friendly environment that promotes seedling growth also provides perfect breeding conditions for common greenhouse pests such as aphids, whiteflies, mealybugs, and spider mites. Aphids are probably the most common insect pest that attacks seedlings. Although spraying with dilute diazinon solution will kill them, it is not the best answer to the problem, because the chemicals can burn the leaves and stems of the seedlings and thus inhibit growth. A nontoxic method is to wash the aphids off the seedlings every day with a stream of water. This procedure is labor-intensive, but it works. Another method is to spray the seedlings with a solution of Ivory soap or Safer's insecticidal soap.

Mealybugs are soft-bodied insects that look like pieces of white fluff. They do not move around much, but once they are established they can suck plenty of sap out of pepper plants. The least toxic way to kill them is to touch them with a swab dipped in isopropyl alcohol.

Whiteflies, another common greenhouse pest, are more difficult to kill because they are so mobile. They can be controlled, but probably not eliminated, by closing up the greenhouse and fumigating it by spraying a flying insect insecticide. The greenhouse should be closed up for 10 minutes, then ventilated. Also useful are the sticky yellow cards that attract the flies and trap them.

By far the most difficult pests to control are spider mites, barely visible eight-legged arachnids that build small webs on the underside of leaves and thus are hard to spot. They can be controlled by spraying the underside of pepper leaves with insecticidal soap or diazinon, according to the manufacturer's instructions. We always prefer mechanical removal of pests by water spraying or gentle scraping to the application of chemical insecticides.

The most devastating problem of the humid greenhouse is damping-off, a fungal disease that causes the stem base to rot and the seedling to topple over. Damping-off can quickly wipe out an entire greenhouse of seedlings. The disease proliferates in still, very moist air, so the first line of defense is good air circulation. In humid growing environments, an extra fan in the greenhouse to blow air around is a necessity. The seedlings also can be treated with the fungicide benomyl according to the manufacturer's instructions.

Hardening off

In the protected environment of a greenhouse or cold frame, or indoors under lights, seedlings tend to grow rapidly and produce large cells with thin walls. This "soft growth," as it's called, has not prepared the pepper seedling for the rigors of the early spring garden. Its leaves are not accustomed to the strong ultraviolet rays of the sun, its stems are not strong enough to withstand high winds, its roots are not established enough for dry conditions, and

Whitefly: enemy of the seedling.

the entire plant is subject to low-temperature shock. Unless properly conditioned for the outside, pepper seedlings may be sunburned, wind whipped, and injured by low temperatures or even heavy rains.

The solution to the problem of shock during transplanting is a process called hardening off, whereby the seedlings are gradually made tough enough for the garden. Technically, hardening off is a physiological process that adds carbohydrate reserves to the plant and produces additional cuticle on the leaves, reducing water loss. Practically, the process slows plant growth while acclimating the seedling to harsher conditions.

A cold frame works best for the hardening-off process. The heating cables are turned off and the top is left open for progressively longer periods of time (all night when the temperatures are warm enough), enabling the seedlings to toughen in the sun, wind, and lower temperatures.

Greenhouse-grown plants, or those grown indoors under lights, are usually taken outside for increasingly long periods of time. Starting

Intercropping: congo peppers between rows of papaya plants, Tobago.

about 2 weeks before transplanting or about the date of the average last frost, move the trays outside to a location where they will receive partial sun. Bring them indoors at night but turn the greenhouse heaters off. Begin with only a few hours a day outside, but as the days go by, increase the amount of sun the seedlings receive and the length of time outdoors until they can be left out all day and night. Reducing the water to seedlings will also "harden" the plants. Allow the seedlings to wilt slightly before watering; after 2 weeks of this treatment they can be transplanted.

Transplanting

When seedlings are ready to transplant, the gardener must decide where to place the peppers within the basic layout planned earlier according to the criteria described under "Garden Design."

PLACING THE SEEDLINGS. Some growers avoid planting peppers in the same location two years in a row, but while crop rotation is crucial for commercial growers, it is merely advisable for home gardeners. If compost is added to the garden each year and there is no sign of disease, peppers can be grown for years in the same locations in the garden.

Many gardening authorities, especially those who favor all-organic techniques, instruct the grower to plant peppers with "companion plants" that are supposedly compatible with them. One book lists basil, carrots, eggplant, onions, parsley, and tomatoes as companion plants for peppers, and kohlrabi as a noncompatible plant. Unfortunately, such claims must be relegated to the domain of gardening lore because of the lack of scientific evidence to support them. In some cases, so-called companion plants for peppers, such as tomatoes and egglants, are closely related and share many of the same diseases and insect pests, so they can hardly be called good companions because one may infect another.

More reasonable is the concept of intercropping, where gardeners take into consideration such factors as how fast the various crops mature, the relative heights involved, and the positioning of light-demanding and shade-tolerant plants. For example, a row of shade-tolerant rocoto chile peppers or chiltepíns might be planted between two rows of corn.

For cultivating large numbers of peppers, the simplest method is to plant them in elevated rows or in clusters in raised beds. Whatever method is used, remember to label each variety or draw a diagram of the relative position of each variety for later use. It is frustrating to lose track of where you have planted a certain variety, especially in the early stages before the pods have matured.

BUYING TRANSPLANTS. Of course, we recommend that gardeners raise their own transplants from seed, but some people will be tempted by the healthy-looking seedlings available from commercial nurseries. The main drawback of nursery-grown transplants is the lack of variety of peppers available—usually only some bells and perhaps jalapeños and yellow wax peppers. However, Cross Country Nurseries (www.chile-plants.com) carries about five hundred varieties, and their bedding plants are large and strong. Also a problem is that some transplants are "forced" with high levels of nitrogen, resulting in tall plants with insufficient root growth. These plants may wilt severely during transplanting.

The opposite problem is too many roots, caused by seedlings that have been growing in cramped containers for too long. It takes longer for potbound seedlings to extend their roots into the garden soil, so they too are subject to wilting until they are established.

Most nurseries indicate that their seedlings are hardened off and ready for immediate transplanting. Instead of taking a chance and being disappointed, harden them off yourself for at least a week.

IN THE GARDEN. The ideal weather for transplanting is cool temperatures, cloudy skies, and little or no wind. After deciding the layout of the peppers, dig a small hole with a trowel slightly larger than the root ball of the seedling. Holding the seedling by its root ball (never by the stem or leaves if it can be avoided), place the seedling in the hole, fill the rest of the hole with garden soil, press the soil around the root ball and stem, and immediately water it.

Plant spacing depends on a number of factors, including the ultimate size of the varieties being grown. Smaller varieties, such as ornamentals, can be planted closer together than, say, ajís, which grow quite large. Arthur Pratt, a professor emeritus at Cornell University, suggests close spacing for peppers, placing them on 1-foot centers. "I do know that pepper plants grow almost twice as tall when they're tightly spaced," he told *Organic Gardening*, "and there's usually less sunscald on the fruit because they're better shaded by the leaves." Some commercial pepper growers space their plants as closely as 4 inches apart. Close spacing also helps to keep moisture under the canopy of leaves.

HOTCAPS. To protect seedlings from insects, wind, and cold temperatures, some gardeners set miniature greenhouses, known as hotcaps, over each seedling. Hotcaps can be purchased at garden stores in the form of waxed paper cones, or they can be fashioned from glass or plastic jugs. The bottoms of the jugs are cut off, and the remainder of the jug is set over the plant and pushed into the soil. The only problem with hotcaps is that on warm, sunny days they can hold so much heat they can cook the seedlings, so they must be removed during the day and replaced in the early evening.

Hotcaps.

BELOW Direct seeding.

John and Ann Swan, pepper growers in West Chester, Pennsylvania, cut the bottoms out of 6-inch plastic nursery pots and place one around each pepper seedling. "They shelter young seedlings not only from cutworms, but also from stem-whipping winds. The pots reflect and concentrate heat, and gives us a reservoir for watering." They also cover the plants with 3-gallon plastic nursery pots if nighttime temperatures fall too low.

Direct seeding

One of the most common weeds in the pepper garden is volunteer hybrid peppers from the previous year's fallen pods, which proves that direct seeding works. This technique is used mostly by commercial growers with acres of pepper plants who don't want to bother with raising transplants.

Direct seeding can be done by the home gardener. However, the technique is not recommended for climates with short growing seasons. The seed should be planted no more than ½ inch below the soil surface, and the row or grouping of peppers should be carefully marked to identify the variety.

THE GROWTH CYCLE

Generally speaking, we use organic techniques as much as possible, particularly by avoiding the use of pesticides and herbicides and practicing composting and mulching. A word of warning: the terms natural and organic are often bandied about in gardening discussions, and people assume that if things come from nature rather than being manufactured, they are obviously better. Here are some "natural" things to avoid:

- Nicotine sulfate, an organic pesticide, is the most hazardous botanical insecticide available to home gardeners.
- Rotenone, a natural insecticide permitted in organic gardening, is highly toxic to fish and is classified by the World Health Organization as a moderately hazardous substance.
- Pyrethrum, widely considered to be the safest organic insecticide, can easily kill bees.

We have some issues about naturally occurring organic fertilizers—including manure, fish emulsion, worm castings, peat, seaweed, sewage, and guano—being considered better than manufactured fertilizers. Our belief is that the essential macronutrients nitrogen, potassium, and phosphorus can be delivered to plants by either natural or manufactured fertilizers, and the plant does not favor one type of fertilizer over the other. That said, organic fertilizers work fine with pepper plants since they do not need a lot of fertilizing anyway, so if you believe that they are better, use them.

The advantages of mulching

Mulch is any material applied to the surface of the soil to retard the growth of weeds, conserve soil moisture, maintain a uniform soil temperature, and improve the appearance of the garden. There is no doubt that mulches increase the yield of pepper plants. Experiments in Canada by Stephen Monette and K. A. Stewart showed

Sign near Hatch, New Mexico.

that black plastic mulch increased bell pepper yield. The increase was due to more fruit being produced per plant rather than a greater weight per pod. Interestingly enough, they also discovered that protecting the pepper plants with a windbreak also increased the yield, but only when the peppers were not mulched.

A wide variety of mulches have been used with peppers, and determining the one that

Straw mulch.

is right for the home garden requires taking a number of factors into account, including climate, decomposition of the mulch, and the use of colored mulches to increase yield. Gardeners should remember that since mulching warm soils keeps them warm and mulching cold soils tends to keep them cold, the mulch should be applied after the soil warms.

ORGANIC MATERIALS. Lawn clippings, leaves, straw, compost, bark, wood chips, and pine needles have all been used to mulch peppers. They do not affect soil temperature very much, but they are effective in controlling weeds and maintaining moisture in the soil. They should only be used in regions wet enough to allow them to decompose into the soil. Otherwise, hard-to-decay materials such as wood or bark chips will have to be raked out of the plot each year before rototilling. Some growers believe that grass clippings are particularly helpful because thick layers of them can be thoroughly saturated to increase the humidity around pepper leaves and flowers in dry weather. However, this practice sometimes promotes pepper diseases.

CLEAR PLASTIC. This mulch warms the soil by about 10 to 12 degrees F but does not control weeds. It should not be used in hot climates. It is not biodegradable and must be removed at the end of the growing season.

BLACK PLASTIC. Excellent for controlling weeds, black plastic also warms the soil (up to 5 degrees F) and is good for moisture control. Most black plastic does not decompose and must be removed at the end of the growing season; however, there are some brands of black plastic that do decompose. Researchers at the University of New Hampshire have developed a black plastic mulch with the heat-transmitting qualities of clear plastic. This so-called IRT (infra-red transmitting) mulch is available from mail-order companies and garden shops.

FOILS AND COLORED PLASTIC. Louisiana researcher L. L. Black discovered that aluminum foil mulch produced higher yields of bell peppers than ordinary black plastic. Reflective mulches also drastically reduced aphid infestations in peppers, thus lowering the incidence of aphid-transmitted viruses, such as tobacco etch. Black's findings showed that plants in plots mulched with aluminum foil yielded 58 percent more than those in black plastic–mulched plots and 85 percent more than unmulched peppers (Black and Rolston 1972).

Further experiments by Wayne Porter and William Etzel (1982) at Louisiana State University confirmed that aluminum-colored plastic works very well as a pepper mulch. "The increased yields were probably due to increased light reflection of the aluminum-painted polyethylene," they wrote. Some gardeners have good luck with laying aluminum foil between their rows of peppers to increase available light. This practice should only be used in humid climates. If used in the Southwest, for example, with its dry air and high levels of ultraviolet light, the plants would bake.

Robert Dufault and Samuel Wiggins of the University of Vermont's Horticultural Research

Center experimented with white plastic mulches on bell peppers and discovered that the yield of white-mulched peppers was 35 percent greater than the yield of those left unmulched.

Decoteau, Kasperbauer, and Hunt of the USDA's Coastal Plains Research Center in Florence, South Carolina, experimented with the effects of black, white, red, and yellow mulches on bell peppers. The plants grown on the red mulch were taller and heavier than those grown on the other plastics. Their theory is that the phytochrome protein in peppers and other plants is a biological light sensor that responds to red light, particularly far-red, which is beyond the range of human vision. Since plant leaves reflect far-red light, when a mulch reflects far-red, the plant reacts as if competing plants are nearby and puts out more leaves and grows taller.

Some mail-order companies and garden shops are selling three-layer weed mats that prevent weeds but let air, water, and nutrients through.

NEWSPAPER AND OTHER PAPER. A favorite mulch that works especially well in the Southwest is ordinary black-and-white newspaper (no colored sheets). Although the sheets must be weighted down with soil to prevent them from blowing away, the newspaper retards weeds, reflects more light than black plastic, holds moisture in the soil, and can simply be rototilled into the soil at the end of the growing season. Use a thickness of at least two sheets after the transplants have been set out.

Some gardeners opt for brown paper from shopping bags, cardboard (which works best in a flat garden), and black, biodegradable paper mulch made from peatmoss and recycled cardboard, which can also be rototilled. The latter works well in cold climates.

Irrigation techniques

Simple experiments have revealed that doubling the water applied to peppers doubles their yield—to a point. If the ground becomes too saturated, it may either suffocate the roots or promote fungal diseases. Adequate watering increases yields and makes the peppers taste better.

Some pepper gardeners are fortunate to live in areas where the only water needed for the garden comes from rainfall. But most gardeners have to irrigate their moisture-demanding peppers. Gardeners should adjust the frequency and amount of watering to rainfall cycles. In other words, do not irrigate if there has just been a heavy downpour. Rainfall can be deceptive, because sometimes it thoroughly wets the mulch but does not penetrate to the deeper roots of pepper plants—some of which are two feet below the surface. Also remember that peppers grown next to large, water-demanding plants, such as corn, may need extra water.

We learned an important lesson about watering in Dave's 1992 home garden. One of the New Mexican varieties wilted and died, apparently from *Phytophthora*, but none of the other thirty plants in the garden showed any wilt symptoms. Dave assumed he was overwatering and restricted the water. The result? Three other plants were stressed from underwatering and nearly died. So the wilting of a single plant misled Dave into a false assumption, and the simple fact remains that occasionally a plant will die from a disease that is not prevalent in the entire plot.

Following are descriptions of some common watering techniques.

SPRINKLERS. Overhead sprinkling works fine when the plants in the garden are small. But once they gain some height, the water from the sprinkler is blocked and the garden is not watered evenly. Because it is awkward to keep raising the sprinkler above the foliage, at this point another watering method should be used.

FLOOD IRRIGATION. This method, which simply floods the garden with water from a hose, works well in a garden with good drainage and is recommended for ridges and furrows, flat beds, and modified irrigated beds (see "Garden Design," earlier). The gardener should carefully watch the amount of time it takes the water to drain from the plot and adjust the amount of water applied to avoid overirrigating. After the hose is turned off, the water should drain from the garden in less than an hour. If it takes any longer, too much water has been applied and the plants will be in danger.

DRIP IRRIGATION. Also called trickle irrigation, this method uses small plastic tubes to apply small but steady amounts of water to each plant in the garden. The main advantages of drip irrigation are that it conserves water because less is lost to evaporation, and it efficiently delivers water to individual plants. However, the system has some drawbacks. It is expensive, and the tubes, valves, and other components are subject to breaking, clogging, getting cut with shovels or hoes, and generally falling apart. The drip system must be constantly checked to make sure it is delivering water; otherwise, the gardener risks severe drying of plants. Master gardener George Brookbank advises: "Use a drip irrigation system like you would any other irrigation system—don't expect too much from it."

A number of studies of trickle-irrigated chile peppers in New Mexico indicated that it is the amount of water applied that increases yield, not the method of applying the water. Gardeners using drip irrigation should take care that the soil around peppers remains moist but not wet. They should also have a backup system in case the drip system fails.

DRIP HOSES. These leaky hoses, usually made from recycled tires, work well because they do not clog up. Often, though, instead of dripping, when the water pressure is too high, they will squirt thin streams of water a long way, sometimes beyond the confines of the garden, thus wasting it. However, there's an easy solution to this problem: place the hoses in the garden plot and then place the mulch over them, keeping all the water in the garden. A word of warning about drip hoses: don't buy the cheapest ones (usually completely round), as they have a tendency to rupture and then do not release the water evenly. Buy the more expensive, flat drip hoses.

Grafting chile pepper plants

Grafting of chile peppers is becoming a more common practice to control soil-borne diseases and nematodes, for both field- and greenhouse-grown crops. Grafting can unite a soilborne-disease-resistant rootstock to the susceptible scion or pod-producing part. In addition, grafted chile peppers can have higher yields and improved tolerance to environmental stresses, soil salinity, and low soil temperatures. In Korea, about 6 million grafted chile pepper plants are grown each year, and it is anticipated that the area of grafted chile peppers will rapidly increase.

The many methods of grafting plants include whip-and-tongue grafting, splice grafting, flat grafting, saddle grafting, and bud grafting. The Japanese top grafting or tube grafting, where a silicon tube is used to hold the scion and rootstock together during healing, is especially popular for chile pepper grafting. The process is fast, and large numbers of grafted seedlings can be managed easily throughout the healing process. Tube grafting makes it possible to graft plants that are small and grown in plug trays. The smaller the plants, the more plants can be fitted into a healing chamber.

Grafting should be carried out in a shady, cool place sheltered from the wind to avoid wilting the grafted plants. Grafted chile pepper plants heal and acclimate best in a healing chamber. A simple healing chamber consists of a frame covered by polyethylene sheeting, which keeps the humidity level high during the healing process, with a shade cloth placed over it to reduce the light level for the grafted plants. The

Chiles grafted onto tomato seedlings.

shading also aids in keeping the healing chamber from getting too hot.

In grafting, it is important to maximize the area of the cut surfaces that are spliced together, in order to increase the chances for the vascular bundles of the scion and the rootstock to come into contact so that water and nutrients can be supplied to the scion. Grafting scions and rootstocks with stems of a similar diameter accomplishes this. The cut surfaces should not be allowed to dry out. After grafting, keeping the grafted plants at about 85°F with more than 95 percent relative humidity for 3 days of healing increases the survival rate. Gradually, the relative humidity can be lowered and the light intensity increased.

The best place for a healing chamber is indoors, in a heated storage area or garage, where lights can be used during the final days of healing. Healing chambers can also be maintained inside a greenhouse as long as sufficient shading is in place to keep the grafts from being exposed to excessive heat inside the chamber.

A water-soluble 20-20-20 fertilizer.

Seed companies are releasing cultivars that have been bred for rootstock use, but their distribution in the United States is limited. Although it is ideal to graft with cultivars bred specifically for rootstock use, typically hybrids or other modern varieties can be valuable sources of disease-resistant rootstocks for susceptible cultivars.

The pros and cons of fertilizing

Opinions about fertilizing pepper plants diverge greatly. D. J. Cotter (1980) of New Mexico State University made a succinct observation: "The chile plant appears to be relatively insensitive to soil-applied nutrients." He cited studies of New Mexican varieties that indicated little or no yield increases when nitrogen was applied during the growing season. He also wrote, "Chile appears to be non-responsive to phosphorous."

Of course, Cotter was referring to the effect of fertilizers on fruit yield. Pepper plants respond very well to fertilizers, but that response is mostly vegetative. One commercial pepper grower told us the story of his attempt to fertilize tabasco plants with large amounts of worm castings. The castings were so loaded with nitrogen that his plants grew 6 feet tall, and not one of them had a single pod!

Excessive nitrogen causes the plant to return to vegetative growth and abort flowers and small pods. Seedlings can be fertilized with fairly high levels of nitrogen to encourage strong vegetative growth, but after the plants have adjusted to the garden, fertilizers should not be applied unless the plants have low-nitrogen symptoms, such as yellow leaves and stunted growth. Then they should be fertilized modestly. That said, a lack of adequate nitrogen can cause poor foliage growth, which exposes pods to direct sunlight and causes sunscald.

For home pepper gardeners, organic techniques seem to triumph over chemical gardening, because the vast majority of growers will be able to raise great pepper crops by simply adding compost and aged manure to the garden each year. By contrast, nearly all commercial growers use a preplanting fertilizer and regular applications of fertilizer throughout the growing season, undoubtedly because the heavy concentration of pepper plants depletes the soil and because manure and compost are not generally added to commercial fields.

Pruning the plants and removing flowers

Several readers of the Fiery Foods and BBQ SuperSite wrote to ask about pruning chile plants during the growing cycle, and one person commented, "I have heard that keeping the blooms trimmed back on my habanero pepper plants will encourage the growth of more peppers." We never prune plants during their growing cycle, as it accomplishes nothing. If you are going to winter them over in pots in a greenhouse, you can prune the plants back in the fall or wait until spring. The only exception would be if you wanted to attempt topiary or even bonsai chiles; in the case of the latter, see "Container Cultivation." And the idea of removing flowers seems wrong; because of flower drop, you need every bloom on the plant.

That said, some experiments have shown that plants recover from flower loss. Dr. William Clapham, a plant physiologist at the University of Maine, recommends pinching off flowers for several weeks to increase fruit dry weight (Clapham and March 1987). He suggests that pepper plants treated this way devote their energy to vegetative growth rather than fruit production, resulting in larger plants that produce more market-sized fruits. In another experiment, plants with all flowers removed as late as mid-July still had good yields. More studies are needed, and this would make a great project for a graduate student in horticulture.

Fighting the weeds

Weeds not only look ugly, they can harbor pests like leafhoppers, which spread curly top virus to pepper plants—something that happened with devastating effect throughout New Mexico in 1995 and the early 2000s. More than 150 types of weeds harbor insect-transmitted viruses that can harm peppers. Weeds often grow faster than peppers and can cut off sunlight, while stealing nutrients and moisture from the soil. They also produce seeds that will sprout in the garden the following year.

Fighting weeds without mulch.

If the garden is mulched properly, weeds will not be a big problem, but vigilance is always necessary in the pepper garden. Some species of weeds grow right next to the pepper stem and can be difficult to see under the canopy of leaves. Some weeds, such as Bermuda grass and bindweed, can invade the garden from other parts of the yard, cross over the top of the mulch, and sometimes establish themselves next to pepper plants.

Early in the season, you can suppress the growth of weed seeds by spreading corn gluten meal over the garden plot. Corn gluten meal, a by-product of corn processing that is often used to feed livestock, inhibits only the germination of seeds. Once the weed seeds have sprouted, corn gluten will not affect them. Also, corn gluten inhibits the germination of *all*

ANATOMY OF A CHILE FLOWER.

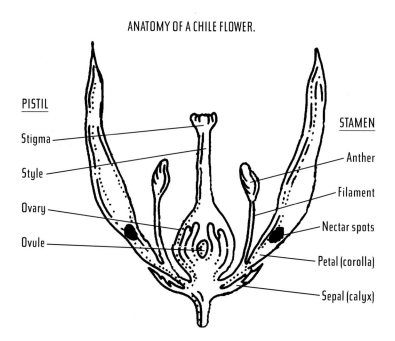

PISTIL

Stigma

Style

Ovary

Ovule

STAMEN

Anther

Filament

Nectar spots

Petal (corolla)

Sepal (calyx)

Courtesy of the Chile Pepper Institute.

Flower, *C. annuum* 'Black Cuban'.

seeds, so if you use it, don't sprinkle any seeds in the garden.

Home gardeners should take pride in their pepper patch and remove the weeds by hand, because hoes and shovels can damage leaves, stems, and roots of peppers and knock pods off the plant. Herbicides such as Roundup should never be used in the home garden, because drifting herbicide spray can kill pepper plants, although some commercial growers need to use these chemicals.

Flowering and pollination

Flowers begin to form when the pepper plant begins to branch. Flowering is dicotamous, meaning that one flower forms, then two, then four, then eight, and so on. The number of flowers produced is very large compared to those that actually set fruit, and a larger percentage of early flowers than of later flowers will set fruit. The key factor affecting fruit set is nighttime temperature, which ideally should be between 65 and 80°F. Fruit will not set when the temperature is above 86°F at night because of excessive transpiration, which causes blossom drop. Other causes of blossom drop are excessive nitrogen, high winds, and lack of pollination. If daytime temperatures exceed 95°F, pollen will abort and the fruit set will be reduced.

In some cases, spraying hormones such as Bloom Set on the flowers may prevent blossom drop. A home remedy calls for spraying the blossoms with a solution of 1 teaspoon Epsom salts in 1 quart of water. According to lore, the magnesium in the Epsom salts assists in the setting of fruit.

FAR LEFT Flower, pasilla pepper.

LOWER LEFT Flower, *C. chinense* 'Bhut Jolokia'.

TOP RIGHT Flower, ají pepper.

LOWER RIGHT Flower, rocoto pepper.

POLLINATION. Peppers are usually considered to be a self-pollinated crop. Pepper plants do self-pollinate, but their ability to cross-pollinate is far greater than expected. As early as 1892, J. H. Hart, the superintendent of the Royal Botanical Gardens in Trinidad, reported: "We do not make any specific distinction between the capsicums from here for the simple reason that they degenerate so quickly to a simple form under cultivation that we cannot refer to them as more than a single species. Some of the finest will in four or five generations be nothing more than 'bird-pepper' of which the forms are as many as the days of the year." Hart, of course,

RIGHT Chile flower releasing pollen.

FAR RIGHT Bee pollinating chile flowers.

Flower nectaries.

was allowing his peppers to cross-pollinate and later planting the seeds of natural hybrids, thus obliterating distinct varieties.

In 1938, M. L. Odland and A. M. Porter of the University of Connecticut suspected that because of fruit variability, a higher percentage of natural cross-pollination took place in peppers than in tomatoes. Their classic study of the crosses produced as a result of different varieties being grown next to each other (Odland and Porter 1941) revealed cross-pollination rates averaging 16.5 percent, with a high of 36.8 percent in an ornamental variety. They noted that "the pepper flower is rather inconspicuous and non-fragrant, a fact that would suggest insect pollination not very likely." But upon close examination of their test plots, they concluded that honeybees were responsible for the cross-pollination and that "the wind accounts for only a very small percent, if any, of the cross-pollination that takes place in this crop." An examination of the flowers of wild species and of wild types of *Capsicum annuum* reveals large drops of nectar that reward bees for visiting the flowers.

In 1984, Steven Tanksley of New Mexico State University found that the rate of natural cross-pollination in New Mexican varieties was far higher than suspected—up to 42 percent cross-pollination. Bees were the culprits again—sweat bees, honeybees, bumblebees, and fruit cutter bees. His findings demonstrated the need for strict isolation conditions for the production of commercial seed. Other insects known to transmit pollen are ants, aphids, and butterflies.

KEEPING SEED PURE. Don't worry about wind pollination—that rarely happens. Most cross-pollination occurs by insects. You can put cheesecloth or other netting over the ends of the branches when flowers just start to form. This is the easiest way to prevent cross-pollination, and the pods will have pure seed through self-pollination. The other method is to build a metal or wood frame capable of holding three or four plants of the same variety and then put netting over it, but cheesecloth is not strong enough. Go to a fabric store and buy netting used to

back draperies. Use a staple gun to affix it if the frame is made of wood.

Gardeners can now determine which peppers will cross and which will not. For example, nothing will cross with a rocoto, so all rocoto seeds produced in a mixed garden will be true. It is somewhat safe to plant ajís next to habaneros, because they only sporadically cross. Likewise, it is somewhat safe to plant tabascos next to jalapeños or habaneros. It is relatively easy to produce hybrids of the *C. annuum* varieties with habaneros. In some cases, the viability of first-generation seed depends on which species pollinates the other. When *C. frutescens* pollinates *C. annuum*, no viable seed results, but when *C. annuum* pollinates *C. frutescens*, a limited amount of viable seed is produced.

Many techniques have been developed for isolating peppers to produce pure seed,

CROSSING POSSIBILITIES

Any two pepper varieties of the same pod type or species will cross, such as jalapeños crossing with piquins. Within *Capsicum annuum*, all varieties of all pod types will cross. Among the five species, the following scenarios occur:

C. annuum: Crosses prolifically with *C. chinense*, sporadically with *C. baccatum* and *C. frutescens*; does not cross with *C. pubescens*.

C. baccatum: Crosses sporadically with *C. annuum*, *C. chinense*, and *C. frutescens*; does not cross with *C. pubescens*. However, *C. baccatum* produces only sterile hybrids with other species.

C. chinense: Crosses prolifically with *C. annuum*, sporadically with *C. frutescens* and *C. baccatum*; does not cross with *C. pubescens*.

C. frutescens: Crosses sporadically with *C. annuum*, *C. baccatum*, and *C. chinense*; does not cross with *C. pubescens*.

C. pubescens: Does not cross with any of the other species.

hydridizing peppers, and developing new varieties. For a discussion of these techniques of pepper breeding, see "Breeding and Hybridization."

Fruiting

Fruit development is enhanced by increased sunlight. More fruit will set near the top of the plant than within the canopy of leaves. The size and shape of the pod is inherited, but it is subject to considerable modification by environmental factors. The size of the pods on the same plant tends to decrease slightly as the growing season progresses. Generally speaking,

fruits are ready for picking in their fresh green stage at about 70 days after planting. Fully mature pods may take 130 days or more for some varieties.

FRUIT LOAD. The maximum weight of fruits that a fruiting plant can bear is known as its fruit load. The fruit load of each pepper plant is dependent on a number of considerations including stem size, amount of foliage, and extent of the root system. When the plant achieves its fruit load, it ceases flowering. Thus a plant will stop producing fruit even though a month or more may be left in the growing season.

IMPROVING THE YIELD. The pepper gardener can increase the yield of plants by picking pods in their largest immature green form. The plant will not have to bear the weight of the pods removed, but it will continue flowering and setting fruit throughout the remainder of the season, and the total weight of pods produced by each plant will be greater. However, the technique of periodic harvesting to increase pod yields only works in long growing seasons or with varieties having very short growing periods. In cooler climates, pepper plants may not reach their fruit load before the first killing frost, so picking pods early will not increase the total yield.

Pepper gardeners have discovered other ways to produce more pods as well. Howard Watson of Houston, Texas, grows his bell peppers in plastic-wrapped wire cages. He makes wire cages 18 to 20 inches in diameter and about 5 feet high and then wraps the

ANATOMY OF A CHILE POD.

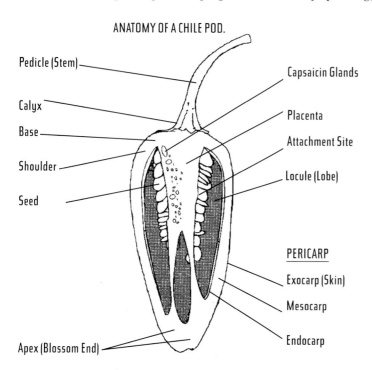

Pedicle (Stem)
Calyx
Base
Shoulder
Seed
Apex (Blossom End)

Capsaicin Glands
Placenta
Attachment Site
Locule (Lobe)

PERICARP
Exocarp (Skin)
Mesocarp
Endocarp

Courtesy of the Chile Pepper Institute.

Capsicum annuum 'Sweet Pickle' at maximum fruit load.

bottom half of the cage with 6-millimeter clear polyethlene. Each cage encloses a single pepper plant in the garden until late May, when the cages are removed. As a result, his pepper plants grow 7 feet tall and are still producing in mid-December. "By my count," wrote Watson in *National Gardening* (1988), "we harvested up to 60 peppers per plant!"

It is ironic that some gardeners use reflective mulches to increase yield while others use shading. Experiments have been conducted to determine the effect of shading on fruit yield in peppers. In the early 1970s, Paul G. Schoch (1972) of the National Institute for Agronomic Research in Guadeloupe, French West Indies, grew two groups of bell peppers in black plastic pots under identical conditions. However, one of the groups was shaded under black cloth between 10 a.m. and 4 p.m. each day. The black cloth permitted only 45 percent of the normal solar radiation to reach the leaves. After 60 days of this treatment, when the first flowers appeared, the plants were transplanted into open fields. The results were that the shaded plants had more fruits per plant, a greater mean weight per fruit, and a much greater total weight of fruits per plant. The results also suggest that pepper plants transplanted from greenhouses, where the light conditions are lower, will yield more than directly seeded plants.

Some peppers grow well in shady conditions all year long. Chiltepíns are usually found beneath "nurse" trees, especially mesquite, so these chile pepper plants are accustomed to low light conditions. However, we have grown Arizona varieties of chiltepíns in full sun in the Southwest with spectacular results. Potted chiltepíns should not be grown in full sun or their leaves may yellow and drop.

Intense sunlight can actually cook peppers (a problem called sunscald) and decrease the yield of usable fruits. If you are gardening in a high-altitude region with intense sunlight, shade the peppers by covering the plants with shade netting (available at garden centers or by mail order). Rig up a makeshift frame over the peppers and drape the shade cloth over this frame so it remains easy to tend the peppers under their "tent." Varieties such as habaneros and rocotos are especially prone to sunscald— and both yield better under netting than they do in open, unshaded plots.

Shading is also useful for some varieties, namely *Capsicum chinense* and *C. pubescens* in the high, dry altitudes of the Southwest that

Placental tissue with seeds and orange capsaicin glands.

have high levels of ultraviolet light. During the 1992 growing season, both these species performed better and had higher yields under netting than they did in open, unshaded plots.

During the hottest days of July and August, many pepper plants experience water loss by transpiration, no matter how wet the ground is. The results are wilting, flower drop, and sometimes even fruit drop. Antitranspirants, oil or wax emusions sprayed on leaves to reduce water loss, are available. They do reduce water loss, but they do not increase yield or pod size. The simplest method of fighting transpiration water loss is to increase the humidity around the plants by wetting thick layers of mulch such as grass clippings.

PUNGENCY. Mature pods are more pungent than immature pods. The reason for this is that capsaicin is present to prevent mammals from eating the pods and destroying the seeds in their intestinal tract. So it makes sense that pungency would be greatest when the seeds are mature and can germinate.

About 50 percent of pungency is genetic and about 50 percent is environmental. Generally

speaking, stressing pepper plants increases their pungency. Both restricting water and overwatering (a dangerous practice) will increase the amount of capsaicin in the pods. Restrict the water until the plants just start to wilt, then water them slightly to perk them back up. Do this several times throughout the growing season and the pods should be hotter. The pungency is also increased when the fruit ripens at higher temperatures. In fact, the pods of New Mexican varieties ripening at temperatures between 86 and 95°F have twice as much capsaicin as those ripening at 59 to 72°F. Applying nitrogen after fruit set can lower the capsaicin levels.

Pepper lore holds that the seeds are the hottest part of the pod, but this is not true. Although the seeds do absorb capsaicin during processing, in the fresh pods they are not very pungent at all. The most pungent part of the pod is the placental tissue, or cross wall, which holds the seeds and produces capsaicin. The pepper pod becomes less pungent toward the apex.

One of the most common complaints about chile fruits in the "Ask Dave" section of the Fiery Foods and BBQ SuperSite is supposedly hot varieties that are not pungent enough. Jalapeños are notoriously mild these days because of the introduction of less pungent varieties into the gene pool as a consequence of the peppers' popularity as a topping for nachos sold at ball games. Apparently the concession people at ballparks wanted milder (and even no heat!) jalapeños and both Texas A&M and New Mexico State universities obliged, with the typical result that farmers did not isolate the pungent

Row covers.

varieties from the mild varieties, causing milder hybrids to develop.

FLAVOR. Each variety of pepper has its own set of aromatic substances that give it a unique flavor. The important flavor component of bells and jalapeños is 2-isobutyl-3-methoxyprazine. This chemical is the most potent aroma known to humankind and is detectable when diluted to one drop in an Olympic-size swimming pool full of water. Tabasco has twenty-three flavor components rather than a single dominant compound. The habanero has a particular, fruity, apricotlike aroma and flavor that is never forgotten. Gardeners should pick fresh pods, cut them open, and smell and taste them to decide which are better for various culinary applications.

Cold-weather growing

Pepper growers in colder climates in the United States and Canada, and at higher altitudes such as in Colorado (with a 56-day growing season at 8500 feet), face many challenges to producing a good crop: a short growing season, low night-time temperatures, unexpected frosts, and high sunlight intensity. Fortunately, there are solutions for these problems.

SITE-SPECIFIC PLANTING. Cold weather gardeners need to pay particular attention to garden planning. Planting the peppers on the south side of ridges that run east and west in the garden will increase the growth rate, because the soil facing the sun will be warmer than level soil. Raised beds that slope toward the south can also be used. Sunken beds covered with polyethylene sheeting that has been cut with slits for ventilation will give plants a good start in cold weather.

ROW COVERS. In Connecticut, the problem is that the growing season for bell peppers is too short to achieve good production of mature red and yellow pods. In 1987 and 1988, Martin Gent (1989) of the Connecticut Agricultural

HINTS FOR COLD-WEATHER GROWING

In his garden in upstate New York (USDA zone 5), Ray Lagoe grows more than fifty varieties of chile peppers—everything from habaneros to tabascos to serranos. Ray, who wrote the article "Chilly Chiles" in *Chile Pepper* magazine (1992), notes: "If you follow these guidelines and don't rush and plant too early, you should have the same excellent results I've had for years." His guidelines are as follows:

- Select early-maturing varieties.
- Start seed indoors 8 to 10 weeks before the last expected frost date.
- Plant seed in a sterile, soilless mix, and keep the seed at 75°F under fluorescent light ten to twelve hours a day.
- Two weeks before transplanting seedlings into the garden, cover the rows with clear plastic mulch to warm the soil.
- Before planting, harden off the seedlings by leaving them outside for 2 weeks or more, for increasingly long periods of time each day.
- Transplant seedlings when daytime temperatures average 70°F and nighttime temperatures stay above 55°F (ideally).
- Soil pH should be 6.5; use a balanced fertilizer (5-10-5 or 10-10-10) but go easy on the nitrogen or you will have great-looking plants with no fruit.
- Cutworms can be a problem in northern gardens, so always protect seedlings with cardboard collars.
- Water during dry spells (at least 2 inches a week), especially after fruit set.

Dick Worth, who grows eighteen varieties of peppers in Dauberville, Pennsylvania (zone 6), says that a head start is the best strategy for gardening in cooler climates. "I planted habanero seeds in flats under grow lights on February 15," he told us, "and transplanted the seedlings into 4-inch peat pots on March 15. I kept the potted plants on a windowsill until the middle of April, when it was warm enough to transfer them into a cold frame. I put the potted plants into the garden on May 15."

The results? "I picked the first edible pods in the middle of August," Dick reported. "The mature plants were about 30 inches high and 30 inches wide, and each of them produced approximately fifty to sixty extremely hot fruits."

Experiment Station used floating row covers made from spun-bonded polypropylene. This light and porous material is draped directly over the plants and traps solar energy, warming the plants by 5°F during the day.

Gent transplanted seedlings of numerous bell varieties on April 20 and covered them for 8 weeks. He also transplanted plants on May 23 and covered them as well. The later transplants did not result in early production, but the results for the April 20 transplanting were good, with several varieties ('Golden Belle', 'Gypsy', 'Canape', and 'Parks Early Thickset') producing early yellow or red pods. Growth under the row covers increased yields (number of pods) by 12 to 19 percent; however, the average weight of each pod decreased between 5 and 15 percent. Gent concluded that row covers work well for gardeners in short growing seasons who need earlier maturing pods.

Polyethylene bed covers worked well at Uvalde, Texas. Researchers from Texas A&M University found that row covers tripled the early yield of New Mexican varieties. Using row covers can bring in a crop between 2 and 3 weeks earlier than normal. Home gardeners can fashion row covers from clear polyethylene stretched over wooden frames, or they can use clear corrugated fiberglass.

Row covers are also available to home gardeners from mail-order companies and garden shops. The manufacturers of Reemay say that their product insulates plants against light frost and enables the grower to plant 10 to 14 days earlier. They also claim that their spun polyester row cover extends the harvest by 2 to 3 weeks and keeps insects out—which would be a perfect way to avoid cross-pollination. Plastic row covers, which are really small row greenhouses called cloches, protect delicate plants from wind, cold, and snow—but not against insects.

WARMING THE GROUND AND EXTENDING THE SEASON. In addition to mulches and row covers, other methods can be used to warm the soil so that peppers can get a head start during a short growing season. Some gardeners grow their peppers inside automobile tires (or inner tubes) that are filled with water. The tire protects small plants from the wind and absorbs heat from the sun. The water warms both the soil and the air around the peppers, releasing heat during cold nights. On the other hand, the open water in a tire may offer breeding sites for mosquitoes, so place a few drops of motor oil on the water. Many nurseries and garden supply shops sell flexible plastic rings that are filled with water, serve the same purpose as tires, and are more attractive.

Another soil-warming technique is to fill one-gallon plastic milk jugs with water and bury them halfway in the ground next to the plants. Solar radiation will heat the water, which will keep the ground warmer near the plants.

Reflector panels made of wood and painted black or aluminum can be mounted on the north side of ridges that run east and west to reflect sunlight onto both the plants and the ground. Such reflectors should be removed later in the summer when the weather heats up.

Microclimates in some regions seriously affect the length of the growing season. For example, in Albuquerque, certain parts of the South Valley are hit by early frosts, but the higher elevations are not (cold air sinks, remember). What often happens is that after an early frost, the weather will warm up sufficiently for another 3 weeks of growing. The problem is to keep the early frost from killing the plants. Short of using heaters, like the citrus growers do, the best and easiest solution is to cover the plants.

Many materials can be used to cover plants, such as cotton bed sheets, clear or black plastic sheeting, nylon netting, plastic row covers, and even large cardboard boxes. The choice for the gardener depends on the arrangement of the plants—and, of course, their size. Ideally, the thickest and most dense material will retain ground heat the most efficiently. However, sometimes thick material is heavy enough (especially if there is rain or snow) to break off branches. Gardeners must make the decision based on available materials, the amount of work involved in covering the plants, and the projected low temperature. If the temperature is expected to hover somewhere between 28 and 32°F, the effort is probably worth it. If the temperature is expected to drop below 28°F, the effort will probably be wasted.

The commercial copy for a product called Wall O'Water claims that this product adds up to 8 weeks to the growing season. Teepees of clear plastic 18 inches high, filled with 3 gallons of water, surround young plants and protect them from the wind and cold. The water teepees absorb heat and release it during the night. When the plants are mature and frost threatens, the water retains heat and releases it at night. In the case of freezing temperatures, the water actually releases heat as it freezes, further protecting the plants.

RECOMMENDED VARIETIES FOR COLDER CLIMATES. We have searched the information sent by various state cooperative extension services in colder states to find the recommended varieties for those areas. Pepper growers in colder regions should contact their extension services for suggestions, then order as many seed catalogs as possible. High Altitude Gardens in Ketchum, Idaho, specializes in seeds and resources for cool weather gardening. The following suggestions from Alaska, Colorado, Idaho, Minnesota, and Vermont are probably the best for cooler climates but are certainly not the only varieties to try. Among bells, try 'Cal Wonder', 'Gypsy', 'Karlo', and 'Mexi-Bell'. Other *Capsicum annuum* varieties to try are 'Yellow Wax Hot', 'Jalapa' jalapeño, 'Long Red Cayenne', and 'Super Chili'.

Harvesting the chile crop

One of the most commonly asked gardening questions in Dave's online Q&A, "Ask Dave," is when to start harvesting. Depending on the geographical area, during the summer and fall pods in every stage of development from recently pollinated to dried will be on the bush. Because of fruit load limits, it is important to harvest the pods as they mature. The pepper plant will continue to flower and produce fruit if the pods are continuously harvested.

WHEN TO PICK THE PODS. Pepper gardening experts recommend the technique of continuous harvesting, which means that the chiles in the garden can be used all season long. Usually the first chiles available are small and used green in fresh salsas—the serranos, jalapeños, and the young green pods of other varieties such as the habanero. Some chiles, especially the New Mexican varieties, can be eaten or processed as soon as they are 4 to 6 inches long, or they can be allowed to turn red before picking and drying. A few varieties are generally used only in their dried state, such as cayenne and pasilla chiles. It is important to continue harvesting the ripe pods as they mature. The best time to pick chiles for drying is when they first start to turn red. This timing will stimulate the plant into further production, and the harvested chiles can be strung to dry and will turn bright red.

Haphazard harvesting can result in waste, so careful plucking is essential to insure the maximum yield of the chile pepper patch. Choose pods that have smooth, shiny skins and are firm to the touch. A good rule to follow is that if the pod comes off the stem easily, the chile is ready. If you have to tug on the pod, it is too early to pick it. The small chiles do not have to be peeled or processed in any way before being used. They can be picked, washed, and used in any recipe. Of course, because of the concept of continuous harvesting to increase yield, it is necessary to pick some peppers a bit early. When harvesting early, it is best to cut the peppers off the plants with a knife or scissors, because the branches are brittle and will often break before the stem of the pepper pod will.

Too many chiles! If, after using the techniques in this book, you have more pods than

ABOVE Hand harvesting chiles near Radium Springs, New Mexico.

LEFT An unnamed *C. chinense* variety matures.

you can use, here are a few suggestions. Despite the fact that many of our friends and neighbors also grow chiles, we have found that most people grow only one or two of their favorite varieties and are therefore quite happy to accept bags of new or different chiles. In addition, we realize that the majority of people do not have a garden, and if we can make contact with them, they will generally be thrilled to take any excess. Organizations that provide food for the

Too many chiles!

homeless generally are happy to accept donations of homegrown produce, although they obviously have limits on the number of hot chiles that they can use or accept.

Over the years, we have found a number of trading partners who know that we always grow chiles, and as a result plant few, if any, chiles of their own. Instead, they rely on us to provide them with chiles, while we in turn depend on them to supply fruits or vegetables that we are unwilling or unable to grow. This works especially well for any plant or variety that tends to overproduce, such as full-sized fruit trees and zucchini patches. Another idea is to find local chefs who use chiles and trade them your excess pods for a dinner or two.

Additionally, you can sell your surplus. These days, nearly every town has a growers' market of some kind. For a minimal fee, growers are allowed to set up a table and sell their crops. So if you have extra chiles and a half day or so to work your table, you can generally sell all your homegrown produce. Your primary goal at these markets is to find a home for your excess, not to get rich. Keep your prices low enough to guarantee that you walk away empty-handed, and enjoy the fact that most buyers are excited and enthusiastic about finding really fresh produce at good prices. These farmers' markets are a good place to trade, and often you will wind up with a load of traded goods but little or no money.

EXTENDING THE HARVEST. Often, the first frost of the year does not signal the end of the growing season. The early frost is followed by an Indian summer that brings enough warm weather to keep peppers growing for another 3 or 4 weeks. But to make use of this extended season, it is necessary to cover the plants. There are many good crop protectors—cotton bed sheets, clear or black plastic, nylon netting, plastic row covers, even large cardboard boxes placed over individual plants. The material should be thick and dense enough to retain ground heat, but not so thick that it will break off branches if it gets weighted down by rain or snow. Place the covers in position as early in the day as possible—say between 4 and 6 p.m. on the evening of the frost—so that there's still some heat to retain (it gets cool fast at night in the fall). And be sure to remove such covers as soon as it's warm enough the following day.

If the temperature is going to drop below 28°F, though, the covering efforts will probably not be enough to protect the plants from freezing. But there are other plants, those peppers that have been growing in pots. Move them indoors before the first frost, and the plants will overwinter nicely. If you have no peppers in pots, dig up a few of the healthiest favorites in the garden (don't dig up a struggler hoping it will recover inside—it won't), pot them in a soil that drains well, and move them inside. These plants may drop most of their leaves over the winter, but most will survive and come back strong—especially if you prune them in the spring, cutting off any branches that look dead and brown, rather than green. The plants will sprout new growth vigorously after such a pruning, even if you cut them back severely.

Gardeners can even make this indoor overwintering and spring pruning a perennial event, because peppers are perennials when grown in frost-free conditions. Wintered-over pepper plants need regular watering, but unless you are actively growing them by providing artificial light, you will not need to fertilize them until they resume growing in the spring. After a few years they will lose vigor and produce fewer pods. The longest we have kept fruiting chiles in pots is twelve years. (See "Container Cultivation" for more detail on potted pepper plants.)

Saving seed

Save seed only from mature pods, never the green ones. Regardless of whether the seeds are produced through self-pollination or cross-pollination, they must be preserved until the next growing season or even later. On the average,

Seed from mature pods, ready for saving.

pepper seeds last two years. However, by using proper techniques, you can extend the viability of pepper seeds dramatically. Seed moisture and storage temperature are the most important factors affecting seed viability, and the longest seed storage life is obtained at low relative humidity and low temperature.

All extraneous pod material should be removed from the seeds, and damaged, discolored, or partial seeds should be culled. Ideally, pepper seeds should be dried to less than 8 percent moisture content. This is easily accomplished by drying the seed at 100°F for 6 hours. Spread the seed on trays and place it in an unlit gas oven, or outside in the shade if the temperature is high and the humidity is low. Or let them dry at room temperature for at least a week. Never use a microwave oven to dry seed. Generally speaking, seeds that are hard and crunchy when they are bitten into are dry enough to store.

Any moistureproof container can be used to store seed, including sealed cans, jars, and even zip bags. Take care that the containers are properly labeled for the variety of seed and, obviously, never mix varieties in a container. Some gardeners place the seeds in moistureproof

Datil peppers growing in pots, Saint Augustine, Florida.

barrier pouches with silica gel and then heat seal the pouches. The containers should be kept cool, so store the seeds in the freezer—that's where most seed banks store their germplasm. When both seed moisture and storage temperature are low, longevity and germination are unaffected by the presence of oxygen. This technique maintains seed viability for up to twenty-five years.

CONTAINER CULTIVATION

With a little foresight and planning, you can grow chile peppers in containers, and the yield will equal that of plants in the garden. Growing chile peppers in containers offers many advantages. Chile peppers grown in containers can be used as patio plants and ornamental houseplants and can even be trained into bonsai. Fresh pods from containerized chile peppers are available all year long. Other advantages to growing chile peppers in containers are that

they are easier to isolate for production of pure seed, and the treasured late-maturing pod types can be overwintered in the house, then set outside in the spring.

Some chile pepper enthusiasts become so fond of their chile peppers in containers that they turn them into pets. They give them nicknames, take pictures of them to send to relatives and friends, and freely share their pods. This kind of behavior seems to be unique to chile pepper gardeners.

Success with container chile pepper plants starts with meeting five basic requirements. First, the container should provide good drainage. The planting medium and holes in the container should release excess water to prevent the roots from drowning. Next, the right size of container is very important. The container must provide enough space for roots so that they can absorb water and nutrients. A third need is for regular watering, and this brings with it the fourth need, regular fertilizing of the plant. Each time the container is watered, nutrients are leached. Over time, the plant will need supplemental feedings to grow vigorously. Last, the chile pepper plant will need appropriate light. Chile pepper plants can take all-day sun and must get at least three hours a day to stay healthy. Artificial lighting can supplement sunshine indoors.

Choosing the container

Virtually anything that will hold a soil medium can be used to grow chile peppers. If the reason for using containers is to expand the size of the garden rather than eventually to bring the plants indoors, then size and appearance are not a problem and the gardener can use fairly large containers such as plastic trash cans, wooden boxes or barrels, styrofoam picnic coolers, and the large plastic, fiber, or metal containers used by greenhouses for shrubs and trees. Depending on the variety, the container size ranges from 4 inches to 5 gallons or larger for outdoor growing. If, however, the chile peppers will be kept for more than a year, a 12-inch deep container is recommended. We have had chile peppers in containers ranging in size from a plastic container with a 4-inch diameter to a barrel with a 22-inch diameter, all grown with success. With a few exceptions, the larger the container, the larger the chile pepper plant will grow. Smaller containers restrict root growth, which limits foliage and flower production, but are recommended for gardeners wishing to grow bonzai peppers. Remember that smaller containers require more frequent watering, and that lighter-colored containers reflect more solar energy and keep the roots of the plant cooler.

Gardeners can use their imaginations when selecting containers. For example, the Chile Pepper Institute has planted strawberry pots with chile peppers, and these make a great patio feature. Strawberry pots are the pots that are shaped like an urn and have pockets up and down the sides. Here is a technique that helps to keep the chile pepper plants watered: before filling the pot with potting mix and plants, cut a length of PVC pipe slightly longer than the height of the pot and drill holes along its sides, about every 2 inches. Center the pipe vertically in the pot while planting. Later, pour water and fertilizer into the PVC pipe; it will seep into the potting mix, and the top of the PVC pipe will eventually be obscured by the plants on top.

Decorative pots for chile plants.

Capsicum annuum 'NuMex Twilight' in a dramatic pot.

Varieties to grow

Any chile pepper can be grown in a container. At the risk of overgeneralizing, we believe that the smaller-podded varieties adapt best to container growing—especially to the smaller containers. The more compact types, like bell peppers, yellow wax, and ornamentals, grow well without needing any pruning. Tall, robust plants like ajís need to be pruned periodically to maintain a coiffured plant.

Container growing of vegetables, including chile peppers, has become so popular that many seed companies are breeding vegetable varieties for container growing. For example, 'Jingle Bells' is a compact plant that will produce a dozen 2-inch pods at a time. These cultivars are labeled as patio or container varieties. Other preferred varieties are just more compact in their growth habit and work well in containers; these include 'Early Jalapeno', 'Thai Chile', 'Big Early', 'Super Chili', 'Tangerine Dream', 'Redskin', 'Mohawk', and of course the ornamentals listed earlier in the book.

Container growing techniques

Container growing techniques involve choosing the right soil, fertilizer, and location, and being aware of potential pests

DRAINAGE AND SOIL. As mentioned earlier, good drainage is essential. Regardless of the type of container chosen for growing chile peppers, the containers should have drain holes. To prevent soil from washing out of the holes, place an irregularly shaped stone or piece of bark over the hole. If the container is placed in a saucer, make sure the container does not sit in water, as this will cause the roots to rot.

One of the biggest problems with container gardening is the tendency for the plants to dry out and wilt between regular waterings. The major cause of quick drying is plant transpiration, which is greater than one might expect when the plant has a well-developed root system. Another cause of drying is evaporation from the top of the soil, which can be controlled with a mulch. Place an attractive mulch, such as finely shredded bark or pebbles, to conserve water and add a handsome touch to the container.

The third cause of quick drying is the type of soil chosen for the container. Commercial soil media for containers is the best choice, because many garden soils are not the right texture for use in containers. However, some commercial potting soils contain so much sand, perlite, and milled sphagnum moss that they drain too fast and dry out too quickly.

FERTILIZING. Chile peppers in containers generally need a little more fertilizer than those growing in the garden. About once a week early in the growing season, use a balanced liquid fertilizer, such as 10-10-10, diluted even more than the instructions suggest. Fish emulsion seems to work well for organic gardeners. A good slow-release fertilizer is Osmocote, which does not burn the plants and provides a steady supply of nutrients. If the growth of the containerized chile pepper seems more vigorous than that of the same variety in the garden, or if blossoms are dropping, stop using the fertilizer. If blossom drop continues, too much nitrogen has been applied, and the container should be flushed by running a lot of water through it.

LOCATION. Outdoors, chile peppers in containers seem to do best in partial shade or in locations receiving full sun only in the morning. There is a tendency for containers in full sun to absorb solar radiation and heat up the roots too much. However, if the containers are quite large, painted white or aluminum to reflect solar energy, and are well mulched, many varieties will thrive in full sun. Indoors, the plants will be partially shaded by the movement of the sun, so place them in the sunniest window. In the summer, it's usually an east or west window; in the winter, a south window is best.

PROBLEMS. One of the biggest problems with growing peppers indoors is pets. The plants are chewed by cats, dogs, and birds. Some gardeners put netting over their chile peppers to keep the cats off, but then they can't see their favorite plants. Another problem with growing chile peppers indoors or in greenhouses is that they are more susceptible to the usual houseplant attackers: spider mites, whiteflies, mealybugs, and aphids. See "Diseases and Pests" for information on dealing with these pests.

Artificial lights

The least expensive way to set up an indoor chile pepper growing area is with fluorescent lights. They are efficient and cost little to set up, and a standard fixture accepts two 40-watt tubes. The number of fixtures to use depends on the size of the growing area, and they can also be placed vertically in corners for side lighting. As with any light source, the intensity of light decreases rapidly as a function of distance. The tops of the chile pepper plants must remain 2 to 4 inches below the tubes. Standard cool-white fluorescent tubes can be used, but many gardeners prefer the Sylvania Gro-Lux with its pink and purplish light, high-intensity output lights, or Vita-Lites, which approach 92 percent of the spectrum of natural sunlight.

However, research has shown that the color spectrum only minimally affects plant growth, if at all. The biggest factor in plant performance is enough light, especially when chile pepper plants are setting flowers and fruit. To avoid the problem of low light levels on lower foliage, serious chile pepper gardeners should use high-

High-intensity discharge (HID) grow lamps in action.

intensity discharge (HID) lamps. They are very similar to the mercury or sodium vapor lamps used to light city streets and come in two basic types, metal halide and high-pressure sodium. They use more electricity than fluorescent tubes.

Metal halide lamps have a spectrum like the bright midday sun, while high-pressure sodium lamps have the spectrum of the early morning or late afternoon sun, which promotes flowering. A high-pressure sodium lamp emits more photosynthetic active radiation (PAR) than a metal halide lamp. One word of warning: this equipment is identical to that used by indoor marijuana growers. The Drug Enforcement Administration has been known to subpoena the records of stores selling indoor growing equipment and to pay visits to indoor gardeners who have ordered it. There will be no problem as long as you grow chile peppers— the legal addiction!

Either paint the plant growing room white or line it with white trashbags to reflect and diffuse light. Aluminum foil and Mylar reflect light but do not diffuse it, causing numerous hot spots unless they are applied evenly, without wrinkling. Line the floors with white plastic to protect them from spills when watering.

Hydroponics

Hydroponics is the cultivation of plants in water instead of soil. Chile pepper growers all over the world use hydroponics to grow chile peppers, for many reasons. There may be a lack of water in the area, too little fertile cropland, a need for a very high quality pod, or a need to grow organically.

Several developments in the past few years have made hydroponic gardening easier for the home gardener. Newer systems are simpler to set up and operate. An increase in suppliers of hydroponic products means equipment and the special fertilizers needed are easier to obtain. The use of lightweight plastics in the newer systems makes hydroponics less expensive. Home gardeners can use hydroponics on a smaller scale to grow chile peppers year-round or to grow them in smaller spaces, such as an apartment or balcony.

Another advantage that hydroponics offers to the chile pepper gardener is fewer weeds. Because a sterile rooting medium is used, no weeds grow, and furthermore, soilborne pests and diseases are minimized, if not completely eliminated. In most situations, the plants mature faster, yielding an earlier and greater harvest of pods. Hydroponic growing uses less space because the roots do not need to spread out in search of nutrients and water. This reduced space need makes hydroponic growing ideal for the home gardener, and it increases the growing capacity of greenhouse space.

One of the biggest advantages to hydroponics is the ability to automate the entire system with a timer. Automation allows the gardener to be gone for long periods of time without having to worry about watering the plants. The automatic system can provide water and nutrients to the plant 24/7. The lighting source can also be automated with a timer, thus completely automating the growing process.

PLANT NEEDS. Whether a plant is grown in soil or in water, four factors affect plant growth and productivity: nutrients, water, light, and air. A plant's roots, whether in soil or in a hydroponic system, absorb the necessary nutrients and water needed. With hydroponics, the water and nutrients are always available to the roots; thus the plant is never stressed for either. In an outdoor hydroponic system, sunlight and air are readily available. However, for an indoor system, one must provide an adequate light source and good air circulation. The light is needed for photosynthesis and can be provided by metal halide lamps, sodium vapor lamps, grolights, or fluorescent lights used in conjunction with incandescent light bulbs.

The chile pepper needs access to air in two ways. First, the roots must have oxygen available to keep them alive. Healthy roots are needed to take up the nutrients needed for plant growth. If the roots die, it is impossible for the plant to survive, even if sufficient nutrients are in the hydroponic solution. Second,

Peppers growing hydroponically at Epcot Center in Orlando, Florida.

air circulation around the leaves is important because it provides the chile pepper with the necessary carbon dioxide to carry out photosynthesis. In addition, good air circulation helps prevent fungal diseases caused by moist, stagnant conditions. Indoor units often have a small fan to circulate the surrounding air.

Even though the soil has been eliminated in a hydroponic system, plants still need a place for their root systems to develop. A hydroponic medium is an inert substance that can provide some support for the root system but has no nutrient value. Almost any inert substance can be used. A few examples include sand, gravel, vermiculite, perlite, lightweight expanded clay aggregate, and rockwool.

A NONCIRCULATING HYDROPONIC SYSTEM. An inexpensive, noncirculating hydroponic system designed by the Asian Vegetable Research and Development

Center can be constructed from a polystyrene container (a soda or beer cooler). This container insulates the nutrient solution and maintains a relatively stable temperature. It holds a large volume of water, which helps maintain pH, nutrient levels, and electrical conductivity.

The combined macro- and micronutrient solution is added to a depth of 4 to 8 inches below the top. A layer of nylon window screening is placed about ½ inch above the surface of the nutrient solution. This screen induces rapid lateral root growth and branching, promotes plant growth, and anchors the plant.

The polystyrene cover is placed on the container to exclude light and prevent algae growth. Fifteen 3-inch holes are made in the cover, and suitable plastic pots, with the bottoms removed and replaced with a circle of nylon screening to hold peat or vermiculite, are set in these holes and rest on the nylon screening in the large container. Chile pepper transplants, grown in peat or vermiculite, are placed in these pots, and the pots are filled with additional peat or vermiculite. Immediately after transplanting, hand water the pots with the nutrient solution to avoid transplant shock and wilting.

The nutrient level in the container will decrease due to evaporation, transpiration, and absorption by the root system. However, do not add large quantities of the nutrient solution at any one time—the level should be increased by no more than 4 inches at a time. Chile pepper plants have grown well with a 6-inch air space below the screen once the roots are established in the nutrient solution. The upper part of the root

system absorbs oxygen for ample aeration, while the lower part absorbs water and nutrients.

If the container is placed outside, a clear plastic cover should be set over it to protect the chile peppers and to prevent rainwater from entering the container. If the container is placed under artificial lights, the lights should be adjusted in the same way they are for chile peppers grown in containers with soil.

The nutrient solution is the most important factor in the success or failure of a hydroponic system. Most fertilizers commonly available in garden centers do not contain all of the thirteen elements necessary for plant growth, because the growing medium usually provides many of them. Hydroponic plants receive nutrients from a different source, so it is necessary to use a fertilizer formulated for hydroponic systems. Hydroponic fertilizers are available from many online companies and a few specialty garden centers. It is important to follow the dilution rate recommended on the label and to test the solution to be sure that the pH (acidity or alkalinity) is between 5 and 6. Simple pH test kits and pH modifiers are available wherever aquarium supplies are sold.

Depending on the stage of plant development, some elements in the nutrient solution will be depleted more quickly than others. Because of this, it is important to change the nutrient solution every 2 weeks. The old solution can be used to water other houseplants or outdoor plants. Also, make sure that the nutrient solution is kept at the original volume. As water evaporates from the nutrient solution, the fertilizer becomes more concentrated and can burn the chile pepper plant's roots. Add water only, not more fertilizer, to raise the nutrient solution back to its original volume.

WATER CULTURE SYSTEMS. Water culture hydroponic growing systems include the nutrient film technique, aeroponics, and the aeration method. The nutrient film technique is the most widely adopted system for commercial solution culture of horticultural crops, chile peppers included, in the world. In this system, the chile peppers are placed in a plastic trough or tube as the container through which a constant, thin film of nutrient solution flows. Plants are suspended through holes in the top of the trough. The trough is gently sloped so gravity pulls the solution back to the nutrient reservoir. There are many variations of this system, making it the most popular for the home gardener, too.

Aeroponics is the growing of plants in a container in which the roots are suspended in a nutrient mist rather than in a solution. The most popular container for aeroponics is an enclosed A-frame constructed of styrofoam boards. The plants are placed in holes along the sloped sides of the frame. The nutrient mist is delivered to the roots by a vaporizer or by special attachments available with drip irrigation kits. The mist clings to the roots. Any excess runs down the inside of the frame, is collected at the bottom, and is recycled back to the nutrient reservoir.

The aeration method, one of the first systems to be developed, uses an aquarium air pump to bubble oxygen to the roots of plants immersed in the nutrient solution. Plants

Water culture at a Korean greenhouse.

are suspended 1 inch above the solution by a 2-inch-deep mesh tray that is set into the container by placing the lip of the tray over the container's edge. A layer of inert material, such as gravel, clay pebbles, or vermiculite, is placed in the tray to provide stability for the plants while allowing the roots to grow down into the nutrient solution.

AGGREGATE SYSTEMS. Aggregate hydroponic growing systems use some form of inert material to support and surround plant roots. The most common materials used are rockwool, clay pebbles, gravel, perlite, vermiculite, sand, or foam chips. The medium provides plant support and allows good oxygen penetration to the roots, yet retains a thin layer of nutrients and water

Plants growing in an aggregate medium.

around the roots. One of the most common systems that uses an aggregate medium is the flood-and-drain method. A water-holding container, such as a plastic dishpan, is filled with the aggregate and chile pepper plants. The container is flooded periodically with the nutrient solution. The solution is drained back into the nutrient reservoir by opening a valve at the bottom of the container. During each cycle, the roots are submerged in the solution for no more than 20 to 30 minutes.

Another common aggregate system is the trickle-feed method. The nutrient solution is continuously pumped from the reservoir through a ½-inch irrigation tube that branches into a number of ⅛-inch tubes. These smaller tubes deliver the solution to the containers. Any excess solution is collected at the base of each container and returned to the nutrient reservoir.

A modification of the trickle-feed method is called tube culture. A 4- to 6-inch plastic tube or bag is filled with a lightweight aggregate.

Holes are made on all sides of the container for the plants. The tube is hung vertically, and an irrigation tube is positioned at the top of the container. The nutrient solution seeps through the container and may or may not be recycled when it reaches the end.

AVOIDING DISEASES AND PESTS. As with any indoor or outdoor garden, a variety of diseases and pests can plague the chile pepper plants in a hydroponic system. Many of the diseases and pests are the same as those described in "Diseases and Pests." However, three are specific to the indoor growing of chile peppers: fungus gnats, *Pythium*, and nitrophilic bacteria.

Fungus gnats are tiny black flies that can become a nuisance for indoor gardeners and may represent a much more serious problem than many gardeners realize. These little flies are believed to be vectors of various fungal diseases. Fungus gnats can carry spores of *Pythium*, *Botrytis*, *Verticillium*, *Fusarium*, and *Thielavaiopsis* as they move from plant to plant. Fungal spores have also been found in their frass (droppings). It is not yet clear how serious this problem is but the potential is certainly there.

Adult fungus gnats do not damage the leaves or roots of chile peppers. Rather, the damage is done by the larvae that live in the medium and feed on any organic matter. These larvae, which can attain a length of about 5 mm, will quickly damage plants by chewing or stripping the roots. Affected plants may lose vigor and the leaves may turn yellow without any visible injury showing on the aboveground parts. Root hairs are eaten off, as are the small feeding roots. In severe infestations, all that is left is the center part of the root.

The damage caused by fungus gnats is often confused with seedling damping-off and other fungal diseases or even with nutritional problems. However, if adult flies are visible, it is highly likely that they are, at least in part, responsible for the declining plant performance.

The best control is to allow the growing medium to dry out between waterings. This will kill the larvae through desiccation. Another option is to drench the growing medium with an insecticide registered for this type of use. An organic approach is to use *Bacillus thuringiensis* H-14 (Gnatol). Drenching the growing medium with the bacteria in weekly applications for 2 or 3 weeks should eliminate the insects.

Pythium is a waterborne fungus, and recirculating hydroponic systems provide it with an ideal environment in which to live and grow. Plants can survive and grow with high levels of *Pythium* in the nutrient solution. However, the fungus will restrict the roots in absorbing water. A sudden rise in air temperature will cause the chile pepper plants to wilt, because they will be unable to increase their uptake of water. For many growers this is the first sign that *Pythium* is active in their system. The most visible symptom of this fungal disease is that the roots will begin to turn brown and lose their healthy white appearance. As the pathogen spreads the roots become soft and mushy, and in the warmer part of the day, the plant has a tendency to wilt.

The first step is prevention. Maintaining a clean growing environment and treating the incoming water minimizes the opportunity for the fungus to enter the system. Second, a well-designed hydroponic system will not allow the fungal spores to germinate and grow. A number of additives and treatments designed to eliminate pathogenic organisms from hydroponic systems are available.

Nitrophilic bacteria can become established in the root zone of hydroponically grown plants. They are most often found in pot culture plants grown in a medium such as perlite or granulated rockwool. These bacterial organisms feed on nitrate ions and excrete ammonia. They are especially favored by cold stagnant liquids in reservoirs. If they become established, the level of nitrate, the form of nitrogen that chile peppers use, in the nutrient will drop very rapidly. This results in decreased growth and a rapid yellowing of the chile pepper leaves. The yellowing will spread, affecting the entire plant, and will eventually lead to necrosis (death) of the plant.

The first symptom is often the yellowing of the foliage, but this may be accompanied by the development of an unpleasant ammonia smell from the reservoir and the root zone. Control measures consist of flushing the pots thoroughly with clean water and washing with hydrogen peroxide. Another precaution is to not allow the reservoirs to be too deep. They should hold only about as much liquid as the plant will draw up in twenty-four hours. Keep the room warm and keep humidity low.

With any disease or pest, the best approach is to contain the outbreak before it becomes large. If one plant is developing symptoms of a bacterial or viral disease, quickly quarantine

Jim Duffy's hydroponic setup.

THE HYDROPONIC ADVENTURES OF JIM DUFFY

Jim Duffy is a chilehead in San Diego who has figured out a way for his hydroponically grown chiles to benefit kids. We decided to let him tell the story in his own words.

"In the late summer of 2005, I wandered into one of our Youth Venture youth centers where a friend was volunteering. As usual I brought chips and salsa with me. I noticed that some of the kids were eating like it was the only food they had had that day. This touched my heart, so I began showing up every Wednesday with meals for them and made spicy dishes with my chiles whenever I could. The kids loved it. They especially requested my spicy chicken soup made with habaneros. By the end of the year I had started going on Fridays to a second youth center where my daughter was volunteering. Now I was feeding kids twice a week. So to fund all these dinners I started doing part-time catering and sometimes sold my chiles and salsa at local farmers' markets.

"In February of 2006, I decided to send some of these kids to local college athletic events. Most of these kids came from single-parent families and had never been to a sporting event. In the summer of 2006, I decided to mostly grow 'Red Savina' and 'Chocolate Habanero' along with some 'Scotch Bonnet'. I could get more money for these. By the end of summer 2006, I had started visiting a third youth center. Now I was feeding kids at three centers a week and sending them in groups to San Diego State athletic events. By the end of 2006 my little journey with chiles had given me the resources to provide more than 800 meals and send more than 400 children to events.

"In the winter of 2007, my close friend Larry Bridgeforth introduced me to hydroponic gardening. I was scared to death to do it. What if I failed and lost all my plants? So in the spring of 2007, I planted 120 plants in my first nutrient film technique (NFT) hydroponic system. Larry was always busy, so with the aid of the Web and many phone calls I got it built and up and running by myself. I planted thirty 'Bhut Jolokia' plants, forty 'Red Savina' plants, and forty 'Chocolate Habanero' plants. The plants had to have the soil washed off their roots before transplanting into small 2-inch pots called net pots that sat in the 20-foot-long tubes. Net pots have slats or open grooves so the roots can grow through the pot down to the water. I used rockwool for a substrate to pack around the roots in the pots. Rockwool is made from volcanic rock but resembles fiber insulation and does hold water. Later I added wicks to draw more water and nutrient up to the roots until they could get down to the water by themselves.

"By July 2007, I had a jungle. The roots had pushed the pots up out of the tubes. I frantically wired down the pots and tried tying the plants to my shade cover, fence, and even other plants. So many chiles caused a lot of plants to fall over and even break. I started selling the chiles in various Web ads, but they were not moving fast enough. Then the famous restaurant in Chicago called Heaven on Seven contacted me and bought almost everything I had. They put on a "Hot as a Mutha Dinner" every year and my chiles were a hit. So I decided that I would be a supplier to them in 2008. Thank God for Heaven on Seven!

"In 2008 I planted the same varieties as I did in 2007. I purchased net pots with larger grooves from City Farmer's Nursery in San Diego. The larger grooves enabled me to pull a few inches of roots down to the water stream while transplanting. I also used the wicks to draw up more water—only this time I used them from the very beginning. In June I knew the plants roots would push the plants up out of the tubes. So I made 2-inch-by-2-inch squares of-inch-thick PVC material, cut-inch slots into them so I could slide them over the base of the stem and cover most of the surface area of a 2-inch net pot, and then fastened down the PVC tightly with coated wire. Now when the roots met resistance at the bottom of the tube, they would not push up the plant; instead they would grow around the surface area of the inside of the NFT tube. The pieces of PVC had other benefits as well. They kept sunlight off the rockwool and prevented surface algae growth, stabilized

the base of most of the plants, and held in moisture.

"The growth was way more than in 2007. I tried telling the plants to grow evenly, but plants do not always listen. Some plants had more branches on one side than the other and that meant more chiles. This monster growth bent over a few plants, and a few just broke in two. So even with the stabilizing at the root base, it looked like I would need to have overhead support in 2009. By the end of August 2008 it looked like I would have at least 30 percent more chiles than in 2007. I could not get between the 2-foot rows; I could only crawl under the system to harvest. As far as I knew, I was the only one growing the world's three hottest chiles in an NFT hydroponic system. So Chef Jimmy Bannos at Heaven on Seven would get plenty."

Jim Duffy's habanero harvest.

Jukka's chile bonsai collection.

has spread throughout the world. Our friend Jukka Kilpinen in Finland is a chile pepper bonsai enthusiast. He has sculptured a wonderful set of chile pepper bonsai. He believes that you do not have to have expert knowledge to make a beautiful and stunning chile pepper bonsai. At his Web site, www.fatalii.net/bonsai, he gives details of the art of growing a chile pepper from a seed to a bonsai tree.

Any of the thousands of varieties of chile pepper will work. The varieties with smaller leaves give better proportions to the bonsai, and many of the wild species have characteristics that lend themselves to bonsai. If a chile pepper plant has been in a container for a year or more, it makes a good candidate to cut back into a bonsai.

Any small container will work. Many hobby shops and upscale garden centers, however, carry the traditional bonsai containers. These pots are designed to add an extra element of beauty to the bonsai.

For soil, Jukka recommends using a peat-based soil. Commercially available soil for houseplants works very well. Remember, the plants are still chile peppers and do not like too much moisture around the root area. The root space is very limited with bonsai plants, so the frequency of watering is critical. Depending on the air temperature and the amount of wind and light, the soil can dry out quickly.

Akadama is good material for maintaining soil moisture. *Akadama* is Japanese for "red" and "ball." It is a claylike mineral that darkens when moist, which can help indicate when to water the chile pepper bonsai. It is more costly

that plant. It may seem like a pain to have to go through the steps necessary to transfer that plant to a new growing area, but it will probably save you a lot of hassle if you can prevent the infection of the entire crop.

Bonsai chiles

The painstaking art of bonsai has enjoyed a huge rise in popularity. Bonsai plants are kept small and trained by pruning branches and roots, by periodic repotting, by pinching off new growth, and by wiring the branches and trunk so that they grow into the desired shape. A bonsai tree should always be positioned off-center in its container, for not only is asymmetry vital to the visual effect, but the center point is symbolically where heaven and earth meet, and nothing should occupy this place. Another aesthetic principle is the triangular pattern necessary for visual balance. Tradition holds that three basic virtues are necessary to create a bonsai: *shin-zen-bi*, standing for truth, goodness, and beauty.

The evolution of bonsai over the past two centuries is truly amazing. It is now a well-known and respected horticultural art form that

than many other soil choices, but it is prized by many gardeners because of its ability to retain water and nutrients while still providing porosity and good drainage. For all of its qualities, many bonsai growers consider the cost of *akadama* prohibitive or unnecessary. Still other growers claim that when subjected to cold and wet climates the granules progressively break down into smaller particles that inhibit drainage, which is an essential characteristic of bonsai soil. This problem can be avoided either by incorporating sand or grit in the soil mix or by using the hardest grades of *akadama*. There are reports that some brands of cat litter work as well and are a much cheaper substitute for *akadama*. Jukka puts *akadama* at the bottom of the container and then uses soil on top.

No special tools are necessary. Tools designed for bonsai growers can make trimming easier, but small pruning shears can do the job.

The five basic bonsai styles are formal upright, informal upright, slanting (or windswept), semi-cascade, and cascade. All have their own individual beauty and serenity. Thus, the first step in making a chile pepper bonsai is choosing a style to aim for as the goal. Next, choose the chile pepper plant. One with a large stem gives the look of a tree trunk. The safest approach is to trim the chile pepper plant only a little at first and to continue the trimming while the plant is forming new foliage lower on the stem. The plant needs the foliage to make food, so cutting back too hard will cause the plant to go into great shock than necessary.

Next trim the roots. The goal is to leave the largest roots visible above the soil level of the

ABOVE **Bonsai containers.**

LEFT **Trimming the roots.**

container to make the bonsai more dramatic. To enhance and encourage woody roots, months before cutting the plant back expose the largest roots to light.

Then trim the stem and limbs. To style the branches, wire is used to shape the plant. Wiring is an important part of the process of styling the bonsai. Nearly all well-designed bonsai have been wired at some point in their

RIGHT Trimming the stems.

FAR RIGHT A finished and decorated bonsai chile pepper.

New growth.

development. Though at first wiring is a daunting technique to master, it gives the bonsai enthusiast better control of the trunk and branches of the bonsai and makes them easier to manipulate.

By coiling wire around the limbs of the bonsai, the gardener is able to bend the plant into a desired position where it is held by the wire. In a matter of weeks or months, the branch or trunk will remain in that position even after the wire is removed. With the use of wire, straight trunks or branches can be given more realistic bonsai movement. Young branches can be wired into a horizontal or downward position to create the illusion of maturity. Foliage or branching can be moved to fill in bare areas of the tree's silhouette. Without wiring, the gardener would otherwise have to wait for shoots to grow in the desired direction. With wiring, existing growth can be manipulated there instead.

Bonsai wire is normally available only from bonsai nurseries and online shops. Anodized aluminum wire and annealed copper wire are generally available; aluminum wire is easier to apply for beginners and can be reused (though this is not recommended), while copper wire is more difficult to apply and cannot be reused but has more holding power. Wire cutters are also necessary for removing wire from branches and for cutting suitable lengths. Bonsai wire cutters are available, but ordinary wire cutters are adequate if the wire can be cut at the very end of the cutter's jaws.

Given proper care, the chile pepper bonsai can live for a decade or more. It is not the age of the bonsai that is important, but its aesthetic effect, its proper proportion to the appropriate container, and its health.

Finally, bonsai are very personal and there are no strict rules to obey. It is a hobby pursued for enjoyment. It does not have to be an expensive commitment, but it is a commitment that requires a great amount of time, patience, skill, and endurance. Although things may not go according to plan, don't give up. Remember that the Japanese bonsai masters were once beginners too, and they have surely had their share of trial and error.

DISEASES AND PESTS

Unfortunately, even a beautiful growing chile pepper garden can expect to have disease and pest problems at some point. Chile peppers are susceptible to several diseases and pests that can reduce yield and quality of fruit. Not all

A field devastated by *Phytophthora* blight.

the diseases and pests occur in the same region or at the same time. Nevertheless, a vigorous, thrifty chile pepper plant can better tolerate or outgrow damage from disease and pests than a weakened one.

The correct diagnosis of a disorder is important in order to choose the proper treatment. A wrong diagnosis means selecting the wrong treatment, which is expensive and unnecessary. As a general rule, most pests cannot be eradicated, but they can be managed so that the risk of occurrence or loss is minimized. Pests are best controlled by taking action before they become serious. Frequent examination of chile pepper plants helps to diagnose potential problems. After a pest problem is well established, it is usually difficult to control.

Disease and insect control must start before seeds are planted or seedlings are transplanted. One of the best ways to avoid chile pepper diseases is to avoid planting in the same spot each year. Rotating where chiles are planted will help to reduce disease, especially root-rot diseases caused by soil-borne pathogens. Proper plant spacing to provide adequate air movement around plants helps reduce foliar disease severity. An equally important disease control method is planting disease-resistant chile pepper cultivars. It is considered the most prudent means of disease control because of its low cost, ease of use, and protection of the environment. In addition, planting healthy seeds and transplants, controlling water in the root zone, controlling insects that carry disease, and cleaning and disinfecting equipment will aid in reducing disease and pests.

Chile pepper plants with root problems normally have nonspecific symptoms, such as wilting, yellowing, or dieback. With general symptoms like these, it may be necessary to send samples to a university agricultural extension service or a diagnostic laboratory for testing. Always follow the laboratory's instructions on how to prepare and ship the sample, and provide a copy of the information collected to the person responsible for your sample. A sample that is improperly collected, packed, and/or shipped and arrives in poor condition may be insufficient for diagnosis.

Each state's agricultural extension service has a plant diagnostic clinic or similar unit designed to provide this information. The clinics provide accurate plant disease diagnosis, quick turnaround time, professional services, and up-to-date control recommendations. Many clinics also facilitate insect and weed identification. A small service fee is normally charged.

For initial assistance with chile pepper problems, contact the local county extension office. The staff can assist with identifying the problem and if necessary can send the sample submission to the appropriate clinic. Some county extension offices have a series of telephone tape recordings on various gardening topics. A caller can request the recording be played, before asking the agent specific questions.

Be diligent and keep records of your observations. Do not depend on memory for important details such as when a symptom first appears, when a problem is treated, weather conditions when the problem is seen, and which cultivars appear more resistant or susceptible. A symptom may be from multiple causes rather than from one isolated pathogen or environmental factor. Therefore, apply integrated diagnostics to diagnose and control the problem.

Both nonliving (abiotic) and living (biotic) agents cause chile pepper disease and injury. Nonliving factors include extreme levels of temperature, moisture, light, nutrients, pH, air pollutants, and pesticides. Living pathogens that cause disease include bacteria, fungi, insects, mycoplasmas, nematodes, and viruses.

There are three approaches to controlling chile pepper diseases and pests: (1) using organic gardening techniques; (2) using synthetic (artificially produced) chemicals; and (3) using integrated pest management (IPM). Both organic and synthetic approaches have merits and can be used independently. However, combining these methods in IPM is often more effective for preventing diseases and pests. IPM programs use current, comprehensive information on the life cycles of diseases and pests and their interaction with the environment. This information, in combination with available control methods, is used to manage the damage by the most economical means and with the least possible hazard to people, property, and the environment. IPM takes advantage of all appropriate pest management options including, but not limited to, the judicious use of pesticides. In contrast, organic food production applies many of the same concepts as IPM but limits the use of pesticides to those that are produced from natural sources, as opposed to synthetic chemicals.

General control measures can be summarized into these key ideas:

- Provide adequate space between plants. This allows good air movement and will help control diseases.
- Plant healthy seeds and transplants. Because disease can be introduced via infested seed or plants, careful inspection is recommended. Purchase seed and transplants from a local, reputable, reliable source, such as a trusted garden center.
- Plant disease-resistant and -tolerant varieties when available.
- Use crop rotation: avoid planting the same or related crops in the same plot in successive years. Do not rotate tomatoes, eggplant, or potatoes in the same spot as peppers. Most pathogens die when suitable hosts are absent.
- Water plants in the early morning hours so that the foliage will dry. Watering plants in the evening creates ideal conditions for disease development and spread.
- Control insects early in the season, because many of them transmit virus and bacterial diseases to healthy plants. Aphids and leafhoppers transmit viruses and mycoplasmas from infected plants to healthy plants. Aphids feed on infected weeds, then move to peppers and introduce viruses that are spread in secondary cycles with the planting. In some instances, it takes only five to ten seconds of feeding by an aphid to infect a pepper plant.
- Use sanitation techniques. Dispose of diseased plants, and frequently clean and disinfect equipment and benches. Control weeds around the garden area, because many disease organisms survive on weeds and can be transferred to peppers by insects, wind, and such. Beware that perennial weeds can overwinter reservoirs of destructive viruses.

Following are descriptions and symptoms of bacterial diseases, fungal diseases, viral diseases, abiotic disorders, and pests affecting peppers.

Bacterial diseases

BACTERIAL CANKER

Causal agent: *Corynebacterium michiganense*

Symptoms: Scabby canker spots on pods. The spots coalesce to form large spots, ¼ inch to 1¼ inches in diameter. The disease may also produce local lesions on fruits, stems, and leaves, but does not induce systemic infection on the plant. It is reported mainly as a problem in greenhouse production and in fields where chile peppers are grown under cover. Infested pods may contaminate the seed with the bacterium.

Control: Use disease-free seed, control bacterial populations present on the leaf surface of transplants in the greenhouse, and plant into a clean field or greenhouse.

BACTERIAL SPOT

Causal agent: *Xanthomonas campestris* pv. *vesicatoria*, which also causes bacterial spot of tomato. A pathovar (pv.) is a subspecific bacteria strain that shares similar pathogenic characteristics with other bacteria. For example, pv. *vesicatoria* is the strain that causes disease in peppers.

Symptoms: Bacterial leaf spot affects the aboveground parts. On young leaves, the spots are small, yellowish green, and slightly raised on the underside of the leaf. On older leaves, the spots are first dark, water soaked, and not noticeably raised. When spots are few, they may enlarge to $\frac{1}{8}$ or $\frac{1}{4}$ inch in diameter. These spots have dead, straw-colored centers with a dark margin. Severely spotted leaves turn yellow and drop. Infected seedlings often lose all but the top leaves of the plant.

The first signs of bacterial spot on fruits are small, raised, dark-colored spots that are often surrounded by a water-soaked margin. The spots appear angular, for the bacteria spread along the veins. As disease progresses, the spots may enlarge, turn black, and become rough, giving the fruit a scabby appearance.

Control: Crop rotation and using disease-free seed is the best approach. The organism is seed-borne and, in some areas, can overwinter on diseased plant refuse in the soil. The main source of infection is infected seed. Infected seedlings carry the disease to the field, where it can spread rapidly during warm, rainy weather, especially when driving rain and wind have caused mechanical injuries to the plants. Marginal success in controlling the disease has come from using copper-based bactericide. However, excessive use of copper can be toxic to the chile pepper.

BACTERIAL SOFT ROT

Causal agent: *Erwinia carotovora* pv. *carotovora*

Symptoms: Rot usually begins in the stem end of the fruit but can also occur through wounds on the pod. The internal tissue softens, and the pod turns to a watery mass. The pod also has a foul smell.

Control: This disease is worst in wet weather because the bacteria are splashed from the ground onto the fruit. It can also be started by insect injury. Therefore, controlling insects helps prevent this disorder.

BACTERIAL WILT

Causal agent: *Pseudomonas solanacearum*

Symptoms: The disease begins with a wilting of leaves. After a few days, a permanent wilt results, with no leaf yellowing. A test for this bacteria is to cut the roots and lower stems and look for an exudate of milky streams of bacteria when suspended in water.

Control: Plant clean seed and transplants and reduce inoculum in the garden by discarding diseased plants.

Fungal diseases

ANTHRACNOSE

Causal agent: Several species of *Colletotrichum*

Symptoms: Small, water-soaked, shrunken lesions appear on ripe pods. The lesions have dark fungal spores in them and a characteristic concentric ring appearance.

Control: Clean seed and crop rotation are important. If the disorder is severe, a fungicide may be needed.

EARLY BLIGHT

Causal agent: *Alternaria solani*

Symptoms: Small, irregular, brown, dead spots with concentric rings form, normally on older leaves. The spots enlarge until they are ¼ to½ inch in diameter. The spots are ridged and have a target pattern. The entire leaf may become yellow. Dark, leathery, sunken spots may form on fruits and cause rot.

Control: Use crop rotation, improve air movement around the plant, manage weeds, use less fertilizer and irrigation, and apply fungicides.

CERCOSPORA LEAF SPOT (frogeye)

Causal agent: *Cercospora capsici*

Symptoms: Brown, circular leaf lesions form, with a small, light gray center and a dark brown margin (frogeye). Leaf drop is common

Anthracnose.

for infected leaves.

Control: Clean seed and crop rotation are important. The disease is worst under humid conditions. Fungicides can help to manage the disease.

DAMPING-OFF

Causal agent: Several fungi, such as *Pythium*, *Rhizoctonia*, and *Fusarium*

Symptoms: Seedlings fail to emerge (pre-emergence damping-off), small seedlings collapse (post-emergence damping-off), or seedlings are stunted (root rot and collar rot).

Control: Treating the seed with a fungicide or treating the soil to minimize the fungi population is the most common method of control. Most commercially prepared soil mixes are safe from these fungi.

FUSARIUM WILT

Causal agent: *Fusarium oxysporum* f.sp. *capsici*

Symptoms: An initial slight yellowing of the foliage and wilting of the upper leaves progresses in a few days into a permanent wilt with the leaves still attached. Cut stem shows a browning, similar to verticillium wilt.

Control: High temperatures and wet soil conditions favor the disease. Most likely to occur in poorly drained areas.

GRAY MOLD

Causal agent: *Botrytis cinerea*

Symptoms: Succulent tissues, such as young leaves, stems, and flowers, suddenly collapse. Gray powdery spore masses of the fungus occur on the surface of dead plant tissues.

Control: High humidity favors the disease. A wide plant spacing so that plants dry quickly helps reduce the disease. A fungicide can be used if the mold is severe.

PHYTOPHTHORA BLIGHT

Causal agent: *Phytophthora capsici*. The fungus can cause four separate disorders: foliar blight, stem blight, fruit rot, or root rot. It spreads rapidly when humidity and temperatures are high and the soil is wet.

Symptoms: Often called chile wilt, it differs from vascular wilts caused by *Verticillium dahliae* and *Fusarium oxysporum*. Large plants wilt and die, leaving brown stalks and leaves and small, poor-quality fruits. If the fungus enters the roots, the plants cannot obtain enough water, may suddenly wilt, and eventually die. When the disease is severe, the fungus may attack main stems and branches, causing brown or black spots that kill that portion of the plant. The disease is most common in overwatered areas, such as low spots, heavy soils, lower ends (tails) of sloping fields, or upper ends (heads) of long fields.

Control: You can prevent chile root rot by avoiding excess water. Do not allow water to stand in the garden and drain the field quickly to avoid infection. One cultural-control measure is cultivating so plants are grown on a high ridge after the last cultivation. Fungicides work against foliar blight and pod rot.

POWDERY MILDEW

Causal agent: *Leveillula taurica*, *Oidiopsis taurica*

Symptoms: Chlorotic blotches or spots that may become necrotic with time. On the lower leaf surface, a white to gray powdery growth may exist. Leaf drop is common.

Control: Fungicides may be needed. Other plants in the garden with powdery mildew should be removed.

SOUTHERN BLIGHT

Causal agent: *Sclerotium rolfsii*

Symptoms: Leaves suddenly wilt with no discoloration but may turn yellow later. The base of the stem is brown and decayed above and below the soil line. White fungus is visible at the base of the stem and on the soil around the base. Sclerotia, small brown spheres about the size of mustard seeds, can be found in the fungal mycelium.

Control: Deep tilling to bury the sclerotia,

removing infected plants, and allowing a plot to lie fallow for a couple of years are helpful control measures. Soil fungicides may provide some control.

VERTICILLIUM WILT

Causal agent: Two species of fungi, *Verticillium dahliae* and *V. albo-atrum*

Symptoms: Plants first show wilting, then usually shed many leaves, and finally die. If the stem is cut, vascular discoloration is seen.

Control: No resistant cultivars nor chemical controls are known. Solarization of garden soil has worked under certain conditions. Rotate crops, but not with eggplant, okra, or tomatoes.

WHITE MOLD (*Sclerotinia* disease)

Causal agent: *Sclerotinia sclerotiorum*

Symptoms: This fungus causes wilt and blighting or rotting of any aboveground or belowground plant parts. At first, the affected area of the plant has a dark green, greasy or water-soaked appearance. On stems, the lesion may be brown to gray in color. If the humidity is high, a white, fluffy mycelial (mold) growth appears. Lumpy areas appear in this white growth, which become hard and black as they mature. The hard, black bodies (sclerotia) form inside the stem or on the outside surfaces of the stem and other plant parts.

Control: Proper plant spacing, well-drained soil, crop rotation, and careful removal of all infected plants as soon as possible are useful control measures. Do not compost or use the plants for mulch.

Brote grande.

Phytoplasma

BROTE GRANDE (big bud)

Causal agent: Phytoplasma (very small bacterialike organisms)

Symptoms: Affected plants have a bushy appearance, develop overly large green buds instead of flowering normally, and fail to set fruit (phyllody).

Control: All known phytoplasmas are spread from plant to plant by insects, mainly leafhoppers. Use insecticides to reduce leafhopper population or cover plants to keep leafhoppers off plants, and plant resistant cultivars.

Viruses

Viruses are extremely small and can be seen only with an electron microscope. Viruses alter the metabolism of plant cells, causing the plants to grow abnormally. One plant can be attacked by many viruses and express many different symptoms. Early detecting and removing

RIGHT Alfalfa mosaic virus.
FAR RIGHT Beet curly top virus.

infected plants helps, but complete control is often difficult. Separating symptoms caused by mosaic diseases from those caused by abnormal pH, herbicide injury, nutritional deficiencies, feeding damage by mites or insects, and the like may be difficult. No viricides exist that control plant viruses.

ALFALFA MOSAIC VIRUS (AMV)

Symptoms: Plants are mildly stunted and have whitish blotches on the leaves. The infected area is white-bleached and mottled. Fruit may be distorted.

Control: Aphids carry AMV. Chile peppers planted near alfalfa have a higher incidence of the disease. Control aphid vectors, avoid planting near alfalfa, and use resistant varieties if available.

BEET CURLY TOP VIRUS (BCTV)

Symptoms: The most striking symptom is stunting and yellowing of the plant. Affected plants are also quite stiff and erect, and the leaves have a leathery feel.

Control: The beet leafhopper (*Circulifer tenellus*) is an effective vector, because it is able to transmit the virus after feeding on an infected chile pepper plant for as little as one minute and can subsequently transmit the virus for the remainder of its lifetime. Fortunately, the virus is not passed on to leafhopper progeny. Because leafhoppers that carry the virus do not feed in shady locations, you can help prevent losses by partially shading plants with muslin tents or by other means early in the season. Spraying or dusting with insecticide can be justified only when control is needed for other insects. If possible, all diseased pepper plants should be removed from the field as soon as they are noticed so that they do not continue to provide a source of virus for transmission to heathy plants. Plant resistant cultivars when available.

CUCUMBER MOSAIC VIRUS (CMV)

Symptoms: Affected plants are severely stunted and have dull light green foliage with a leathery appearance but no distinctive foliar markings. Leaves may become narrow and no longer expand, while in other cases, small necrotic specks or ring spots with oak-leaf patterns develop. Sometimes a necrotic line develops across the leaf. Affected leaves may drop prematurely. Older plants that are infected may show foliar mottling or no symptoms on foliage or fruit.

Control: Aphids carry the virus, so their control is paramount. Avoid growing near plants in the gourd family, and plant resistant cultivars.

GEMINI VIRUSES

Several new viruses have been detected. Local names for the viruses are *chino del tomate* (tomato crinkle), serrano golden mosaic, sinaloa tomato leaf curl, pepper mild tigre, and Texas pepper virus. The viruses cause similar symptoms but are biologically distinct.

Symptoms: The common symptoms are stunting, curling, or twisting of the leaves; bright yellow mosaic; distorting of leaves and fruit; and reduced yield.

Control: The viruses are spread by whiteflies (*Bemisia tabaci*). Control of gemini viruses is difficult once plants become infected. Destruction of perennial weeds that harbor whiteflies and crop rotation are currently the only control measures.

Tobacco etch virus.

PEPPER MOTTLE VIRUS (PEMV)

Symptoms: Stunted plants, distorted fruit, and low pod set indicate this virus.

Control: Aphids carry PeMV. Control aphid vectors, practice good sanitation, and plant resistant cultivars if available.

POTATO Y (PVY)

Symptoms: Plants are stunted, and leaves show mosaic and dark green vein-banding, crinkle, and distortion.

Control: This has been called the most common pepper virus. Plant resistant varieties and control aphid vectors.

SAMSUN LATENT TOBACCO MOSAIC VIRUS (SLTMV)

Symptoms: Leaves show mild mosaic and distortion. Pods develop rings, line patterns, necrotic spots, and distortion. Plant stunting may also occur.

Control: SLTMV is spread mechanically, by hands touching an infected plant and then

Tomato spotted wilt virus.

later may show chlorotic line patterns or mosaic with necrotic spots. Fruit of infected plants has chlorotic spots, streaks, mosaic, and ring patterns. On ripe fruit, yellow spots with concentric rings or necrotic streaks may be present.

Control: TSWV is carried by thrips that feed on various virus-infected perennial flowering plants commonly grown around homes. Use clean seed and control thrips.

touching an uninfected plant. Plant clean seed, use crop rotation, and wash hands after handling infected plants.

TOBACCO ETCH VIRUS (TEV)

Symptoms: Leaves show mosaic and dark green vein-banding and distortion, and plants are stunted. Tabasco plants wilt and die.

Control: Plant resistant varieties and control aphid vectors.

TOBACCO MOSAIC VIRUS (TMV)

Symptoms: Plants show mosaic and systemic chlorosis and leaf drop.

Control: TMV is spread mechanically, by hands touching an infected plant and then an uninfected plant. Plant clean seed, use crop rotation, and wash hands and equipment after handling infected plants.

TOMATO SPOTTED WILT VIRUS (TSWV)

Symptoms: Young pepper plants are stunted and exhibit yellowing and/or necrotic spots on the leaves and terminal shoot. Leaves infected

Insects

Insects are not usually a big problem for chile peppers. Early in the season, cutworms are the most damaging pests to both seeded and transplanted chile peppers. Seeded chile peppers are also subject to attack by flea beetles when the cotyledons emerge. Green peach aphids can become numerous at any time but are probably more prevalent during the warmer weather. Besides the stress created by aphids feeding on plant sap, their honeydew gets on the fruit and leaves. Its presence on the leaves, if heavy enough, can decrease photosynthesis from sooty mold growth. Problem insects differ in each region. To control the insect population, keep seedlings insect-free, inspect plants daily, weed well around the chile pepper plants, dispose of diseased plants immediately, and use an insecticide if necessary.

CUTWORMS

Description: Many species of cutworms exist. They are dull gray, brown, or black, and may be striped or spotted. They are stout, soft-bodied, smooth, and up to 1¼ inches long. When disturbed, they curl up tightly.

Damage: Cutworms attack only seedlings. They cut off the stems above, at, or just below the soil surface.

Control: Tilling disturbs the overwintering places of the cutworm. When setting out chile pepper plants in spring, place cardboard, roofing paper, plastic, or metal collars around the young stems, and push the collar 1 inch into the ground to stop cutworms. Treat the soil with Sevin before planting.

EUROPEAN CORN BORERS (*Ostrinia nubilalis*)

Description: Corn borer moths are active at night and hide during the day. Normally, the European corn borer does not prefer chile peppers as a host. Infestations in chile peppers usually occur when corn becomes relatively unattractive to egg-laying moths as a result of plants reaching maturity and females lay eggs on chile pepper plants as an alternative.

Damage: Egg masses usually are deposited on leaves. The eggs hatch in 3 to 7 days, and the larvae disperse over the plant. First instars enter the upper part of the fruit by crawling under the calyx and boring into it or into the fruit wall. First and second instars feed on the calyx, on the flesh around the calyx, or in the placenta. Third instars may continue feeding on the chile pepper fruit or may leave the pod. Those leaving the pod commonly bore into uninfested pods or into stems. Larvae continue to develop and may pupate in pod or stems. Late in the season, larvae may go into

diapause and overwinter in stems and fruit pedicels. Pods infested early usually rot and drop off the plant. Pods infested late in development may appear healthy or show premature coloring. Damage from feeding around the calyx also may reduce the size and quality of pods that escape internal infestation.

Control: Remove plant debris, especially cornstalks. The borer overwinters in corn stubble and emerges in the spring. *Bacillus thuringiensis*, rotenone, and Sevin are effective against the caterpillars.

FLEA BEETLES

Description: These beetles are about 1/16 inch long.

Damage: Young plants are severely damaged, chewed full of holes.

Control: Rotenone or Sevin dust is effective. The flea beetle is repelled by shade.

FRUITWORMS

Description: Fruitworms include the fall armyworm, the beet armyworm, and the tomato fruitworm / corn earworm. At the larval stage, the worm is green, brown, or pink, with light strips along the sides and on the back. It grows to 1¾ inches long.

Damage: The fruitworm eats holes in fruits.

Control: Fruitworms can be removed by hand. Rotenone, *Bacillus*, or Sevin dust is also effective.

GRASSHOPPERS

Description: Adults have front wings that are larger than the body and are held rooflike

Hornworm.

over the insect. The hind legs are long and adapted to jumping.

Damage: Grasshoppers eat pepper foliage. They may destroy complete plantings.

Control: Soil cultivation is useful because grasshoppers lay their eggs in the top 3 inches of soil. Birds often eat grasshoppers. Sevin dust is also effective.

GREEN PEACH APHIDS OR PLANT LICE (*Myzus persicae*)

Description: These pests are usually light green and soft-bodied. They cluster on leaf undersides and on stems.

Damage: Aphids excrete a sticky liquid called honeydew, which creates spots on the foliage. A black fungus, sooty mold, may then grow on the honeydew. Severe infestations can cause wilting, stunting, curling, and leaf distortion.

Control: Normally, aphid predators and parasites keep the aphid numbers low, but the aphids can multiply quickly. Spray with insecticidal soap.

GRUBS

Description: Grubs are white to light yellow with dark brown heads. They are the larvae of June beetles, May beetles, and Japanese beetles. There are more than one hundred species of white grubs. They are curved (C-shaped) and ½ inch to 1½ inches long.

Damage: The larvae feed on roots and underground parts. Root-feeding can cause wilting, stunting, and death of the plant.

Control: Till the soil repeatedly to uproot the grubs so the birds can eat them. Apply insecticide.

HORNWORMS (*Manduca sexta* and *M. quinquemaculata*)

Description: These worms are the larval stage of the sphinx moth. A green body with diagonal lines on the sides and a prominent horn on the rear end distinguishes these worms. They can be up to 4 inches long.

Damage: Foliage is eaten, and these worms can strip a chile pepper plant quickly.

Control: Hornworms are large enough to be removed by hand. Rotenone, *Bacillus*, and Sevin dust are also effective.

LEAFHOPPERS

Description: These bugs are green, wedge-shaped, and up to ⅛ inch long. They fly quickly when disturbed. Nymphs resemble adults but are smaller.

Damage: The leafhopper spreads curly top virus and can cause hopperburn. Hopperburn is rare in chile pepper, but the symptoms are tips and sides of chile pepper leaves turning yellow to brown and becoming brittle.

Control: Remove infested plants or plant parts immediately to reduce overwintering sites. Use floating row covers as a physical barrier to keep leafhoppers from damaging plants. Beneficial insects such as ladybugs, lacewings, and minute pirate bugs are all voracious predators of both the egg and young larval stage. If leafhopper levels become intolerable, spot spray with insecticides as a last resort.

LEAF MINERS *(Liriomyza trifolii)*

Description: The larva is yellow, about ⅛ inch long, and lives in pods and leaves. The adult is a tiny black-and-yellow fly.

Damage: The infected leaves are blotchy. The larvae make long, slender, winding tunnels under the epidermis of the pod and the leaf.

Control: Natural enemies, primarily parasitic wasps, often control leaf miners. When natural enemies are killed by pesticides, leaf miner outbreaks are common. Remove infested leaves. Sabadilla dust will control leaf miners.

PEPPER MAGGOTS *(Zonosemata electa)*

Description: The maggot is the larva of a fly. The pepper maggot is white or yellowish-white and ¼ to ½ inch long. Adult flies are yellow-striped, about ¼ inch long, with dark bars on the wings.

Damage: The pepper maggot feeds inside the pod by tunneling underneath the calyx. The damage appears very similar to that of the European corn borer. The first sign of a pepper-maggot infestation is the appearance of tiny elliptical holes in pods. The female's ovipositor creates these holes as she inserts her eggs just beneath the skin of young pods. As infested pods enlarge, the egg punctures become shallow depressions. Pods damaged by the pepper maggot are susceptible to premature pod ripening and rotting, as a result of pathogens such as *Erwinia carotovora* entering through the feeding wound. Although external damage to the pod is not always easily discernible, considerable internal tunneling and discoloration is caused by the maggot.

Control: Field sanitation and rotation typically are used to control pepper maggot. Adult flies are attracted to rotting pods, so removing rotting pods from fields reduces the fields' attractiveness to egg-laying flies. Destroying infested pods, which act as reservoirs, can help minimize future infestations. Insecticides can be applied to reduce the incidence of damage.

PEPPER WEEVILS *(Anthonomus eugenii)*

Description: The adult pepper weevil is a small beetle, about ⅛ inch long, with a dark body that has a brassy luster to it. Larvae are

Pepper weevil.

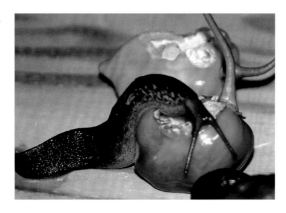

Slug having a pepper pod lunch.

off-white grubs with a brown head and are about ¼ inch long when mature.

Damage: The larvae and the adult weevil cause damage. Adult weevils feed on pods and leaf buds. Larvae feed inside the pods and cause young fruit to drop prematurely, reducing yields. Weevil larvae and frass are left in the chile pepper pod.

Control: Once the larvae are inside the pod, practical control is impossible. Control of pepper weevils is based on frequent and accurate scouting. Destroy chile pepper residue and weeds of the nightshade family to reduce the possibility of adult weevils overwintering. Remove infested fruit from the field and destroy. Regular applications of insecticides are recommended. Sprays of pyrethrin are acceptable for use on organically certified produce.

ROOT-KNOT NEMATODES

Description: Nematodes are microscopic worms that feed on plant roots. Three species of root-knot nematodes cause serious damage to chile peppers: *Meloidogyne incognita, M. hapla,* and *M. arenaria.*

Symptoms: Aboveground symptoms include plant stunting, leaf wilting, and plant unthriftiness. Roots infected with root-knot nematodes have obvious swellings or galls. Injury is more severe in sandy soils.

Control: Use resistant cultivars, crop rotation, and/or soil fumigants.

SLUGS AND SNAILS

Description: Snails differ from slugs in that snails have shells.

Damage: Plant parts are missing, and a shiny trail from the pest is left.

Control: Slugs and snails can be trapped under boards. Pans of fresh beer can be placed in the garden to attract and kill the pest. Chemical bait (metaldehyde) is also available.

SPIDER MITES

Description: Spider mites are almost too small to be seen with the naked eye, looking like tiny moving dots; however, they are easily seen with a 10X hand lens. Adult females, the largest forms, are less than ½ inch long. Spider mites live in colonies, mostly on the undersurfaces of leaves; a single colony may contain hundreds of individuals. The name "spider mite" comes from the silk webbing most species produce on infested leaves. The presence of webbing is an easy way to distinguish them from all other types of mites.

Damage: Mites cause damage by sucking cell contents from leaves. At first, the damage shows up as a stippling of light dots on the leaves; sometimes the leaves take on a bronze color. As feeding continues, the leaves turn yellow and drop off. Often leaves, twigs, and fruit are covered with large amounts of webbing. Damage is usually worse when compounded by water stress. They can kill the plant if left uncontrolled.

Control: In the early stages, these mites can be eliminated by washing the plant with a mild soap solution, then spraying the plant with water, including the undersides of leaves where the mites usually congregate. Repeat this process weekly until the mites are gone. If the mite problem is very severe, a miticide can be sprayed.

STINKBUGS

Description: Adults are ½ inch long and shield shaped. Crushing one releases a "stink." This smell enables them to avoid getting eaten by several species of birds and lizards.

Damage: Adults and nymphs pierce plant tissue with needlelike mouth parts and suck out plant juices from buds, blossoms, pods, stems, fruit, and seeds. Immature fruit and pods punctured by stinkbugs become deformed as they develop, or drop off the plant. Seeds within pods turn brown and become flattened and shriveled, and fruit becomes unpalatable. Fruits have a cloudy spot or whitish area with indistinct borders. Damage is similar to hail damage on fruit, but hail damage tears leaves.

Control: Sabadilla dust or Sevin.

TARNISHED PLANT BUGS (*Lygus lineolaris*)

Description: These bugs have a greenish-yellow to brown body ¼ inch long with a distinctive triangular pattern on the back, and they show rapid movement in both the adult and immature stages. They fly away if disturbed, making monitoring difficult. Nymphs are small, green, and wingless. Their quick movements help to distinguish them from aphids.

Damage: They inject a toxin causing flower bud drop, and occasional damage can occur to the pod, resulting in indentations and yellowing beneath the skin.

Control: Synthetic pyrethroids and carbamates can be applied. Organic growers can use pyrethrum.

THRIPS

Description: There are many species of thrips and all are extremely small. They can produce a new generation every 2 weeks. The mouth parts are classified as rasping-sucking. Thrips of the species *Frankliniella tritici* are the vector for tomato spotted wilt virus.

Damage: Leaves are distorted and curl upward (boat-shaped). The lower surface of the leaves develops a silvery sheen that later turns bronze.

Control: Insecticides, insect growth regulators, and biological controls such as predatory mites and ladybugs can be effective.

WHITEFLIES

Description: These pests are white and about 1/16 inch long. Whiteflies are harmful because they fly from one plant to another and quickly attack all chile peppers. They can also carry viruses to plants.

Damage: Adult and young whiteflies feed on the undersides of leaves. They suck the juices from the leaves, causing the leaves to shrivel, turn yellow, and drop.

Control: Remove infested plants. Insecticides have only a limited effect on whiteflies. Most kill only those whiteflies that come in direct contact with them. For particularly troublesome situations, try insecticidal soap or an insecticidal oil such as neem oil or narrow-range oil. Because these products only kill whitefly nymphs that are directly sprayed, plants must be thoroughly covered with the spray solution. Be sure to spray undersides of all infested leaves; usually these are the lowest leaves and the most difficult to reach. Use soaps when chile pepper plants are not drought-stressed and when temperatures are under 80°F to prevent possible damage to plants. Avoid using other pesticides to control whiteflies; not only do most of them kill natural enemies, but whiteflies quickly build up resistance to them, and most are not very effective in garden situations.

Abiotic disorders

BLOSSOM-END ROT

Causal agents: Root pruning, fluctuations in water supply, and heavy applications of nitrogen fertilizers cause blossom-end rot. Wilting, lack of soil moisture, and lack of calcium encourage the problem.

Symptoms: This disorder first appears as a water-soaked area. The tissue near the blossom end of pods has a brown discoloration. Spots elongate and become brown to black, dry, and leathery. Discolored tissue shrinks until the affected area is flat or concave. Blemishes range from ¼-inch spots to 3-inch-long elongated spots. Pods affected with blossom-end rot usually ripen prematurely. Fungi growing on and within the infected pods is common. The fungi, however, are not the cause of the initial problem.

Control: Maintain a uniform supply of soil moisture through irrigation and avoid large amounts of nitrogen fertilizer. If manure is applied, turn it under in the fall (as early as possible) so it will be well rotted before planting time. Irrigate when necessary during rapid pod development.

EDEMA

Symptoms: Numerous small bumps appear on the lower sides of leaves and sometimes on the leaf petiole. The cause is most likely to be overwatering. High humidity can also contribute.

Control: Reduce watering and create better air circulation around the plant.

HERBICIDE INJURY

Symptoms: Contact with hormone-type herbicides, such as 2,4-D (Weed-B-Gon), can cause distorted leaves. Other herbicides may cause chlorosis, necrosis, or lesions.

Control: Control spray drift of herbicide application.

MUTATIONS

Symptoms: Symptoms include leaf distortion, variegation in leaves, fruit deformity, and the like. Mutations can be mistaken for herbicide or virus infection.

Control: No control is necessary, but interesting mutants should be sent to the Chile Pepper Institute, P.O. Box 30003, Dept. 3Q, NMSU, Las Cruces, NM 88003.

SALT PROBLEMS

Symptoms: Young seedlings can be "pinched off" at the soil line from heavy amounts of salt in that area. A young seedling can die when light rains move the salt to the young tender roots.

Control: Avoid planting in fields with severe salt problems and irrigate so that salt is moved below root areas.

STIP (blackspot)

Symptoms: Gray-brown to greenish spots on fruit, most noticeable on red fruit that matures in the cooler weather. The disorder affects only some chile pepper cultivars. It can occur in the interior tissue of fruit as well as on the external surface.

Control: Plant resistant cultivars; for example, 'King Arthur' and 'Galaxy' are resistant bell pepper cultivars.

SUNSCALD

Symptoms: A necrotic or whitish area on the fruit, on the side exposed to afternoon sun, indicates sunscald. Often fungi, such as *Alternaria* spp., grow on the affected area of pods.

Control: Keep pods shaded by the plant's

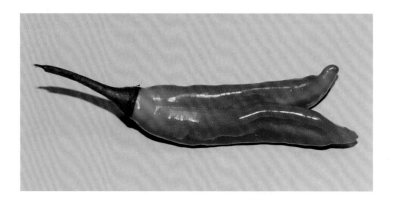

ABOVE **Mutant pod.**
LEFT **Salt burn.**

Sunscald.

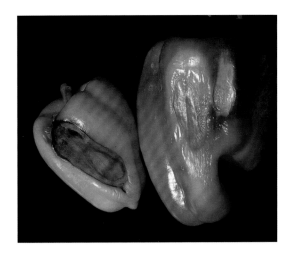

leaves. Harvest the fruits carefully and avoid stress to the plant from water, nitrogen, or nematodes.

VIVIPARY

Symptoms: Seeds sprout in the chile pepper pod while it is still attached to the plant.

Control: Increase the level of potassium available to the plant. Tissue analysis can evaluate the potassium content in the leaves.

WIND INJURY

Symptoms: In most cases, pepper plants can withstand strong winds without significant injury. However, some larger plants may snap off at the soil line, where callus tissue has formed from wind whipping the plant back and forth in hard, crusty soil.

Control: Control the injury by erecting wind screens.

BREEDING AND HYBRIDIZATION

The indigenous peoples of the Americas were the first chile pepper breeders. They selected and developed many of the pod types of chile peppers known today. These include ancho, chilhuacle, costeño, de árbol, jalapeño, mulato, pasilla, and serrano, and many others. Breeding chile peppers to create new varieties is an enjoyable and easy task. The hybridization technique is straightforward and easy to learn. One can produce offspring with new trait combinations never seen before. An understanding of flower morphology is necessary, but a detailed discussion of plant reproduction is beyond the scope of this book. The simple techniques to produce new chile pepper varieties are described and illustrated here.

Flower morphology

Understanding flower morphology is a basic necessity for the chile pepper breeder. The salient feature of the flower is that it is complete, meaning it has a calyx, a corolla, and male and female sex organs. Chile peppers can be considered self-compatible, meaning that only one plant is necessary for fruit and seed set. The stigma (the part of the flower that receives the pollen grains for reproduction and on which germination takes place) can be positioned slightly below the level of the anthers (the reproductive parts that produce and contain pollen) or exerted beyond, in which case the chances for cross-pollination become greater. Honeybees and other pollinating insects are common visitors to gardens and will pollinate

FAR LEFT **Hand pollination.**

LEFT **Flower of** *Capsicum chinense* **'Multicolor'.**

chile peppers. Research indicates that chile peppers can cross-pollinate up to 90 percent, depending on location and season. Therefore, when making hybridizations care must be taken not to allow foreign pollen to fertilize the eggs.

The plant breeder must transfer the pollen from the anther of the male parent to the stigma of the female parent to make a controlled hybridization. Hybridizations can be made at any time during daylight, but the best time is between one hour after sunrise and approximately 11:00 a.m. To prevent self-pollination, flower buds that are unopened and where the anthers have not shed pollen should be chosen. The best flower buds are 1 to 2 days from opening. These buds are plump and white. With forceps dipped in alcohol for sterilization, the petals are carefully removed to expose the reproductive organs. The flower is then emasculated by removing all anthers. The stigma is then examined with a magnifying glass for any pollen "contamination." Pollen is collected from the open flower of the male parent with a small paintbrush or a bee stick, or by removing the anthers. The pollen is gently transferred to the stigma of the emasculated female plant.

Label the pollinated flowers with a string tag. Record on the tag the mother plant, the father plant, and the pollination date. After 5 to 7 days, the flower will fall off if the hybridization was not successful. Otherwise, the fruit will grow and mature and can be picked when it has reached its mature fruit color. Several flower buds should be pollinated at one time to increase the chance of a successful hybridization. After the fruit ripens the seed is collected.

Many bacterial, fungal, and viral pathogens can be transferred from the mother chile pepper plant to the seed. Careful inspection of the mother plant is essential for producing pathogen-free seed. Usually, seed crops are grown in arid areas where insects that carry pathogens are very scarce, and bacterial and fungal diseases are minimal.

Plants in cages to prevent insect cross-pollination.

Inheritance

Plants inherit traits from both parents. The laws of heredity explain how different traits are inherited. These laws make it possible to predict the number of offspring that will inherit a certain trait. When the gametes unite in the ovule, each contributes one gene for each trait, so the new seed has two genes for each trait. Various combinations of many genes determine the traits that will be expressed in the following generations.

Once a trait is fixed (the plant breeds true for a specific trait), selfing the plant and its offspring will cause that trait to continue to appear. Sometimes a trait, such as yield, earliness, or level of heat, cannot be fixed. This is because the traits are governed by many genes. With two genes for each trait in each parent, many offspring will have to be grown before one will appear with all the desired traits. Many plants may have to be grown to produce a few plants showing the desired trait.

Sometimes a person will want the chile pepper plant to self-pollinate, instead of making a hybrid. To "self" a chile pepper plant requires keeping insects away from the flower. Growing the chile peppers in a greenhouse is the simplest method. Insect-isolation cages can also be used to self chile peppers outdoors. A simple technique is to enclose a branch of the chile pepper plant that has flowers in a small paper bag for a week. After the flower has selfed, remove the bag. Another technique is placing a gelatin capsule over the flower bud. This will keep the flower closed until it has selfed. As the fruit grows, it pushes the capsule off. In fact, any netting material, including drapery backing and nylon window screening, can work. The entire plant can be covered or just a branch. Again, tag the selfed pods to separate them from others that might be insect-pollinated.

Hybrids

Hybrid seed is the seed of an F_1 (first filial) generation sold for commercial production of the crop. Chile peppers grown from hybrid seed are highly uniform and usually higher yielding. The production of chile pepper hybrids relies on making hybridizations by hand between the two parents, a very labor intensive and expensive process. Seed from the hybrid will not produce true-to-type offspring. Therefore, saving seed from hybrids is seldom worthwhile.

Tools

Equipment required for plant breeding is relatively inexpensive and easy to find. Basic items include rubbing alcohol, a pair of narrow-pointed forceps, a spear needle, a hand lens, a pencil, string tags, and a notebook. The notebook is used to record each parent's characteristics, as well as how the resulting seedlings perform. The tools must be disinfected with rubbing alcohol between different hybridizations to reduce cross-pollination. The alcohol must be allowed to dry on the tools before they are used, or the alcohol will kill the pollen or ruin the stigma.

Biotechnology

Biotechnology is being used in chile peppers to develop new cultivars, map genomes, and evaluate genetic resources. Presently, genetically engineered chile peppers are not commercially available because of the lack of an efficient transformation system. However, several areas of biotechnology are aiding in the development of improved chile pepper cultivars.

Molecular markers have proven invaluable for understanding the genetic makeup of agricultural crops. Molecular markers take advantage of technologies that allow scientists and plant breeders to observe genetic differences between two or more individuals. In general, molecular markers are commonly used to examine genetic diversity, systematics, and phylogeny. They are used in combination with other markers to construct genetic maps, and they are used in linkage studies. Markers linked to a desired trait can be used by plant breeders in marker-assisted selection. When markers are identified with a gene or genes of interest, the markers can be used as a selection criterion by plant breeders. Selection via molecular markers eliminates the need for costly and sometimes inefficient screenings and speeds up the process of cultivar development. Several different types of molecular markers have been used successfully in chile peppers.

Tissue culture

Tissue culture of chile peppers can be divided into different areas of research: anther culture, protoplast regeneration, and embryo rescue. Anther culture involves regenerating plantlets from pollen microspore tissue. Plantlets produced from pollen microspores are haploid. Using colchicine, the chromosome number can be doubled. The benefit derived from double haploid plants, as they are called, is that these plants are homozygous at every loci. Many generations of self-pollination would be required to produce this same effect. Plants that are homozygous at all loci are invaluable for a variety of research and plant-breeding needs.

Embryo culture is useful when "embryo rescue" is required. Embryos from interspecific hybridizations often abort before seed development is complete. Some interspecific hybridizations may produce viable plants if the embryo is rescued at an early stage of development. This technique of excising the embryos and placing them on a nutrient medium has been use to transfer genes from *Capsicum baccatum* to *C. annuum*.

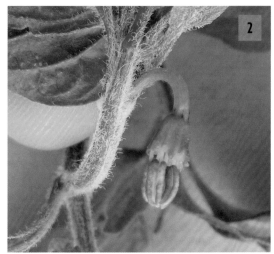

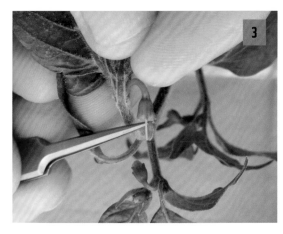

Making your own chile pepper hybridizations

Chile breeders make controlled hybridizations between chile pepper plants in order to combine genes of interest, and with a little practice you too can make your own hybridizations. Follow the steps outlined here.

1. **SELECT THE FLOWER BUD.** Select a flower bud that has not opened. A chile pepper flower has both male (stamens, consisting of anther and filament) and female (pistil) reproductive organs. Selecting an unopened flower bud reduces the chance for cross-pollination.

2. **OPEN THE FLOWER BUD.** Using forceps or tweezers, carefully remove the petals from the flower buds to expose the reproductive organs.

3. **EMASCULATE THE FLOWER.** The male parts of the flower are composed of anthers attached to small filaments. Pollen is produced in the anther. In order to prevent self-pollination, the anthers must be removed. Remove them but be sure to leave the central pistil in place.

4. **COLLECT POLLEN.** Collect pollen from the open flower of another chile pepper plant. A small paintbrush or a bee stick can be used to collect and transfer the pollen.

5. **POLLINATE THE FLOWER.** Transfer the pollen to the tip (stigma) of the pistil.

6. **LABEL THE HYBRIDIZATION.** Label the hybridization so that it can be identified as the fruit matures. The fruit will look like all the other fruit on the plant, because the new genes reside in the growing seeds, not in this year's pod shape. After the fruit ripens, harvest the seed and plant it as you would any seed. Remember to label the hybridization in the garden. Results will become visible as the seeds grow into mature plants.

CAPSAICIN AND THE QUEST FOR THE WORLD'S HOTTEST PEPPER

The active principle that causes heat in chile peppers is a crystalline alkaloid generically called capsaicin. It is produced by glands at the junction of the placenta and the pod wall. The capsaicin spreads unevenly throughout the inside of the pod and is concentrated in the placental tissue.

Capsaicin is an incredibly powerful and stable alkaloid, seemingly unaffected by cold or heat, which retains its original potency despite time, cooking, or freezing. Because it has no flavor, color, or odor, the precise amount of capsaicin present in chiles can only be measured by a specialized laboratory procedure known as high performance liquid chromatography (HPLC). Although it has no odor or flavor, it is one of the most pungent compounds known, detectable to the palate in dilutions of one to seventeen million. It is only slightly soluble in water but very soluble in alcohols, fats, and oils.

P. A. Bucholtz in 1816 first discovered that the pungent principle of peppers could be extracted from the macerated pods with organic solvents. In 1846, L. T. Thresh reported in *Pharmacy Journal* that the pungent principle could be extracted in a crystalline state. It was Thresh who named the substance capsaicin. In 1878, the Hungarian medical scientist Endre Hogyes extracted capsaicin, which he called "capsicol," and discovered that it stimulated the mucous membranes of the mouth and stomach and increased the secretion of gastric juices. Capsaicin was first synthesized in 1930 by E. Spath and F. S. Darling.

The word *capsaicin* actually describes a complex of related components named capsaicinoids by Japanese chemists S. Kosuge and Y. Inagaki in 1964. Capsaicinoids are the chemical compounds that give chile peppers their bite. Scientists have identified and isolated twenty-two naturally occurring members of this fiery family and one synthetic cousin, which is used as a reference gauge for determining the relative pungency of the others. The major capsaicinoids contained in the crystalline extract and their percentages are capsaicin (69 percent), dihydrocapsaicin (22 percent), and three minor related components: nordihydrocapsaicin (7 percent), homocapsaicin (1 percent), and homo-dihydrocapsaicin (1 percent).

Capsicum chinense 'Bhut Jolokia'.

The synthetic capsaicinoid vanillylamide of n-nonanoic acid (VNA) was administered to sixteen trained tasters by researchers Anna Krajewska and John Powers at the University of Georgia (1988). The tasters compared the heat of VNA to the four natural capsaicinoids, and the results were as follows: The mildest capsaicinoid was nordihydrocapsaicin (NDHC), which was described as "the least irritating" and "fruity, sweet, and spicy." Next was homodihydrocapsaicin (HDHC), a compound described as "very irritating," and one that produced a "numbing burn" in the throat, which also was the most prolonged and difficult to rinse out. The two most fiery capsaicinoid compounds were capsaicin (C) and dihydrocapsaicin (DHC), which produced burning everywhere from the mid-tongue and palate down into the throat. Evidently, all of the capsaicinoids work together to produce the pungency of peppers, but capsaicin itself is still rated the strongest.

Capsaicin is so powerful that chemists who handle the crystalline powder must work in a filtered "tox room" in full body protection. The suit has a closed hood to prevent inhaling the powder. Said pharmaceutical chemist Lloyd Matheson of the University of Iowa, who once inhaled some capsaicin accidentally: "It's not toxic, but you wish you were dead if you inhale it!" Capsaicin expert Marlin Bensinger noted: "A one milligram dose of pure capsaicin placed on your hand would feel like a red-hot poker and would surely blister the skin."

Did capsaicin evolve to protect chile peppers from mammalian predators? That's the theory of Dr. Michael Nee of the New York Botanical

Rezolex oleoresin extraction plant, Radium Springs, New Mexico.

Garden. Scientists have long speculated that plants produce secondary metabolites, chemicals that are not required for the primary life support of the plant. These metabolites fight off animal predators and perhaps even competing plant species.

Nee speculates that the capsaicin in chiles may be such a metabolite. It prevents animals from eating the chiles, so that they can be consumed by fruit-eating birds that specialize in red fruits with small seeds. Mammals perceive a burning sensation from capsaicin, but birds do not. The seeds pass through the birds' digestive tract intact and encased in a perfect natural fertilizer. Many experts believe that the wild chiltepín (*Capsicum annuum* var. *glabriusculum*) was spread by this method from South America to what is now the United States-Mexico border.

It has long been believed that capsaicin is

present only in *Capsicum* pods and in no other plant or animal material. However, during our research we uncovered a quote from W. Tang and G. Eisenbrand in *Chinese Drugs of Plant Origin* (1992): "Capsaicin, the pungent principle of *Capsicum* species, was isolated from ginger rhizomes." Chemical engineer and capsaicin expert Marlin Bensinger strongly believes this finding to be in error. He says the proper chemical precursors are simply not found in ginger.

Which is the world's hottest pepper?

Chileheads and pepper gardeners are captivated by the largest and hottest peppers. Contests are held to see who can grow the largest chile pepper, usually 'NuMex Big Jim', and there is a huge international reaction when a new super-hot variety is found. With pure capsaicin at about 16,000,000 Scoville heat units (SHUs), everyone wants to know what chiles come closest to this heat level.

In September 2000, we received a newspaper clipping from the *International Herald Tribune* headlined "Assam Chile Named Hottest in the World." It was a brief story about a chile pepper variety grown in the northeastern hills of Assam, India. At 855,000 SHUs, it would outperform the much-quoted (and never duplicated) heat level of *Capsicum chinense* 'Red Savina': 577,000 SHUs. (Regular red and orange habaneros are typically in the range of 150,000 to 300,000 SHUs.) The source given for that newsbyte was S. C. Dass, deputy director of the Defense Research Laboratory in the Assamese town of Tezpur. The pepper, 'Naga Jolokia', also named 'Tezpur' in some reports, was said to be a member of *Capsicum frutescens*, the same species as the 'Tabasco' chile.

The news story about the Indian "hottest pepper" reached Frank Garcia of GNS Spices, the California developer and grower of 'Red Savina', listed at that point as the world's hottest pepper in *Guinness World Records*. "It would be highly unusual for a *C. frutescens* to be that hot," Garcia said in an interview with fiery-foods.com. Along with some 'Red Savina' record challengers, Garcia also questioned the reliability of the test results: "In some cases labs have discovered that the challengers' samples have been adulterated with oleoresin," the extremely hot capsaicin extract, thus disqualifying them. "But anything's possible," he said of 'Naga Jolokia', "so, bring it on and let's get some American laboratories to test samples of both the Indian chile and 'Red Savina' and see which is the hottest."

Skepticism abounds

The cited heat level of 855,000 SHUs came from the August 2000 report published by Mathur et al. in the journal *Current Science*, giving somewhat more detail. As DeWitt noted, the report was interesting for the lack of detail about the methodology used to calculate Scoville heat units through high performance liquid chromatography (HPLC). He asked Bosland to read the report in *Current Science* and to give an opinion. Bosland pointed out that while the high-performance liquid chromatograph should be calibrated first by using a known concentration of capsaicin solution, there was no mention of such a procedure. This alone could account for measurement of an extra 100,000 SHUs. He also questioned the preparation of the chiles—Did they weigh the chile sample before extracting? Were the seeds, pericarp, and placenta ground together, or did they just pick the hot parts?

In light of Bosland's skepticism, DeWitt emailed a challenge to the Indian scientists, Ritesh Mathur, R. S. Dangi, S. C. Dass, and R. C. Malhotra of the Defense Research Laboratory in Tezpur, India, to send him samples of 'Tezpur' pods for testing by two U.S. labs, at New Mexico State University and at Analytical Food Laboratories. Frank Garcia agreed to provide his samples for a "hottest chile test-off." The Indian scientists never responded.

A first clue that the infamous 'Naga Jolokia' had to be a member of *Capsicum chinense*, too, came in 2003. For a special issue on international chile peppers, the Japanese magazine *Paper Sky* sent a reporter to Tezpur to check out the claim about this pepper. The reporter, Graham Simmons, soon discovered that the chile was named after the ferocious Naga warriors who once inhabited Nagaland in Assam, one of India's most fertile regions.

Accompanying the article was a photo of a rather dried-out plant that still had some orange-red pods on it. The pods were clearly *Capsicum chinense*, the species containing the habaneros. So at least the species mystery was solved—but what about that HPLC test? Unfortunately, Simmons did not speak directly to the Indian scientists, and even if he had, it would have been too much to hope that he quizzed them about their testing methodology.

More indications that 'Naga Jolokia' was most likely a *C. chinense* chile came from a 2004 fiery-foods.com reader. He reported that the numerous curry houses in Japan would make some extremely spicy dishes, many with Indian 'Tezpur' chiles. Some of these restaurants even had jars of whole Indian 'Tezpur' chiles sitting on shelves, he went on, looking much like a Caribbean habanero, just a little bigger.

Meanwhile, the Chile Pepper Institute grew out and analyzed all sorts of *Capsicum* varieties that were supposed to be "the world's hottest." Most of the time, the results were rather disappointing. One variety showed potential, though. In 2001, the Institute received seed of a chile named 'Bhut Jolokia' from a member who had collected it while visiting India. Because of poor fruit and seed set, it took Bosland several years to have sufficient seed on hand for an extensive field trial. 'Bhut Jolokia' was grown under insectproof net cages to produce the bulk seed, and by 2004, enough seed was available for the test.

Extensive field trials and tests in New Mexico

Bosland and his colleagues were ready for a large-scale experiment. An extensive study was undertaken, with three goals:

1. Compare the heat level of 'Red Savina', 'Bhut Jolokia', and orange habanero in a replicated field trial.
2. Find out whether 'Bhut Jolokia' truly had a higher heat level than 'Red Savina'.
3. Determine the species designation of 'Bhut Jolokia'.

Pods of 'Bhut Jolokia'.

The comparison experiment was conducted in 2005 at a plant science research facility close to Las Cruces, New Mexico. On heat pads in a climate-controlled greenhouse, seeds of all three varieties were started and thinned after germination. When the seedlings had developed eight to ten true leaves, they were transplanted to field plots or to 1-gallon plastic pots and grown in the greenhouse for DNA extraction. In the field, they were planted in a sophisticated, randomized pattern, forming blocks of thirty-six plants each. A single line of plants was spaced about 1 foot apart within the row and with 3 feet between rows. The plants were grown using standard cultural practices for growing chile peppers in southern New Mexico. As customary in the Chile Pepper State, the plots were furrow irrigated throughout the season to maintain optimal plant growth. Fortunately, 2005 weather conditions proved to be favorable for this sort of field test.

Once the fruit had matured, harvest also followed a scientific plan. To get a good fruit average of each variety, the scientists harvested twenty-five random mature fruits from at least ten plants. To prepare for HPLC Scoville testing, the whole sample pods were dried and ground.

'Bhut Jolokia' was also used for DNA testing. So-called RAPD (random amplification of polymorphic DNA) markers show a typical pattern of stripes that can be matched against other samples. To be able to create such fingerprints of various *Capsicum* species as a reference, the scientists at the Chile Pepper Institute obtained various samples of *C. annuum*, *C. baccatum*, *C. chinense*, and *C. frutescens* from germplasm collections like the National Plant Germplasm System. For DNA isolation, samples of leaf tissue were taken.

By comparing the 'Bhut Jolokia' RAPD markers with the reference markers, it was possible to determine which species' genes are part of this particular pepper variety. That method, of course, is much more accurate than just observing how many pods per node are growing or comparing flower types, which was still done in addition. Both the HPLC test and the DNA analysis brought valuable insight into this chile pepper from India.

Besides the makeup of a pepper cultivar's genes, environmental factors are known to increase or decrease the heat level, but being able to compare the samples with standard control cultivars from field trials increases the confidence of the heat level measurements. The HPLC data were converted from parts per million to SHUs by multiplying by 16. For example, if a total capsaicinoid content of 36,000 mg/kg is determined, multiplying this value by 16 gives 576,000 SHUs. (For SHU measurements, capsaicinoids like capsacin and dehydrocapsaicin are included.)

The HPLC analysis revealed that 'Orange Habanero' had a mean (average) heat level of 357,729 SHUs. That's quite a bit, but according to Bosland, this is in the range normally seen for this cultivar in Las Cruces, New Mexico. For 'Bhut Jolokia', the analysis revealed an extremely high heat level indeed, an incredible 1,001,304 SHUs. That's a heat level normally seen only for ultra-hot sauces using pepper extract (oleoresin capsicum). A different kind of surprise was the test result for 'Red Savina'—it scored a rather low heat level of just 248,556 SHUs. This means the SHU value for 'Bhut Jolokia' was four times higher than for 'Red Savina'. So much for "the world's current hottest chile pepper"!

In 2004, Assam-based pepper grower Frontal Agritech also had their 'Bih Jolokia' chiles HPLC-tested and reported 1,041,427 SHUs, which means two independent results for 'Jolokia' are similar. The northeastern Indian region allows for two harvests per year, though, and there seems to be a certain seasonal heat fluctuation between the two. Two U.K. growers reported quite similar results for 'Naga Jolokia'-type peppers grown in greenhouses.

DNA results

Now let's take a look at the DNA test of 'Bhut Jolokia', researching its species. From the nineteen samples of *C. annuum*, *C. frutescens*, *C. chinense*, and 'Bhut Jolokia', the scientists obtained 136 reproducible and reliable polymorphic RAPD markers to work with. To sum up the rather complex test results, the researchers found eight RAPD markers specific to *C. chinense*, as well as three markers specific to *C. frutescens*. No *C. annuum*–specific patterns were detected in this Indian chile, but a pattern that was specific to 'Bhut Jolokia' was detected. The genetic similarities among and within the species were calculated by applying some sophisticated algorithms that would be beyond the scope of this summary. At the bottom line, the experts obtained a so-called "similarity index value." A totally pure species would mean a value of 1.00, which is rather rare, as most cultivated varieties contain genes from more than one species through breeding. The average genetic similarity between *C. chinense* and 'Bhut Jolokia' was 0.79, which means this chile clearly belongs to *C.chinense* but has some *C. frutescens* genes as well.

According to Bosland, such a genetic species mix—interspecific hybridization—is not uncommon. For example, 'Greenleaf Tabasco' was developed by interspecific hybridization between *C. frutescens* and *C. chinense*, followed by repeated backcrossing to *C. frutescens*. DNA analysis reveals that 'Greenleaf Tabasco' indeed contains some *C. chinense* genes.

Considering that various *C. frutescens* peppers are cultivated in northeastern India as well ('Indian PC-1', for example), the presence of some *C. frutescens* genes in this *C. chinense* cultivar should be no surprise. In Assam, plants of *C. chinense* and *C. frutescens* could have been grown near each other, allowing for hybridization between them. Quite possibly, local farmers knowingly selected for a higher heat chile pepper, eventually leading to the ultra-hot 'Bhut Jolokia'.

But what about all the confusing Indian names for these super-hot chiles, like 'Bhut Jolokia', 'Bih Jolokia', and 'Naga Jolokia', our friend Harald Zoschke asked Leena Saikia of Frontal Agritech. Leena told him: "All these chiles are from Northeast India. They belong to *Capsicum chinense*. In fact, they are all the same chile but named differently at different places. For example, the Assamese community calls it variously 'Bih Jolokia' (poison chile), 'Bhut Jolokia' (ghost chile), and 'Naga Jolokia' (extreme heat representing the aggressive temperament of the warriors of the neighboring Naga community)."

Despite slight differences, all those varieties of 'Naga Jolokia' seem to have basically the same genetics and origin, and if heat level claims differ, it might be due to environmental influences, growing seasons, or nonstandard HPLC tests. Expect any of those peppers to be in the same range—very, very hot. The chile community will greatly benefit from their widened availability through various sources, including the Chile Pepper Institute.

A new heat champion

At the 2007 New Mexico Chile Conference, held in Las Cruces, Paul Bosland proudly presented a document he had recently received from Guinness World Records, Ltd.—the certificate that officially declares 'Bhut Jolokia' to be "hottest of all spices." Since the *Guinness World Records* entry for 'Bhut Jolokia' made worldwide headlines, the "ghost chile" has gained incredible popularity. Thanks to the research by NMSU and the Chile Pepper Institute (and the resulting news stories), the Indian growing regions could enjoy an enormous increase in demand for the now-famous pepper. This was more than welcome in a region that has to cope with political instability, high crime rates, a tea industry suffering from falling prices and rising costs, and a large part of the population living below poverty level. An expanding business of growing 'Bhut Jolokia' means a lot of new jobs in agriculture, processing, and administration. According to an Associated Press report published in the summer of 2007, one Assamese company shipped barely 1 ton of the various 'Naga' chiles in 2006, but in 2007 it was more like 10 tons, exported to nearly a dozen countries around the world. And that's just one company.

During the 2007 growing season, Harald Zoschke grew out 'Bhut Jolokia', 'Bih Jolokia', and 'Naga Morich' to compare and contrast them. His report, published on fiery-foods.com, confirmed that they are slightly different varieties of the same pod type, much like the different cultivated varieties of jalapeños. All were, of course, extremely hot.

HEAT SCALE FOR CHILE VARIETIES AND COMMERCIAL PRODUCTS

1,000,000 SHUs

C. chinense 'Bhut Jolokia', 'Bih Jolokia', 'Naga Morich'

100,000–500,000 SHUs

C. chinense 'Orange Habanero', 'Scotch Bonnet', South American varieties of *C. chinense,* African birdseye

50,000–100,000 SHUs

C. annuum 'Santaka', chiltepins, rocotos, Chinese kwangsi peppers

30,000–50,000 SHUs

C. annuum 'Cayenne Long', 'Prik Khee Nu', piquins; *C. frutescens* 'Tabasco', Pakistan dundicut peppers

15,000–30,000 SHUs

C. annuum de árbol peppers, crushed red pepper, habanero hot sauce

5,000–15,000 SHUs

C. annuum 'Early Jalapeno', serrano peppers; *C. baccatum* ají amarillo, Tabasco sauce

2,500–5,000 SHUs

C. annuum 'Large Red Thick', 'Mild Jalapeño', mirasol, Louisiana hot sauce

1,500–2,500 SHUs

C. annuum 'Sandia', 'Cascabel', 'Yellow Wax Hot'

1,000–1,500 SHUs

C. annuum 'Española Improved', ancho, pasilla, Old Bay seasoning

500–1000 SHUs

C. annuum 'NuMex Big Jim', 'New Mexico No. 6-4', chili powder

100–500 SHUs

C. annuum 'NuMex R-Naky', 'Mexi-Bell', cherry, canned green chiles, Hungarian hot paprika

10–100 SHUs

C. annuum pickled pepperoncini

0 SHUs

C. annuum 'Sweet Banana', bell peppers, pimiento, U.S. paprika

Processing and Preservation

WE LOVE CHILES IN WHATEVER FORM we can get them, but there is something special about fresh chiles—their flavor and texture cannot be duplicated by canned, dried, or frozen chiles, and they bring bright colors to summertime meals. So naturally, the first way to handle a megaharvest is to consume as many of the fresh chiles as possible.

Fresh chiles straight from the garden can be used many ways. Obviously, they can just be eaten raw, although many of the really hot varieties such as bird peppers and members of *Capsicum chinense* are simply too hot to be eaten by themselves. But the larger, milder ones can be sliced up for use in sandwiches as well as on hot dogs and burgers. They can also be added to salads of all kinds.

PROCESSING AND FREEZING FRESH CHILES

Only the larger chiles, especially the New Mexican ones, need to be roasted and peeled before use. The small ones are best preserved by freezing them whole, as described here.

Roasting and peeling the pods

The poblanos and New Mexican varieties have tough skins that are usually blistered and peeled before the chiles are used in recipes that require cooking. Blistering or roasting the chile is the process of heating the fresh pods until the transparent skin separates from the meat

A truckload of fresh cayennes arriving at the mash plant.

ABOVE A chile roaster at the Hatch Chile Festival.

RIGHT A roasted pod.

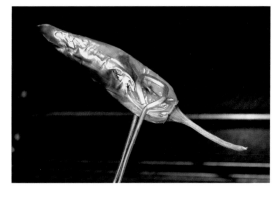

grill. Place the pods on a grill 5 to 6 inches from the coals or gas flames and turn them often. Blisters will soon form, indicating that the skin is separating. Be sure that the pods are blistered all over before you take them off the grill or they will not peel properly. The pods may burn slightly, but take care that they do not blacken entirely or they will be overcooked and will be nearly impossible to peel. The idea is to use intense heat for short periods of time rather than low heat for a long time.

During the charcoal roasting process, the sugar and starch caramelize in the chile, which imparts a cooked flavor, while a rapid roasting over high heat leaves the chile tasting more raw. And, during the roasting process, why not save a few perfectly formed pods and make a classic dish of chiles rellenos—stuffed peppers? Remove the pods from the grill with tongs, then immediately wrap the chiles in damp paper towels and place them in a plastic bag to steam for 10 to 15 minutes. For a crisper, less-cooked pepper, plunge the pods in ice water to stop the cooking process.

Chile roasters have become commonplace in the Southwest, and these cylindrical cages with gas jets below can roast a 40-pound sack of chiles in a lot less time than it takes to roast pods on the grill. Although this method is a more convenient way to process large quantities of pods, there are some drawbacks to using a roaster. Occasionally the pods are roasted unevenly, and some are difficult to peel. The pods are usually placed in a large plastic bag to steam after being roasted and must be processed as soon as they have cooled enough to handle.

of the chile so that it can be removed.

To roast and peel pepper pods, first cut a small slit in the pod close to the stem end so that the steam can escape. The pods can be placed on a baking sheet and put directly under the broiler, or on a metal screen on top of a burner. They can also be plunged into hot cooking oil to loosen the skins, but that method is messy and not recommended.

The easiest method is to use a barbecue

If allowed to sit for too long, the pods can be spoiled by bacterial growth.

After the chiles have cooled down, it's time for the final step. If you've done a good job of roasting your chiles, peeling them is fast and easy. Simply start at either end and pull off the skin—wearing gloves, of course. We generally pull from the tip back toward the stem, but it depends on the roasting job. Occasionally, you will run into problems with the deep indentations, or valleys, on the pod; it is difficult to blister those valleys without burning the surrounding areas. In these cases, you simply have to go in with a knife and scrape off any remaining skin.

Because the hotter varieties of green chiles have thinner flesh than the mild ones, it is difficult to peel them and come up with an intact pod. They tend to tear and split apart during the peeling process. If you are going to chop the chiles before using, it really doesn't matter if the pods split. If you want chiles to stuff, however, this can be a disaster. To keep roasted and peeled green chile pods intact, simply start with mild chile pods, which have much thicker flesh.

At this point, most people like to cut off the stem and remove the seeds. The easiest method is to simply cut off the very top of the chile along with the stem and then scrape the seeds out of the open end. If you really want to reduce the firepower, you can also remove the veins (the placental tissue) that run the length of the pod and serve to attach the seeds to the pod. You've now completed the whole process and have a chile pod that is ready to eat, cook with, or freeze.

Peeling the pod.

Our readers over the years have come up with some unusual methods for removing the skins of New Mexican chiles. One person wrote to say that he used a small propane torch to blister each pod individually and added that the flame can easily be directed into the creases. Perhaps the most unusual method was sent to us by Chris Mathews of Marquette, Michigan. He wrote: "Freeze the little buggers solid. Using a dry rag to hold one end of the frozen pepper, use a vegetable peeler to peel the skin off, then a small knife or garnishing tool to scrape in the crevices that the peeler missed."

Fresh red chiles

Of course, those green chiles are the immature stage of the New Mexican red chiles, which are used to make chile ristras and when dried are ground into red chile powder. Many people swear that the stage between fresh green and dried red, known as "fresh red," is the most delicious stage. It has a fresh taste like fresh green but also includes the rich, mature flavor of dried

Fresh red chile almost ready to pick.

red pods. For those who have never tried it, it is a deliciously new chile flavor sensation.

Green chile, like many other chiles, undergoes a substantial chemical transformation as it turns red and matures, as the sugars and vitamin A increase. As soon as the pods turn red, they start to dry out. Fresh red is the stage where the pods have just turned red and are as fat as fresh green. In fact, fresh red is handled just like fresh green—that is, roasted and peeled. Many people use fresh red just like fresh green, for chiles rellenos and red chile stew, and chopped on sandwiches, steaks, hamburgers, and eggs, just to name a few possibilities. Personally, we prefer to use fresh green for most of those foods; we use fresh red to prepare a base for some wonderfully tasty red chile sauces that can be eaten as soups.

Dave's Fresh Red Chile Sauce

¼ cup vegetable oil

8 (or more, to taste) fresh New Mexican red chiles, seeds and stems removed, chopped

1 large onion, chopped

3 cloves garlic

4 cups water

¼ teaspoon ground cumin

1 tablespoon minced fresh cilantro

½ teaspoon Mexican oregano leaves

   Salt to taste

MAKES ABOUT 3 CUPS

HEAT RATING: MILD TO MEDIUM

Dave's method of making chile sauce differs from others using fresh New Mexican chiles because these chiles aren't roasted and peeled first. Because of the high sugar content of fresh red chiles, this sauce is sweeter than most. Dave harvested some chiles from his garden one late summer day, made a batch of this sauce, and ate every drop as a soup! It makes a tasty enchilada sauce, too.

Heat the oil in a large saucepan over medium heat and saute the chiles, onion, and garlic until the onion is soft, about 7 minutes.

Add the remaining ingredients, bring to a boil, then reduce the heat and simmer for 1 hour, uncovered.

Puree the sauce in a blender in batches and return to the saucepan.

Cook over medium heat until the sauce thickens to the desired consistency. Add salt to taste.

Iced heat: Freezing chiles

Freezing chiles is an excellent way of preserving them. Chiles that have been frozen retain all the characteristics of fresh chiles except for their texture. Since the individual cell walls have been ruptured by the freezing of the water within each cell, frozen chiles lose their crisp texture.

Another result of the freezing process, according to one source, is to spread the capsaicin throughout the chile. This occurs with the rupturing of the cell walls and can actually make some chiles seem hotter after freezing than they were beforehand. Research to date indicates that freezing chiles does not actually make them hotter. There is simply nothing that the freezing process alone can do, either physically or chemically, to increase the heat of a chile.

There are different requirements for freezing chiles, depending on the size of the chile. Large chiles can be frozen at any stage once they have been roasted. That is, they can be frozen before peeling (freezing actually makes them easier to peel) or after peeling and deseeding. They can be frozen whole or chopped.

The easiest way to freeze large chiles is to put them into freezer bags, double-bag them, and place in the freezer. You can also wrap them in heavy foil or freezer wrap, or you can pack them in rigid plastic containers. A handy way to freeze chopped New Mexican green chiles is in plastic ice cube trays. After the trays are frozen, the chile cubes can be popped out and stored in bags. The cubes can then be used when making soups or stews, or in other recipes, without having to pry apart blocks of frozen chiles.

Smaller varieties, including habaneros, serranos, jalapeños, and Thai chiles, can be frozen without processing. Just wash off the chiles and allow them to dry. Then place them on a cookie sheet or other flat surface, one layer deep, and put them in the freezer until frozen solid. They can then be stored in double freezer bags and will keep for nine to twelve months at 0°F. Sometimes they dry out a bit and need to be soaked in water during defrosting to rehydrate them. When these peppers are chopped into a salsa, for example, few people can tell that they have been frozen. Some sources call for blanching fresh peppers first, but in our experience, this step is not necessary.

Fresh red chile paste can be stored in plastic containers or zip bags and frozen to use all year long. The paste holds up well in the freezer and really helps to cut meal preparation time.

Chopped chiles frozen in an ice cube tray.

Asian Chile Paste

1   cup small fresh red chiles, such as Thai, serrano, or piquin, stems removed

⅓   cup white vinegar

8   cloves garlic, chopped

3   tablespoons vegetable oil

1   teaspoon salt

Water as needed

MAKES 1 CUP
HEAT RATING: HOT

Popular throughout Southeast Asia, this garlic and chile–based paste is used as a condiment that adds fire without greatly altering the taste of the dish. It is especially good in stir-fry dishes. To use up a lot of chiles, triple the recipe. It will keep for up to three months in the refrigerator. It can also be frozen.

Combine all the ingredients in a blender or processor and puree, adding enough water to form a thick paste.

Making mash

Chile mash is the foundation of commercial hot sauce production. It is a combination of crushed chiles, salt, and often vinegar which is then fermented and stored in barrels and huge tanks.

Since Tabasco sauce is the longest continually produced hot pepper sauce, let's start with their procedure, which the McIlhenny Company has used for more than 125 years. After harvest, whole tabasco chiles are crushed in a hammer mill; salt is added in the amount of 8 pounds for every 100 pounds of chiles. This mash is placed in Kentucky white oak barrels with salt-sealed wooden lids that have tiny holes that allow the gases of the peppers to escape during fermentation. The wooden tops are secured and placed on the barrels with stainless steel hoops (iron hoops disintegrate in the air of the salt and chile mash).

Each 400-pound barrel is aged for three years. Carbon dioxide is released for the first two years, but after this time the fermentation process ceases, and the salt topping hardens and naturally seals the barrel. The mellowing and aging process, called steeping, permits the flavors and colors to intermingle and mix naturally. Then the barrels are uncovered, and oxidized mash is removed from the top of the barrels. The mash is inspected for aroma, color, and moisture. Upon being accepted under McIlhenny standards, the mash is pumped into large blending vats and mixed with

Freshly ground mash ready for fermentation.

is sold to crawfish boil and hot pepper cream manufacturers.

Making mash at home really isn't necessary, as you can just make chile paste using our recipe and freeze it. But many chile growers like to experiment, so here is the process. Use freshly roasted and peeled green chile, or the fresh pods of any variety or color, but remember that the mash will be the color of the chiles. Remove the seeds and stems of the pods; wash and dry them. Weigh them on a scale and keep close track of the weight of the total pods used. Process them in a food processor or blender until you have a coarse mixture. Transfer the processed chiles to a container large enough to hold all of the mixture. Add salt 10 to 12 percent by weight of the peppers and blend thoroughly. Some methods add 10 percent vinegar by weight at this point, too. Place this mixture in large, heavy jars. Over time, the mash will ferment, releasing gases, so remove the top(s) every couple of weeks and immediately recap. Let sit in a cabinet or closet for six months to a year. Hot sauce is made by mixing the mash with vinegar and spices and then straining it; however, there are easier ways to make hot sauce without waiting six months. For example, you can freeze the mash using the following technique.

distilled, all-natural white vinegar in the ratio of two-thirds vinegar to one-third mash. For a month, this mixture is stirred for 5 minutes every hour. Finally, the vinegar-mash solution is strained, filtered, and bottled under the familiar trademarked diamond-shaped white, green, and red label. The strained mash residue

Frozen Chile Mash

Fresh small chile pods, such as jalapeño, habanero, or rocoto, seeds and stems removed

Water as needed

YIELD VARIES
HEAT RATING: HOT TO
EXTREMELY HOT

Here is one of the best methods for processing and preserving large quantities of small chile pods quickly. The method is so basic that it is sometimes overlooked among preservation methods. You should have a powerful blender or food processor for this. To use, defrost the cubes and estimate two to three pods per cube. Use in recipes calling for minced or chopped small chiles.

Place the chile pods in a food processor or blender with a little water and process to a medium-thin puree. Take care not to breathe the fumes from the pureeing.

Pour the puree into plastic ice cube trays and freeze solid.

Pop the cubes out and double bag them in zip bags. Label and date them and place them back in the freezer.

Salsas and sauces

Another way to use up a bumper crop of peppers is to make salsas and sauces and then freeze them. Numerous cookbooks have recipes for salsas (uncooked sauces), but the concept is simple. Favorite peppers are chopped with tomatoes, onions, garlic, and spices such as fresh cilantro, Italian parsley, or oregano. The usual proportion is two large tomatoes per onion, one to three garlic cloves, and peppers to taste, depending on heat level. The key to making good salsas is to hand-chop all ingredients; do not use a food processor. Ideally, salsas should be used fresh, but they can be frozen. However, the consistency will suffer, and the vegetables will not be as firm.

Cooked sauces freeze better than salsas. Roasted and peeled New Mexican peppers are chopped coarsely and cooked with chopped onions, garlic, and a little cooking oil for about 30 minutes. Then the sauce is cooled and frozen. Dried New Mexican red pods (or anchos) can be softened in water, pureed in a blender, and then cooked with chopped onion and garlic for about an hour. The sauce is pureed again and then frozen. The gardener can use up a lot

Make your own
custom hot sauce.

of pods by making sauces.

Another sauce that doesn't use as many pods but is still fun is a traditional bottled hot sauce. Sometimes these hot sauces have a vegetable base, and sometimes they consist entirely of peppers. For a vegetable base, cook together in a little cooking oil ½ cup chopped onions, the same amount of carrots, and two minced cloves of garlic. When the vegetables are soft, puree them in a blender with the fresh peppers of choice. Combine this mash with ½ cup vinegar and ¼ cup lime juice and simmer for 10 minutes. Strain the mixture into sterilized bottles and seal, then refrigerate.

For a Louisiana-style bottled hot sauce, take a pound of fresh red peppers such as tabascos or cayennes and chop them coarsely. Combine them with 2 cups vinegar and 2 teaspoons salt and simmer for 5 minutes. Remove from the heat and puree the mixture in a blender. Let this mixture sit in the refrigerator for a couple of weeks, then strain into sterilized bottles and keep refrigerated. Remember, this is a bottling process, not a canning process, and the bottles require refrigeration.

Salsa Fresca

4 serrano or 2 jalapeño chiles, stems and seeds removed, minced

2 yellow wax chiles, stems and seeds removed, minced

2 large tomatoes, finely diced

1 medium purple onion, finely diced

2 cloves garlic, minced (optional)

2 tablespoons vegetable oil

2 tablespoons fresh lime juice or cider vinegar

¼ cup chopped fresh cilantro or parsley

1 large avocado, diced (optional)

MAKES 2 CUPS
HEAT RATING: MEDIUM

Fresh salsas are a must during the summer and are a great way to use the earliest pods such as jalapeños and serranos. Vary the flavor of the salsa by using different chiles as they become available. Keep a supply on hand to serve with chips as a dip, as an accompaniment to grilled poultry or fish, or with burritos, fajítas, or even hamburgers. This salsa will keep for 2 or 3 days in the refrigerator.

Combine all the ingredients in a bowl except the cilantro and avocado and let the salsa sit for at least an hour to blend the flavors.

Mix in the cilantro and avocado before serving.

Belizean Habanero Hot Sauce

1 small onion, chopped

1 tablespoon vegetable oil

1 cup chopped carrots

2 cups water

2 habanero chiles, stems and seeds removed, minced

3 tablespoons lime juice, fresh preferred

3 tablespoons white vinegar

1 teaspoon salt

MAKES 2 CUPS
HEAT RATING: HOT

In order to preserve the distinctive flavor of the habanero chiles, we add them after cooking the other ingredients of this delicious but fiery hot sauce. To cut the heat, add more carrots or decrease the number of chiles. To use up a lot of habaneros, triple the recipe, as this sauce will keep for months in the refrigerator.

Saute the onion in the oil in a saucepan over medium heat until soft.

Add the carrots and the water. Bring to a boil, reduce the heat, and simmer until the carrots are soft. Remove from the heat.

Add the chiles, lime juice, vinegar, and salt to the carrot mixture. Place in a blender or food processor and puree until smooth.

Pour into sterilized bottles and close with lids.

CANNING AND PICKLING

Generally speaking, canning is not the best way to preserve chiles at home, because the texture of canned chiles is very soft. That said, over the years so many people have asked us how to do it that we have compiled the information here. Canned chiles—especially the New Mexican varieties—are readily available in supermarkets.

Pressure canning

Because they are a low-acid fruit, chiles canned at home must be pressure-canned to be safe. If the canning is done improperly, botulism can develop. Therefore, home canning of chiles is not to be considered unless one has a pressure canner. If you have the proper equipment, follow the manufacturer's instructions to the letter to insure safe results. The following description will take you through the basic steps, but again, it is imperative that you follow the instructions for your particular canner.

To begin, blister and peel the chiles you plan to can and remove all stems and seeds. Pack the prepared chiles loosely into hot, clean jars, leaving an inch of headroom. Add salt (½ teaspoon per pint) and add boiling water up to the 1-inch headroom level. Put on lids, tighten well, and place the jars in the canner according to the manufacturer's directions. After letting steam escape from the canner for 10 minutes, close the petcock and process half pints for 30 minutes, pints for 35 minutes.

When finished, remove the canner from the heat and let the pressure fall to zero, which

Pickled chiles and mixed vegetables.

A pressure cooker, the only way to can chiles.

will take up to half an hour. When the pressure reaches zero, open the petcock, wait 5 minutes, then open the canner and remove the jars to a draft-free location to cool. Be sure to check the seals on the jars the next day to be sure that they remain tight, before storing the jars in a cool, dry, and preferably dark location.

Water-bath canning

One way to avoid having to use a pressure canner is to can chiles along with high-acid vegetables or liquids, as in salsas. For example, adding vinegar, lemon juice, or lime juice can raise the acid level to a pH of 6 or lower, the point that makes it safe to use the water-bath method of canning. If the addition of these ingredients raises the acid level to unpalatable levels, the amount of vinegar or lemon juice can be reduced, but if the pH is 7 or higher, the product must then be either pressure-canned or frozen.

Water-bath canning can be done in a special pot or in any large metal container that is deep enough so that the water will be at least 2 inches over the tops of the jars and can boil freely. A rack of some kind is also necessary to keep the jars off the bottom of the pot during vigorous boiling.

After preparing the salsa, bring it to a boil and then simmer it for 5 minutes. Pour it into hot, clean jars, being sure to use all the liquid, which is the high-acid portion of the salsa. Put on the lids and put the jars into the water bath. After the water comes to a boil again, process for 30 minutes. Add boiling water during the process to keep the jars covered. When the processing time is finished, remove the jars to a draft-free location to cool.

When you use the water-bath method, you can add equal parts of lemon or lime juice to replace the vinegar if you prefer. You can use fewer chiles in the salsas but not more, since that would reduce the acid content of the final product. Additional salt can be safely added. And finally, additional seasonings such as oregano or cumin are best if added when serving the salsa rather than before canning.

Green Chiles and Tomatoes

3 cups peeled and chopped tomatoes

3 cups chopped New Mexican green chiles, roasted, peeled, seeds and stems removed

1½ teaspoons salt

1¼ cups white vinegar

MAKES 4 PINTS
HEAT RATING: MEDIUM

Before serving this cooked salsa, add 1 teaspoon cumin powder and stir in chopped cilantro. Serve as an all-purpose sauce with chips for a dip or with enchiladas or tacos, or as a relish or condiment with grilled meats, poultry, or fish.

Combine all of the ingredients in a saucepan, bring to a boil over medium-high heat, cover, reduce the heat, and simmer for 5 minutes.

Pack in hot, clean, sterilized jars, taking care to use all the liquid. Process according to the water-bath directions.

Picante Chile Ketchup

6 pounds tomatoes, peel and seeds removed, chopped

2 stalks celery, chopped

1 large onion, chopped

4 jalapeño or serrano chiles, or 2 habanero chiles, stems and seeds removed, chopped

1 red bell pepper, stem and seeds removed, chopped

1 cup brown sugar

1½ cups cider vinegar

2 teaspoons dry mustard

1 teaspoon ground cinnamon

½ teaspoon ground cloves

¼ teaspoon ground allspice

1 to 2 teaspoons salt

MAKES 4 PINTS
HEAT RATING: MEDIUM

Use this fiery version in place of regular ketchup to spice up sandwiches, meatloaf, hot dogs, and hamburgers. It also tastes great in salad dressings and on french fries. If you wish, after pureeing, you can freeze the ketchup instead of canning.

Cook the tomatoes in a pan on low heat for 15 minutes, then drain off the juice. Add the celery, onion, chiles, and bell pepper and simmer for 1 hour.

Add the sugar, vinegar, and spices and simmer for an additional hour.

Remove from the heat and puree until smooth.

Pour into sterilized jars and process according to the water-bath directions.

Pouring chile ketchup into the jar before processing.

A peck of pickled peppers

One of the best ways to handle an overwhelming chile crop is to pickle them. Pickling the peppers will preserve them at least until next year's crop comes in, and it makes "almost fresh" chiles available throughout the year. They can be pickled by themselves or in combination with other chiles or other vegetables. With just a little imagination, you can easily turn out attractive, multicolored jars of pickled peppers. Although pickling does require some time at the stove, it's an easy way to put up a lot of chiles.

There are a few basic rules to follow when pickling:

- Sterilize the jars and lids in a boiling water bath for 10 to 15 minutes. We generally bring 1 to 2 inches of water to a boil in a large pot with a folded dish towel in the bottom. We then place jars into the water mouth down, along with the lids, which can just be set between the jars. We turn down the heat just enough to keep the pot slowly boiling or simmering.
- Use pickling salt rather than table salt, which contains undesirable (for pickling) additives.
- While cider vinegar is more flavorful, 5 to 6 percent distilled white vinegar should be used to avoid discoloring the chiles. Note that we do use cider vinegar when discoloration is not a problem.
- Do not boil the vinegar for a long period of time, as that will reduce the acidity.
- Poke or cut a hole in each chile to keep it from floating and also to allow the pickling solution to work into the entire chile.

- After filling each jar, remove any trapped air with a spatula or knife blade inserted between the chiles and the wall of the jar, or by gently tapping the jar.
- After processing in a boiling water bath, remove jars to a draft-free location and allow to cool for 12 hours before handling.

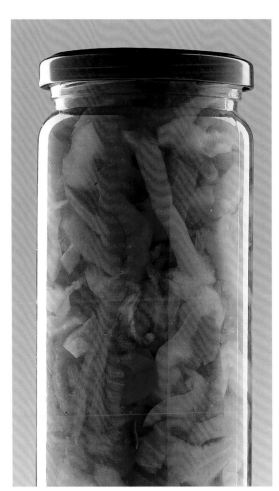

Mixed pickled peppers.

Pickled Green Chiles

2 cups white vinegar

2 cups sugar

1 teaspoon salt

1 teaspoon dill seed

½ teaspoon mustard seed

8 to 10 New Mexican green
chiles, roasted and peeled,
cut in strips

3 cloves garlic, cut in slivers

MAKES 2 PINTS
HEAT RATING: MEDIUM

These chile strips are great on sandwiches or chopped and mixed with salads such as tuna or shrimp. **NOTE** *This recipe requires advance preparation.*

Combine the vinegar, sugar, and spices in a pan and simmer over low heat for 5 minutes.

Put the chiles into small, sterilized jars, cover with the liquid and add some garlic to each jar.

Cover tightly and refrigerate for 3 days before using.

Pickled Habanero Chiles

3 dozen fresh habanero chiles
or enough to fill the jars

2 sterilized pint jars

PICKLING SOLUTION

3 cups 5 to 6 percent distilled
white vinegar

3 cups water

To insure the best pickled chiles, choose only the freshest ones and those with no blemishes. Bruised fruits will produce mushy chiles. You can also soak the chiles overnight in a brine of 3 cups water and 1 cup pickling salt to crisp them before pickling. Be sure to rinse them well to remove excess salt before processing. **NOTE** *This recipe requires advance preparation.*

Poke a couple of small holes in the top of each chile and pack tightly in sterilized jars, leaving ¼ inch headroom.

Combine the vinegar, water, and salt in a pan and bring the solution to a boil over medium-high heat.

1½ teaspoons pickling salt

MAKES 2 PINTS
HEAT RATING: EXTREMELY HOT

Pour over the chiles. Remove trapped air bubbles by gently tapping on the sides of the jars. Add more of the pickling solution if needed; close the jars.

Store for 4 to 6 weeks in a cool, dark place before serving.

Pickled Peppers

2 pounds jalapeño, serrano, yellow wax, cherry, habanero, or pepperoncini chiles, whole

4 sterilized pint jars

BRINE

3 cups water

1 cup pickling salt

PICKLING SOLUTION

3 cups water

3 cups 5 to 6 percent distilled white vinegar

3 teaspoons pickling salt

MAKES 4 PINTS
HEAT RATING: VARIES

This recipe works well with a variety of chiles. So if you're a lover of pickled peppers, mark this recipe, as you'll be using it a lot. **NOTE** *This recipe requires advance preparation and does not have to be processed in a water bath.*

Combine the salt and water and cover the chiles with the mixture.

Place a plate on the chiles to keep them submerged in the brine.

Soak the chiles overnight to crisp them. Drain, rinse well, and dry.

Poke a couple of small holes in the top of each chile and pack them tightly in sterilized jars, leaving ¼ inch headroom.

Combine the water, vinegar, and salt in a pan. Bring the solution to a boil and pour over the chiles, leaving no headroom. Remove trapped air bubbles.

Store for 4 to 6 weeks in a cool, dark place before serving.

Sun-Cured Pickled Jalapeños

1 cup jalapeño chiles, stems and seeds removed, cut into slices

1 tablespoon coarse salt

1 tablespoon mustard seeds

1 teaspoon cumin seeds

¼ cup oil, peanut preferred

1 teaspoon chopped fresh ginger

¼ cup freshly squeezed lemon juice

MAKES 1 PINT
HEAT RATING: HOT

These pickled chiles have an East Indian flavor because of the mustard seeds and ginger. Any small green chiles can be substituted for the jalapeños. Serve these unusual chiles on sandwiches or hamburgers, or as a side relish for grilled or roasted meats. **NOTE** *This recipe requires advance preparation.*

Sprinkle the chile slices with the salt; toss and let them sit for 10 minutes.

Toast the mustard and cumin seeds on a hot skillet, stirring constantly, for a couple of minutes until the seeds begin to crackle and pop.

Heat the oil until medium hot, remove from the heat, stir in the ginger, and let it simmer for 2 minutes. Remove the ginger and discard.

Stir in the chiles, cumin seeds, and lemon juice and pack in a sterilized jar.

For 5 days, set the jar in the sun in the morning on days when it is at least 70°F and bring it in at night. Shake the jar a couple times each day.

Harvest Bounty

Chiles: yellow hots, jalapeños, serranos

Cauliflower, broken into florets

Broccoli, broken into florets

Zucchini, unpeeled and thinly sliced

Carrots, baby or cut into coins

Pearl onions, peeled and left whole

Garlic cloves, whole

Small button mushrooms, whole

½ part water

½ part vinegar

1 teaspoon salt per pint of liquid

YIELD VARIES

HEAT RATING VARIES

This recipe can be used for pickling a combination of vegetables, including chiles and bell peppers. Choose whatever mixture you desire, as well as the amount and type of chiles, and arrange them attractively in a jar before covering with the pickling solution. Be aware that some vegetables such as olives and mushrooms absorb capsaicin well and can become quite hot. **NOTE** *This recipe requires advance preparation.*

Wash the chiles and prick with a toothpick. Arrange your choice of vegetables and chiles in sterilized jars.

Bring the water, vinegar, and salt to a boil and allow to boil for 1 minute. Pour over the vegetables, leaving no headroom, and cover.

Allow the mixture to pickle for at least 2 to 3 weeks in a cool, dark place before serving.

Jalapeños in Escabeche

1 pound jalapeños, whole, holes poked in pods

¼ cup olive oil

1 medium onion, thinly sliced

2 small carrots, thinly sliced

4 cloves garlic

12 whole black peppercorns

¼ cup salt

3 cups white vinegar

3 cups water

MAKES 4 PINTS
HEAT RATING: MEDIUM

Escabeche *means "pickled" in Spanish, and this recipe is a way of pickling chiles that is popular in Mexico and other Latin countries. This particular method requires that the peppers be cooked and packed with several other vegetables. A variety of small hot chiles can be used, so don't limit yourself to only jalapeños.* **NOTE** *This recipe requires advance preparation.*

Saute the chiles in the oil in a pan over medium heat until the skin starts to blister. Add the onion and carrots and heat for an additional minute.

Pack the chile mixture into sterilized pint jars, leaving ½ inch headroom.

Add a clove of garlic, 3 peppercorns, and 1 teaspoon salt to each of the jars.

Combine the vinegar and water in a pan and bring to a boil. Pour over the chiles.

Seal and process the jars in a boiling water bath for 15 minutes.

Store for 4 weeks in a cool, dark place before serving.

One final method of "pickling" chiles is to preserve them in liquor. This method has several advantages to it, including the fact that the process can be completed without using the stove. Also, alcohol tends to change the chiles less than vinegar. Simply cut or poke a hole in each chile and cover with your preferred liquor. Vodka, gin, vermouth, and rum all produce tasty results. Not only does this process preserve the chiles, it also produces some very interesting drinks!

The process is simple. Just clean the chiles and remove all the seeds and stems. Slice them in quarters lengthwise and place them in jars. Fill the jars with the liquor of choice and place in a cool, dark area for a minimum of 2 weeks.

DRYING, SMOKING, POWDERS, AND SPICE BLENDS

Drying is the oldest and most common way to preserve pepper pods and works well for most peppers—except for the very meaty ones such as jalapeños, which are smoke-dried and called chipotles. To dry peppers, select those that have reached their mature colors or are just starting to turn. If picked while still green, these peppers are unlikely ever to turn the mature color. Avoid any pods that have black spots, because these will mold or rot.

On dry days, the peppers can be placed on metal racks and set in the sun. Placing them on a surface that collects heat, such as a car hood or roof, accelerates the process. They can also be hung individually on a clothesline. Another method to use is a home dehydrator—just follow the manufacturer's instructions. Jalapeños and several other chiles will dry well in a dehydrator. Cutting the thick-fleshed chiles in half or into several pieces helps to speed up the process. Some of the larger growers use forced convection solar dryers, which reduces the time for sun drying by 65 percent.

Dehydration also works for fresh New Mexican or poblano peppers, which are first roasted and peeled (either green or red) and then placed in the sun to dry. Lay long strips of the peeled pods on nylon window screening, cover them with cheesecloth, and place them in a semi-shady location with good air circulation. The more humid the climate, the more sun should be applied to the drying pods. This

process makes *chile pasado* (chile of the past), which will turn an unappetizing dark color, brown or almost black. However, when the chile pasado is rehydrated in water for about 30 minutes, it regains its green or red color. One ounce of this chile pasado is equivalent to ten to twelve fresh pods.

Chiles drying on the roof of a store, Mesilla, New Mexico.

Ristras and wreaths

The long red ristras (strings) of New Mexican chiles are seen everywhere in that state in the early fall. They provide decoration but are also the centuries-old method of preserving red chile peppers for later culinary use. To make a ristra, you need a supply of freshly picked red (or just turning red) New Mexican chile pods; three-fourths of a bushel of chiles will make a ristra about 3 feet long. Don't bother using green chiles in the belief they will turn red, for many will be immature pods that will shrivel and turn a dull white. Ristras and wreaths can be made

Ristras drying in the sun.

out of any elongated pods, so try making them with cayennes or mirasols.

Besides the pepper pods, you will need a ball of lightweight cotton string and some baling wire or heavy twine. The first step is to tie clusters of three pods together with the cotton string. Hold the three pods by their stems, wrap the string around the stems twice, bring the string upward between two of the pods, and pull tight. Then make a half hitch with the string, place it over the stems, and pull tight. Continue this process with sets of three pods until there are several clusters of pods tied to the cotton string, or until the weight of the pods makes the string difficult to handle. At that point break the string and start again, continuing until all of the pods have been tied into clusters of three.

The next step is to attach the clusters of pods to a stronger length of twine or wire. Suspend the twine or wire from a rafter or the top of a door and make a loop at the end to keep chiles from slipping off. Starting from the bottom, braid the pods around the twine in a manner similar to braiding hair. The twine serves as one strand and two pods in the cluster serve as the other two strands. As you braid the pods, keep the center pushed down to insure a tight fit and be sure that the pods protrude evenly from the ristra. These days, some ristra makers have resorted to using rubber bands to tie up groups of three chiles, and then they slip each group over a wire to form the ristra. This method is considerably faster than the traditional method, but the disadvantage is that the ristras tend to be a bit thin or skinny and last only as long as the rubber bands hold out.

One final method to make a ristra is to use a large needle threaded with string. Push the needle through the bottom of the stem where it widens out, pushing the chiles up tightly against each other. Again, this tends to produce thin-looking ristras, but this can be overcome by hanging several strings together. It is also a handy way to handle smaller chiles such as cayennes or piquins, which require a lot of time and dexterity to string in the traditional way.

To make a wreath, use smaller pods such as cayennes, braid the pods around a straightened-out coat hanger, and then bend the wire into a circle. When you have completed the braiding, hang the ristra or wreath in full sun from a clothesline or rafter where air circulation is good. The chiles should dry in the sun before the ristra is brought inside, or else they may turn moldy and rot. Do not spray the ristra with lacquer to make it shiny—all that will do is make the peppers inedible. Dry red peppers have their own natural luster and do not need an artificial shine.

Making chile powders

Although whole pods keep best because they best retain color and flavor, another way to store peppers is to grind them into powders. Powders are concentrated and take up less storage space than whole pods. All dried chiles can be ground into powder—and most are, including the habanero. Remember, though, that chile powders oxidize more easily than pods, so they must be stored properly. Crushed chiles, or those coarsely ground with some of the seeds, are called *quebrado*. Coarse powders are referred to as *caribe*, while the finer powders are termed *molido*. The milder powders, such as those made from New Mexican chiles, can also be used as the base for sauces, but the hotter powders such as cayenne and piquin are used when heat is needed more than flavor.

To turn fresh pods into powders, use a food dehydrator to dry them out before grinding them. If they are dry enough to snap in half and not bend, they are ready for grinding. The seeds should be removed for purer powder colors.

A shortcut for drying pods that will be turned into powder immediately is to cut fresh pods of any size in half, remove the seeds, chop them coarsely, and then microwave small quantities on low power until most of the moisture is gone. Place these microwaved pepper pieces in a food dryer or under the sun until they break

Use a food dehydrator to dry pods before grinding.

when bent. They can also be dried in a 200°F oven for 6 to 8 hours. Remember that drying fresh peppers in the oven for long periods of time tends to darken them, and they have a tendency to lighten under full sun.

The next step is to grind the peppers into powders. The fresher the powders, the better they taste, so don't grind up too many pods. Use an electric spice mill and be sure to wear a painter's mask to protect your nose and throat from the pungent powder. Store the powders in small, airtight bottles.

Adventurous cooks can experiment with creating powders of specific colors. For example, collect the different varieties of green, yellow, orange, red, and brown chiles and separate them into their respective colors. The colors of the powders vary from a bright, electric

Grinding chiles.

red-orange (chiltepíns) to light green (dried jalapeños) to a dark brown that verges on black (anchos). The colored powders can then be combined with spices, as in our recipe for chili powder, or they can be stored for later use.

Another use for the powders is to turn them into green, yellow, orange, red, or brown chile pastes. Since some of the colors of the powders tend to be a bit dull, they can be brightened up by adding a few drops of the appropriate food coloring when making the pastes.

Chile pasado

The most ancient method of preserving green chiles—the method used before the advent of refrigeration and freezing—is chile pasado, or "chile of the past." Chile pasado is roasted and peeled green chiles that have been dried in the sun. Since a chile is 90 percent water, when dehydrated the chile is lightweight and very easy to transport. The only problem is its appearance—it dries to an unappealing brownish or blackish color, although it rehydrates to a dark green. Chile pasado is expensive, if you can find it, and this method has been replaced by using modern technology.

In 2008, AEI International Laboratories in Las Cruces, New Mexico, introduced InstantChile Futuro. Following the concept that cooking should not precede consumption by more than an hour to achieve the best combination of roasted and cooked flavors, the lab developed a new peeling process called MicroRoasting. MicroRoasting is a computer-controlled system that automatically adjusts the roaster to peel areas on a single chile no larger than a dime. In this way, MicroRoasting is able to produce chiles that are peeled but not cooked. Like a gem cutter working to bring out the beauty of each individual stone, the MicroRoasting process is forty thousand times more selective than steam peeling.

With the skin removed and a smoky flavor left in its place, the chile is ready for the dehydration process to begin. Dehydration parameters are tightly controlled to insure that the chile's firmness and smoky flavor from MicroRoasting are preserved. The result is an emerald green InstantChile Futuro pod that is light and shelf-stable for two years. These dried pods can be carefully packaged and shipped worldwide, so now cooks and chileheads everywhere can enjoy the unique flavor of fresh roasted chiles all year long. Because the process leaves the chiles supple, they arrive as whole pods even if the package has been crushed.

Chile Pasado (Chile of the Past)

2 pounds New Mexican green
   chile pods (about 20 pods)

String

MAKES ABOUT 3 OUNCES
HEAT RATING: VARIES BUT USUALLY
MEDIUM

Here is the way green chiles were preserved before the invention of canning and freezers. This method assumes that you live in a dry climate like New Mexico or Arizona. If not, remove the stems from the chile pods and place them in a food dehydrator until brittle. You can alternatively place them in an oven set at the lowest heat possible, but you must monitor them carefully.

Roast the chile pods on a charcoal or gas grill until the pods blister and start to turn black, turning often. Remove them from the grill and place in a plastic bag with a wet paper towel for a half hour.

Remove and carefully peel the skin off, leaving the stem and seeds intact.

Tie four pods together by wrapping string around the stems and place over a line outside in the sun. Do not let the chiles get wet. You can protect them from flies and other insects by wrapping them lightly in cheesecloth.

Drying time varies with humidity levels, but dry them until they are very dark and brittle.

To store, break off the stems and place the dried pods in a zip bag and then place in a second zip bag. Place in the freezer for optimum results, especially if you live in a humid climate. Because the pods are brittle, breaking off the stems will sometimes cause them to break into strips and other pieces.

To reconstitute the pods, place them in a pot of boiling water for 1 minute. Remove from the heat and let stand for 5 minutes. Remove from the water and drain. Use them in any recipe calling for green chile in any form except whole pods.

Smoked chiles

Why did Native Americans smoke chiles in the first place? Perhaps some thick-fleshed chiles such as jalapeños were dropped near the communal fire and later salvaged as leathery, preserved chiles. Since smoking (along with salting) is believed to be one of the earliest preservation methods, it would make sense that the "meaty" chiles could be smoked right along with the meat.

In the town of Delicias in northern Mexico, red jalapeños are smoked in a large pit on a rack that can be made out of wood, bamboo, or metal. Another nearby pit contains the fire and is connected to the smoking pit by an underground tunnel. The pods are placed on top of the rack, and drafts of air pull the smoke up and over the pods. A farm may have a smoker of a different design at the edge of the fields, and it may be a fireplace of bricks with grates at the top and a firebox below.

Traditional chipotle (smoked red jalapeño) supplies from Mexico are often unreliable, can be of poor quality, and are sometimes difficult to get through customs. Gale Carr, a farmer with a master's degree in business, runs the Chipotle Texas operation in the tiny town of Fort Hancock, Texas, near El Paso. He believes that American-made chipotles offering quality, consistency, and cleanliness will soon take over from the imports—and he has the lab reports to prove the higher quality of his chipotles. "Basically, we are taking two by-products that nobody wants–red jalapeños and pecan tree trimmings–and turning them into a gourmet product," he says. He dries the red jalapeños before smoking them, as that technique reduces the time for a finished product.

Chilehead hobbyists can smoke their own chiles, although the process is time-intensive. It is not difficult to make chipotles in the backyard with a meat smoker or Weber-type barbecue unit with a lid. The grill should be washed to remove any meat particles, because any odor in the barbecue will give the chile an undesirable flavor. Ideally, the smoker or barbecue should be new and dedicated only to smoking chiles. The result of this type of smoking is a chipotle that more resembles the red *morita* than the classic tan-brown *típico*.

There are five keys to the quality of home-made chipotles: the maturity and quality of the pods, the moisture in the pods, the type of wood used to create the smoke, the temperature of the smoke drying the pods, and the amount of time the pods are exposed to the smoke and heat. But remember that smoking is an art, so variations

Chile drier at Chipotle Texas, purveyor of traditional dried and smoked chile pepper products.

are to be expected and even desired.

Recommended woods are fruit trees or other hardwoods such as hickory, oak, and pecan. Pecan is used extensively in parts of Mexico and in southern New Mexico to flavor chipotle. Although mesquite is a smoke source in Mexico, we prefer the less greasy hardwoods. Mesquite charcoal (not briquets) is acceptable, especially when soaked hardwood chips are placed on top to create even more smoke. It is possible, however, that the resinous mesquite smoke (from the wood, not charcoal) contributes to the tan-brown coloration of the típico variety of chipotle.

Wash all the pods and discard any that have insect damage or bruises, or are soft, and remove the stems from the pods. Start two small fires on each side of the barbecue bowl, preferably using one of the recommended hardwoods. If you are using a meat smoker with a separate firebox, simply build the fire in the firebox and smoke the chiles until they are pliable but not stiff.

Place the pods in a single layer on the grill rack so they fit between the two fires. For quicker smoking, cut the pods in half lengthwise and remove the seeds. Keep the fires small and never directly expose the pods to the fire, so they won't dry unevenly or burn. The intention is to dry the pods slowly while flavoring them with smoke. If you are using charcoal briquets, soak hardwood chips in water before placing them on the coals, so the wood will burn more slowly and create more smoke. The barbecue vents should be opened only partially to allow a small amount of air to enter the barbecue, thus preventing the fires from burning too fast and creating too much heat.

Check the pods, the fires, and the chips hourly and move the pods around, always keeping them away from the fires. Be sure to stand upwind as you open the smoker; that smoke could be "hotter" than you think! It may take up to 48 hours to dry the pods completely, which means that your fire will probably burn down during the night and will need to be restoked in the morning. When dried properly, the pods will be hard, light in weight, and reddish-brown in color. Ten pounds of fresh jalapeños yield just 1 pound of chipotles, but a pound of chipotles goes a long way, as a single pod is usually enough to flavor a dish. After the pods have dried, remove them from the grill and let them cool. To preserve their flavor, place them in a zip bag and freeze them.

Chipotle (morita) pod.

A quick smoking technique involves drying red jalapeños (sliced lengthwise, seeds removed) in a dehydrator or in an oven with just the pilot light on until they are dessicated but not stiff and then smoking them for three hours over fruitwood in a traditional smoker with a separate firebox, or in the Weber-style barbecue described earlier. This technique separates the drying from the smoking, so you spend less time fueling the smoker.

Although jalapeños are the most popular chile for smoking, many people have started to smoke-dry a variety of peppers including haba-neros, serranos, and even yellow wax varieties. Experiment with your favorite varieties, and you will be in for a real treat.

Ancho Chile Dry Rub

4   ancho chiles, stems and seeds
    removed, dried in the oven

2   teaspoons whole white
    peppercorns

1   teaspoon whole black
    peppercorns

½ teaspoon celery seed

3½ teaspoons cumin seed

1   teaspoon thyme

1   small bay leaf

1   teaspoon annato seeds

1½ teaspoons salt

MAKES ABOUT ½ CUP
HEAT RATING: MILD

Here's a great rub to use on meats that will be smoked or grilled. Since anchos are sold in fairly pliable condition, place them in the oven on low heat until they are brittle.

Blend all the ingredients together in a spice mill or blender. Store in a glass jar.

Dry Jerk Seasoning

1   teaspoon dried ground
    habanero or cayenne

2   tablespoons onion powder

2   teaspoons ground thyme

Jerk seasoning is actually a delicious, tropical way to season either pork or poultry; simply rub into the meat, marinate overnight in the refrigerator, grill (or bake), and then enjoy!

2 teaspoons ground allspice

1 teaspoon coarsely ground
   black pepper

½ teaspoon ground nutmeg

½ teaspoon ground cinnamon

½ teaspoon garlic powder

¼ teaspoon ground cloves

MAKES ABOUT ¼ CUP
HEAT RATING: HOT

Combine all the ingredients and mix well. Store in a glass jar.

Chili Powder

5 tablespoons ground New
   Mexican red chile

1 tablespoon ground hot chile,
   such as piquín or chiltepín

1½ tablespoons ground cumin

1½ tablespoons ground oregano

1½ tablespoons garlic powder

1 teaspoon salt

MAKES ½ CUP
HEAT RATING: HOT

This powder is used to make chili con carne and replaces the commercial type; experiment with the ingredients and adjust them to your taste.

Mix all the ingredients together and process in a blender or spice grinder until fine. Store in a glass jar.

Chile and Herb Salt Substitute

4 tablespoons dried parsley

4 tablespoons dried basil

2 teaspoons dried rosemary

1 tablespoon dried tarragon (or pineapple sage)

2 tablespoons dried thyme

1 tablespoon dried dill weed

2 tablespoons paprika

1 teaspoon celery seed

1 teaspoon crushed, dried red chiles such as piquins, or 2 teaspoons New Mexican red chile powder

MAKES ½ CUP

HEAT RATING: MILD TO MEDIUM

Use this recipe to replace salt in your diet or in any recipe you cook from. It tastes best, of course, when you grow and dry your own herbs, but commercially purchased dried herbs will work as well. Try this mixture on baked potatoes, pasta, and vegetables—and especially on corn on the cob.

Place all ingredients in a mini-food processor and blend for 10 seconds or so. Put the mixture into a glass shaker jar and cover tightly until ready to use.

CREATIVE PRESERVATION

In addition to the more traditional means of preserving the chile pepper harvest, creative cooks use such diverse techniques as juicing and candying and also create chile vinegars, butters, jellies, oils, liquors, and condiments.

Juicing chiles

Putting chile pods through a juicer removes all the solids and leaves the flavor and heat embedded in the juice. In 2003, Nancy Gerlach, former *Fiery Foods and BBQ* magazine food editor, experimented with the process while wearing protective gear, including a mask. First, she removed the stems from fresh pods and cut the pods into pieces that would fit into the feed tube of the juicer. The first pass through the machine yielded a quantity of juice, but the pulp had rather large pieces of flesh, so she ran the pulp through a second time before measuring either the juice or the pulp. Nancy juiced the milder chiles (the poblano and Anaheim) first and then the jalapeños. She was a little disappointed in the results. They all juiced well enough, but they tasted about the same and didn't have much heat, so she was stuck with a very mild jalapeño juice.

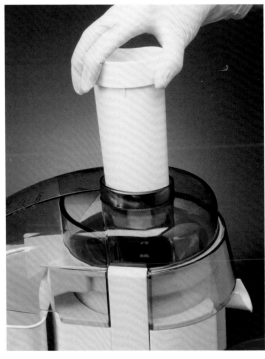

Jalapeños ready for juicing.

Pushing the pods into the juicer.

Since the chiles were producing such mild juice and pulp, and because it was getting hot under her protective gear, she took off the mask before proceeding to the serranos. A big mistake, as the fumes drove her from the room. And after tasting the juice, she had to run to the refrigerator and grab something dairy to quell the fire. After that experience, she didn't do any more chile juicing without a mask. The remainder of the chiles produced very hot to blistering juice, and the pulp was full of heat, though the juice was definitely hotter.

Nancy wondered if dried varieties would also work. She rehydrated a few of the larger, more flavorful varieties (ancho and New Mexican) in hot water for 30 minutes to insure that they were fully softened. She drained and then juiced them. No liquid was produced and the pulp was such a thick paste it had to be scraped out of the machine. Reconstituted dry chiles obviously did not work in a juicer.

First she used the juice as a condiment to spice up simple recipes. A squeeze of lemon or lime, some coarsely ground black pepper, a little salt, and chile juice was all that was needed to turn tomato juice into a tasty vegetable juice. She tried the serrano juice in her version of a Bloody Maria, and it was wonderfully hot without being thick and pulpy. It also turned out to be a good way to control the amount of heat in a recipe, as you can add a little at a time, actually drop by drop, until the desired heat level is reached.

Adding the pulp to salsas seemed fairly obvious, but Nancy experimented anyway. She removed the big pieces from the jalapeño pulp and added the remainder to a simple pico de gallo. Since the pulp was more of a mash, it was a little harder to get it mixed into the salsa, but once it was mixed in it was fine. She reported that the salsa was milder than if the whole chile had been used, but it still had the flavor.

Next she wondered if the pulp would work in baking. She tried the jalapeño pulp in Blue Corn Chile Cheese Muffins but was disappointed. Even though these jalapeños were mild, she thought that the pulp would be more evenly distributed and maybe more of the chile taste would be apparent. The muffins were good, but they had only a hint of chile taste and no heat. Next she tried a tablespoon of habanero juice in the Spiced Cranberry Pumpkin Muffins recipe.

Jalapeño juice.

JUICING RESULTS

Chile Type	Amount	Amount Liquid	Amount Pulp	Heat Rating
Anaheim	½ lb.	⅓+ cup	2 tablespoons	mild
jalapeño	¾ lb.	⅔ cup	6 tablespoons	mild
rocoto	15	½ cup	1 cup	very hot
serrano	15 (2 ounces)	¼ cup	5 tablespoons	hot
poblano	1 (3 ounces)	¼ cup	3 tablespoons	mild
yellow hots	6 (3 ounces)	¼ cup	5 tablespoons	hot
habanero	6 (3 ounces)	1 tablespoon	¼ cup	fiery

The result was muffins with heat that seemed to increase the longer they were stored, but the muffins didn't have anywhere near the fire you would expect if you had used six habaneros in the recipe.

Since the juice wasn't working all that well in baking, the next step was to experiment with a direct heat method. She substituted the hot serrano juice for green chile in her clam chowder. The soup had some heat but no serrano flavor. It appeared that cooking on top of the stove was also having an effect on the capsaicin. She had more serrano juice, so she tried another approach to confirm that heat was indeed the culprit. She prepared Creamy Asparagus Rosemary Soup, but instead of adding the chile while the soup was cooking, she removed the pot from the heat and stirred in the serrano juice before serving. It worked. The soup was hot and had a nice serrano flavor.

Nancy's conclusion was that this method of handling chiles works in recipes that do not require cooking, such as in drinks and salsas. She also wouldn't juice the large, milder chiles, as their distinctive flavors and any heat appear to get lost in the process. The pulp worked well in salsas, but she wouldn't juice the chiles just to produce the pulp. She thinks that juicing works well with the smaller, fleshy, super-hot chiles such as habaneros and rocotos. She tried freezing the juice as well as the pulp, and both were fine when defrosted; so she has decided to juice her habaneros, freeze the juice in ice cube trays, and use it in fresh salsas, uncooked hot sauces, and drinks.

Bloody Maria

8 ounces tomato juice

2 ounces tequila

1 teaspoon rocoto juice (or
⅟₂ teaspoon habanero juice)

½ teaspoon lime juice

Dash Worcestershire sauce

Dash celery salt

Freshly ground black pepper

Salt to taste

Lime wedge

SERVES 1
HEAT RATING: HOT

This is a "south of the border" Bloody Mary substituting tequila for vodka. But if you are a purist, use vodka or leave out the alcohol altogether and have a great morning wake-up drink. Adding rocoto juice, rather than Tabasco, adds flavor as well as warming the drink nicely. The heat comes on slowly and lingers. This is one of the best uses for chile juice.

Combine all the ingredients in a pitcher and mix well. Fill a tall glass with ice, pour the juice over the ice, garnish with a lime wedge, and serve.

Belizean Habanero Hot Sauce Made with Juice

1 small onion, chopped

2 cloves garlic, chopped

1 tablespoon vegetable oil

1 cup chopped carrots

¼ cup lime juice, fresh preferred

2 tablespoons distilled vinegar

1 teaspoon salt

2 tablespoons habanero juice

MAKES 1½ CUPS

HEAT RATING: HOT

In our original Belizean Habanero Hot Sauce recipe we never cook the habaneros in order to preserve their distinctive flavor, so it was a perfect choice for the first experiment with juicing chiles. After cooking and pureeing the sauce, stir in the habanero juice. The final consistency of the sauce is very smooth, with lots of heat and a strong habanero flavor.

Saute the onion and garlic in the oil in a saucepan over medium heat until soft.

Add the carrots and 2 cups of water and bring to a boil. Reduce the heat and simmer until the carrots are soft.

Remove from the heat and transfer the mix to a blender or food processor. Add the lime juice, vinegar, and salt, and puree until smooth. Add the habanero juice and mix well.

Store the hot sauce in a glass bottle.

Candied capsicums

Candying is one of the most ancient forms of preserving the harvest. When chile fruit is placed in syrup and the sugar content is gradually increased, the pods' cell liquid gets replaced by sugar. This migration through semipermeable cell walls is called osmosis. Typically, 70 to 75 percent of the extracted cell liquid, mostly water, will be replaced by sugar, while shape, color, and a good portion of the flavor will be preserved. That way, candied chile fruit will keep almost indefinitely. The ways you can use these sweet peppers are almost limitless, and the same is true for a by-product of the process, spicy syrup.

In 2007, Harald Zoschke, then webmaster of the Fiery Foods and BBQ SuperSite, experimented with candying chiles. Be forewarned: candying chiles is not for the impatient. The process spreads over 6 days, taking about 30 minutes every day, not counting cleanup of sticky utensils and pots. While the sophisticated approach of French confectioners aims for soft fruit, Harald was aiming for crunchy chiles with a transparent, almost glasslike appearance, so we can take a simpler approach. Harald advises: "Most important, take your time and allow this to be a fun project."

REQUIRED EQUIPMENT

Medium-sized saucepan
Wooden spoon
Mason jar (1 quart or 1 liter) or similar glass container with lid
Small glass bowl that just fits into the opening of the jar, to hold down the peppers in the liquid
One or two clean marmalade jars and lids
Heat-resistant strainer
½ quart jars (for example, jam jars) to keep excess syrup
Cookie cooling rack
Baking oven or electric dehydrator
Old newspapers to put under pots and jars

INGREDIENTS

½–¾ pound fresh chile pods rinsed and cut in half or strips
2⅔ pounds regular white sugar
1 quart water

INSTRUCTIONS: DAY 1

Start by preparing the peppers. As with all preserving techniques, use only the freshest, spotless chiles. Rinse and pat dry. Cut the pods of thin-walled varieties like habanero, cayenne, or Thai peppers in half to ease the syrup penetration, and deseed them. Fleshier chiles like jalapeños are better cut into strips. Keep

Candied chiles.

Cleaned chiles.
Pouring the syrup.

sections of pods uniform in size for each batch.

Then cook the syrup. In a large saucepan, combine 1 quart water and 2 pounds sugar. Using the wooden spoon, mix well, then bring to a rolling boil. Keep boiling and stirring until the mixture takes on a syrupy consistency but still stays clear and colorless. This takes about 30 minutes. If you are using a ceramic stovetop, watch out not to spill any sugar or syrup on it, as this stuff burns in fast.

Put the cut chiles into the mason jar or other glass container and pour the boiling-hot syrup over them (caution—don't burn yourself). Leave enough room to put a small bowl as a weight on top to keep the peppers down, all covered with the liquid. Close the container and keep the remaining syrup in marmalade jar(s). Let the chiles sit in the closed container for 24 hours. To minimize spill cleanup, put a newspaper underneath your jars. Rinse and clean all cooking utensils right after work.

Various candying instructions recommend that you start the pouring with syrup that has cooled down first. We found that pouring the liquid while piping hot helps prevent spoilage of peppers by fermentation while sitting in the liquid for days. You could also boil the pods quickly first, but that might make them soft and mushy, losing their shape.

DAY 2

On the second day, drain the chiles in a strainer, letting the syrup flow into your saucepan. Put the chiles back into the glass container.

Bring the syrup to a boil and stir in an additional 1¾ ounces sugar. Add also the syrup you

Chiles candying in the syrup.

Finishing the candying in a dehydrator.

saved in the marmalade jars. Keep boiling at high heat and stirring with your wooden spoon for about 10 minutes. Pour the hot syrup over the chiles again and put on the weight to keep them all covered in liquid. Save the remaining syrup again. Let the chiles sit in their closed container for another 24 hours.

DAY 3 TO DAY 6

Repeat the second day's procedure on days 3, 4, and 5, including the addition of 1¾ ounces more sugar every day. Both the sugar addition and the reduction by cooking will cause the syrup to become thicker and thicker. And it's getting hotter, too, as some of the capsaicin dissolves from the peppers into the liquid. After day 5, let the chiles sit for 48 hours and have a rest on day 6.

DAY 7

Pour the syrup and chiles into a saucepan and bring to a brief boil for just 1 minute, then take off the heat. Drain the chiles through the strainer and catch the syrup in jars. There are great uses for the sticky, spicy liquid as well. Arrange the chiles on a cookie cooling grid or a grid from your oven. Be sure to put parchment paper or newspaper underneath to catch drips of excess syrup. Let them sit for 2 hours.

Finish the sticky pieces off in the oven or a dehydrator. Harald used his dehydrator, and the chiles were nice and dry after just 4 hours. In the oven, drying should take about 15 minutes at 210–300°F with the door slightly open. Check after 10 minutes, and drying should be finished no later than another 10 to15 minutes. (To keep the peppers as they are, the airflow and lower temperature offered by a dehydrator works best.)

Let the chiles cool to room temperature, then store them in an airtight container. Flat containers like Tupperware or Gladware allow to you place the pieces side by side rather than stacking them and potentially having them stick together. If the chiles are still a little sticky, you can coat them with powdered sugar (also called confectioner's sugar). The French confectioners glaze their fancy fruits with a thin sugar coating after candying to prevent them from drying out and keep them soft and moist. But since Harald's goal was to produce crunchy chiles, he didn't need to do that. His candied chiles didn't stick after weeks of storage, and they kept their shape, color, heat, and aroma.

If you store the candied chiles in a dark place, they should keep their colors nicely without any additives. The colors of the mature pods survive the syrup treatment and cooking really well. In fact, the colors seem to come out even more vibrantly on the translucent pods. But the green color of immature pods tends to darken to a brownish tint during candying.

We found it very important to get rid of all humidity and to store the candied peppers tightly closed in a cool place, preferably in the refrigerator. Fleshy peppers, especially, can get moldy after a couple of months if not dried well and/or if stored too warm. Since the thin-fleshed varieties get dry more easily, we have found that small hot red peppers as well as *Capsicum chinense* varieties like habanero and 'Caribbean Red' are best suited for candying. The syrup is stored best in marmalade or mason jars. Strain

Candied chile cheesecake.

to keep out seeds and chile particles.

Here are a few suggestions for using candied chiles:

- Spice up fruitcake, muffins, and other cakes like Bold Banana Bread.
- Add to habanero cheesecake, with bits in the dough and matching decoration on top.
- Decorate cakes, ice cream, and other desserts.
- Use as a spicy snack (optionally covered with chocolate).

Try using the spicy syrup in these ways:

- Sweeten tea and hot chocolate, especially during the cold season.
- Use in cocktails that call for syrup as an ingredient, like our Blue Lagoon.
- Pour over waffles and pancakes.
- Add to spicy toffee, caramels, or our Belligerent Butterscotch.

Bold Banana Bread

1¾ cups all-purpose flour

2¼ teaspoons baking powder

½ teaspoon salt

⅓ cup shortening (or butter)

⅔ cup sugar

½ teaspoon lemon zest

2 eggs

2 soft, ripe bananas

½ cup chopped walnuts or pecans

1 cup coconut flakes

1 tablespoon mixed candied chiles, chopped

MAKES 1 LOAF

HEAT RATING: MILD, PUNCTUATED WITH HOT PEPPER BITS

Credit for this tasty recipe goes to Mary Jane, Dave's wife, who originally made this banana bread with a chopped fresh habanero. Harald Zoschke came up with the idea of using a colorful mix of chopped candied peppers instead, making it look almost like a fruitcake.

NOTE All ingredients should be at room temperature.

Preheat the oven to 350°F.

Sift the flour with the baking powder and salt into a bowl. In another bowl, blend the shortening, sugar, and lemon zest to a creamy consistency. In two other bowls, beat the eggs, mash the bananas, and blend both well with the shortening or sugar mixture.

Add the sifted ingredients in three batches, beating the batter after each addition until smooth. Fold in the chopped nuts, coconut flakes, and candied chiles.

Pour the batter into a well-greased loaf pan. Bake for about 1 hour, or until a toothpick inserted in the center comes out clean. Let cool before slicing.

Blistering Blue Lagoon Cocktail

2 ounces vodka

½ ounce Blue Curacao

1 ounce Captain Morgan's Coconut Rum

¼ ounce lemon juice

2 ounces pineapple juice

½ ounce chile syrup

Candied habanero half

Crushed ice

SERVES 2

HEAT RATING: MEDIUM (DEPENDING ON THE HEAT OF THE SYRUP)

Here's Harald's kicked-up version of this classic Caribbean cocktail.

Blend liquors, juices, and syrup in a blender.

Fill two 12-ounce glasses with crushed ice and pour blended liquid over ice.

Garnish with candied habanero half and serve with straws.

Chile vinegars

Chile vinegars are a great way of using some of the chiles that are left after drying, freezing, and pickling your crop. Use these flavored vinegars for marinades, with oil for salad dressings, or to deglaze pans. We have included a couple of recipes, but use your imagination in combining your favorite herbs with chiles and vinegar, using the basic instructions as a guideline.

This is probably the easiest way to put up chiles. Simply pack chiles and herbs in sterilized jars and cover with vinegar. Place the jars in a cool, dark place and leave undisturbed for 3 to 4 weeks. Strain the mixture. You can speed up the process by heating the vinegar and pouring it over herbs that have been chopped and crushed. Let the mixture steep for a couple of days before straining and rebottling.

Rosemary Chile Vinegar

2 tablespoons minced fresh small chiles

1 cup fresh rosemary leaves

3 cloves garlic

1 quart white vinegar

MAKES 1 QUART

HEATING RATING: VARIES

This is our favorite vinegar. Recommended chiles include serranos and habaneros, but it can also be made with dried pasillas for a raisiny flavor. **NOTE** *This recipe requires advance preparation.*

In a large jar, cover the chiles, rosemary, and garlic with the vinegar, and put the lid on. Place the jar in a cool, dark place and leave it undisturbed for 3 to 4 weeks. Strain and pour into clean, sterilized jars.

Oregano-Garlic Green Chile Vinegar

1 cup fresh oregano leaves

10 peeled garlic cloves, whole

2 fresh green chiles such as serrano or Thai, cut in half lengthwise

1 quart white vinegar

MAKES 1 QUART

HEAT RATING: MILD

The combination of oregano and garlic imparts an Italian flavor to this vinegar, which we keep on the mild side so that the heat doesn't mask the flavor of the garlic. **NOTE** *This recipe requires advance preparation.*

Cover the oregano, garlic, and chiles with the vinegar in a large jar. Store in a cool, dark spot and leave the bottles undisturbed for 3 to 4 weeks. Strain and pour into clean, sterilized jars.

Chile oils

Any of the preceding vinegar recipes can also be used to make flavored oils. Be aware that fresh herbs will cloud the oil as they break down, so remove them as soon as the flavor has developed. Basil is the worst offender and will turn black in the oil. If you use garlic, thread the cloves on wooden skewers, because if a fuzzy haze develops around them they need to be removed and removing a skewer is easier than removing individual cloves. Do not attempt to preserve fresh chiles in oil as there is a risk that the jars will develop botulism.

Asian Chile Oil

4 cups vegetable oil, peanut preferred

1 cup small dried red chiles, such as piquins

MAKES 4 CUPS
HEAT RATING: HOT

Bottles of chile oil decorated with ribbons and tiny paper-mache chiles make nice gifts for anyone who likes to cook. Include an Asian stir-fry recipe along with each gift bottle. **NOTE** *This recipe requires advance preparation.*

Heat the oil to medium hot in a saucepan over medium heat, remove from the heat, and add the chiles.

Cover the pan and let it stand for 12 to 24 hours (the longer it steeps, the hotter the oil). Strain the oil into clean, sterilized jars or bottles.

Tie a few dried chiles to the jars for decoration.

Sichuan Ginger Oil

2 cups vegetable oil,
  peanut preferred

2-inch piece fresh ginger, sliced

3-inch cinnamon stick

4 small dried red chiles, such
  as piquin, Thai, or cayenne

1 teaspoon lightly crushed
  Sichuan peppercorns

MAKES 2 CUPS
HEAT RATING: MILD

This oil adds a lot of flavor to any dish and especially Asian fare, but don't limit its use. It's also great on a simple salad of mixed greens and bean sprouts. **NOTE** *This recipe requires advance preparation.*

Heat the oil to medium hot in a saucepan over medium heat, remove from the heat, and add the ginger, cinnamon stick, chiles, and peppercorns.

Cover the pan and let it stand for 12 to 24 hours (the longer it steeps, the hotter the oil). Strain the oil and pour in clean, sterilized jars.

Piri Piri Oil

3 cups extra virgin olive oil

2 habanero chiles, cut in half

1 teaspoon lemon zest

2 bay leaves

MAKES 3 CUPS
HEAT RATING: HOT

This interesting sauce is the Caribbean, oil-based variation on the African sauce from Angola, which was transferred to the region by Portuguese immigrants working the cacao plantations in Trinidad and Guyana. Use it to spice up soups and fried fish. Pimento leaves are traditionally used in this recipe, but they are hard to find. **NOTE** *This recipe requires advance preparation.*

Combine all the ingredients in a jar and seal tightly. Place in the refrigerator and let steep for 2 weeks. Remove the top and stir every 2 or 3 days. The longer it steeps, the hotter the sauce will become. Remove the chiles when the heat is at the desired level.

Chile condiments

Virtually any condiment you can think of can contain chiles—sometimes in fairly large quantities. Mustard, chutney, and jelly are just a few of the condiments you can add chile to.

Fiery Fruit Chutney

1 cup pitted prunes, chopped

1 cup seedless raisins

1½ cups cider vinegar

1 tablespoon lime juice

1 cup brown sugar

1 teaspoon dry mustard

1 teaspoon ground cinnamon

½ teaspoon salt

¼ teaspoon ground cumin

6 small fresh red chiles, such as jalapeños or serranos, stems and seeds removed chopped

2 cups chopped tart apples

1 cup chopped onions

1 cup peeled, chopped tomatoes

MAKES 2 PINTS
HEAT RATING: MEDIUM

Chutneys are the Indian version of a highly seasoned relish or ketchup and are usually sweet and spicy. Serve this one as an accompaniment to shrimp, poultry, or curries.

Cover the prunes and raisins with very hot water and let steep for 10 minutes to soften. Drain.

Combine the vinegar, lime juice, sugar, mustard, cinnamon, salt, and cumin in a large kettle and bring to a boil over medium heat. Add the prunes, raisins, chiles, apples, onions, and tomatoes.

Cover and boil the mixture, stirring frequently, for 20 minutes or until the mixture has attained the desired consistency.

Pour into clean, sterilized jars and seal.

Jalapeño Jelly

8 red jalapeño chiles, stems and seeds removed

2 medium red bell peppers, stems and seeds removed

1¼ cups white vinegar

¼ cup lemon juice

5 cups sugar

6 ounces liquid pectin

Green food coloring

MAKES 5 CUPS
HEAT RATING: HOT

This jelly goes well on crackers with cream cheese or as a basting sauce for grilled poultry.

Place the jalapeños and bell peppers in a blender or processor and chop, being careful not to grind the peppers too finely.

Combine the vinegar, lemon juice, and sugar in a large kettle and bring to a rolling boil over medium heat. Add the chiles, along with any juice, and boil rapidly for 10 minutes, stirring occasionally and removing any foam that forms.

Add the pectin and food coloring. Bring back to a boil and while stirring constantly, boil for an additional minute.

Skim off any foam that forms and bottle in clean, sterilized jars.

Jalapeño Mustard

½ cup yellow mustard seeds

¾ cup yellow mustard powder

1 cup flat beer

⅓ cup vinegar, cider or
chile-herb flavored

½ teaspoon salt

4 jalapeño chiles, stems
and seeds removed, minced

MAKES 1 PINT
HEAT RATING: HOT

Replace mundane yellow mustard with this spicy version. Use a chile-herb vinegar for an even hotter, more flavorful mustard. For a smoother mustard, grind all the seeds to a fine powder. **NOTE** *This recipe requires advance preparation.*

Grind half of the mustard seeds to a fine powder. Coarsely grind the remainder of the seeds.

Combine the mustard seeds and powder, beer, vinegar, and salt, and mix well. Stir in the chiles and pack in clean, steril-ized jars.

Allow the mustard to sit in a cool, dark place for 2 weeks before using. Be sure to refrigerate after opening.

Mustard seeds
and chile
mustards.

Compound butters

Compound butters are a combination of herbs, spices, and butter that can be used in a variety of ways—on vegetables, potatoes, and pasta or with grilled meats, poultry, or fish. Use these butters for sauteing foods or even cooking an omelet. They will keep indefinitely in the freezer, so make several variations to keep on hand.

Cinnamon Chipotle Chile Butter

1 medium chipotle chile, stem and seeds removed

2 teaspoons ground cinnamon

1 pound unsalted butter, softened

2 teaspoons lime juice

MAKES 1 POUND
HEAT RATING: MEDIUM

This butter adds a great touch to vegetables, fish, and even a grilled steak.

Cover the chipotle with very hot water in a bowl and let it sit until soft, about 60 minutes. Drain the chile and place in a blender or food processor along with some water, and puree until smooth.

Mix all the ingredients together and allow to sit at room temperature for an hour to blend the flavors. Wrap in plastic or wax paper and freeze.

Orange Zest Red Chile Butter

2 tablespoons grated orange zest

2 teaspoons orange juice

2 teaspoons ground red chile, such as New Mexican, piquin, or de árbol

1 teaspoon onion powder

1 pound unsalted butter, softened

MAKES 1 POUND
HEAT RATING: VARIES

Serve this on breakfast toast or a bagel.

Mix all the ingredients together and allow to sit at room temperature for an hour to blend the flavors. Wrap in plastic or wax paper and freeze.

Cooking with Chile Peppers

CHILE PEPPERS DON'T HAVE TO BE HEALTHY to be fun to eat, but fortunately, they are. Chile peppers contain only a few calories (37 per 100 grams of green chile, about 3½ ounces) and possibly enhance the body's ability to burn off those calories and others as well. This intriguing possibility comes from researchers at Oxford Polytechnic Institute in England, who conducted an experiment in TEF, an acronym meaning "thermic effects of food."

Twelve volunteers ate identical 766-calorie meals. On one day, 3 grams each of chile powder and mustard were added to the meals; on the next day, nothing was added. On the days chile and mustard were added, the volunteers burned between 4 and 76 additional calories, with an average of 45. The researchers concluded that the test was "a possible lead to a different approach to weight reduction" but also warned that the effect had been demonstrated in only one small test. They also cautioned that 6 grams (⅕ ounce) of the chile-mustard mixture "may be a large amount for the average American. If you are used to Mexican, Spanish, or Indian food, though, it's reasonable."

A possible explanation for the process is the fact that certain hot spices—especially chiles—temporarily speed up the body's metabolic rate. After we eat, our metabolic rate increases anyway—a phenomenon known as "diet-induced thermic effect." But chiles boost that effect by a factor of 25, which seems to indicate that increasing the amount of chiles in a recipe could reduce the effective caloric content—provided, of course, that one does not drink more beer to counter the added heat.

Nutritional properties

Most of the research on the nutritional properties of hot peppers has been conducted with the New Mexican pod types, because they are consumed more as a food than a condiment. The long green pods are harvested, roasted, and peeled, and are stuffed or made into sauces. Some of the green pods are allowed to turn red on the bush; after harvesting, the red chiles are used as the primary ingredient in red chile sauces. The green chiles are quite high in vitamin C, with about twice the amount by weight found in citrus, while dried red chiles contain more vitamin A than carrots.

Vitamin C is one of the least stable of all the vitamins; it will break down chemically by heat, exposure to air, solubility in water, and by dehydration. A high percentage of vitamin C in fresh green chiles is retained in the canned and frozen products, but the vitamin C content drops dramatically in the dried red pods and powder. Each 100 grams of fresh ripe chile pods contains 369 milligrams of vitamin C, which diminishes by more than half to 154 milligrams in the dried red pods. Red chile powder contains less than 3 percent of the vitamin C of ripe pods, a low 10 milligrams.

Vitamin A is one of the most stable vitamins and is not affected by canning, cooking, or time. The amount of vitamin A dramatically increases as the pod turns red and dries, from 770 units per hundred grams of green pods to 77,000 in freshly processed dried red pods. This hundred-fold rise in vitamin A content is the result of increasing carotene, the chemical that produces the orange and red colors of ripe peppers.

The recommended daily allowances for these vitamins are 5000 International Units (IUs) for A and 60 milligrams for C. These allowances can be satisfied daily by eating about a teaspoonful of red chile sauce for A and about 1 ounce of fresh green chile for C.

Each hundred grams of green chile contains less than .2 gram of fat—a very low amount. Since no cholesterol is found in vegetables or fruits, peppers are free of it. The fiber content of fresh hot peppers is fairly high (between 1.3 and 2.3 grams per 100 grams of chile), and many of the dishes prepared with them use starchy ingredients such as beans, pasta, and tortillas. And the sugar in chiles is in the form of healthy complex carbohydrates.

Fresh green chiles contain only 3.5 to 5.7 milligrams of sodium per 100 grams—a very low amount. We suggest that chile peppers can be very useful for the low-sodium dieter. The substitution of hot peppers for salt makes gustatory sense because the pungency of the peppers counteracts the blandness of the meal that results from salt restrictions. In other words, the heat masks the absence of salt.

However, canned green chile peppers should be avoided because of the salt used in the canning process, which can be more than a hundred times the amount in fresh or frozen chiles. For people on a potassium-restricted diet, the opposite is true: canned chiles have half the potassium content of fresh ones. Some experts blame this anomaly on the hot lye bath method of removing the tough pepper skins, a technique that provides additional sodium by absorption and reduces the potassium through

HANDLE WITH CAUTION!

Capsaicin, the alkaloid responsible for the heat in chiles, is wonderful for making bland foods interesting, but it is far less welcome in large doses on the skin, or in any amount in your eyes. We urge everyone who processes chiles in any form to wear gloves while handling them. This is especially important when handling the hotter varieties, because chile burns can be extremely painful and can even cause contact dermatitis, redness, and blistering of the skin. This condition is difficult to treat, but the burning eventually goes away.

If you burn your hands, remember that capsaicin is soluble in oils and alcohols, meaning that water will have no effect on it. So if you have "Hunan hand," which is the official name for capsaicin-burned hands, the best remedy found by researchers at the University of New Mexico is to coat your hands in vegetable oil, rub them together for about 30 seconds, and then wash with a strong detergent and water. Even this will not completely eliminate the heat, but it will reduce it. Probably the best treatment is to rub the burning area with isopropyl (rubbing) alcohol. Then rub a salve such as Preparation H over the burned area.

When you burn your mouth and tongue, eat a thick dairy product like cream, sour cream, yogurt, or ice cream and swirl it around in your mouth before swallowing. A protein in the dairy product, casein, effective strips the capsaicin molecules from the capsaicin receptors in your mouth and on your tongue.

If you get capsaicin in your eyes, about the only thing you can do is flush with eyedrops, keep blinking, flush some more, and wait. You will think you are going blind, but after a few minutes the pain and irritation will diminish.

Additionally, be careful where you put your nose while cooking chile. It's not wise to stick your nose right over the top of the blender as you remove the lid after grinding up a batch of chiles, or over a pot of chiles that is being cooked on the stove. Whenever you're working with or cooking chiles, it's a good idea to keep your face away from any concentrated chile combinations.

leaching. It should be noted that some processors have switched to a high-pressure steam treatment to remove skins—a far healthier and tastier method.

During steam peeling, the outer third of the pods is liquefied to remove the peel. In this step, the flavor and texture of the chile decreases dramatically from the fresh values. The pods are then packed into a can and pressure-cooked to sterilize the chile for shelf stability. This second thermal process further degrades the chile flavor and leaves a metallic taste. Using fresh or frozen chiles is clearly preferable to using canned, for reasons of taste as well as nutrition.

Medicinal properties

In addition to their nutritional qualities, chile peppers have quite a long history as a folk remedy for all kinds of ailments, from anorexia to vertigo. Some of the more scientifically recognized medical applications of chile peppers include topical treatments for the pain of arthritis, cluster headaches, and post-herpetic neuralgia (shingles). Capsaicin depletes substance P from nerve endings, thus short-circuiting pain signals to the brain.

Chile-Flavored Vodka

1 liter vodka

1 pasilla chile, seeds and stems removed, cut into thin strips

½ dried New Mexican red chile pod, seeds and stems removed, cut in fourths

¼ habanero chile, seeds and stems removed, left whole

MAKES ABOUT 1 QUART
HEAT RATING: VARIES

When we write "flavored," we mean it, as we have chosen the chiles that we think impart the most distinct flavors. The raisiny flavor of the pasilla melds with the apricot overtones of the habanero and the earthiness of the New Mexican red chile to create a finely tuned, fiery sipping vodka. Of course, use an excellent vodka like Stolichnaya or Absolut.

Open the bottle of vodka and drink some of it to make room in the bottle. Add the chiles and recap. Let sit for at least 3 days to generate some heat, and the vodka will get progressively hotter over the weeks. As you drink the vodka, replace it with more fresh vodka, and the process will go on for some time.

Satan's Blood

1 cup tomato juice

1½ ounces good-quality vodka

2 teaspoons juice from canned jalapeños

2 teaspoons finely minced jalapeño, optional

2 teaspoons Worcestershire sauce

Pinch of caribe (dried pepper flakes), optional

Jalapeño for garnish

SERVES 1
HEAT RATING: MEDIUM

This is Satan's version of the popular Bloody Mary.

In a separate container mix together the tomato juice, vodka, jalapeño juice, jalapeños, Worcestershire sauce, and caribe (this is optional as it will make the drink very hot). Pour into a tall cocktail glass filled with ice and garnish with a jalapeño or the traditional celery stick.

Dante's Martini from Hell

2½ ounces gin

Dry vermouth to taste

Crushed ice

Olive stuffed with a slice of
your fresh chile of choice

SERVES 1
HEAT RATING: MILD

Freeze the martini glasses before making the drinks. Martinis are best served very cold. Dave even keeps the gin in the freezer as well. You can vary the flavors by using different garnishes. There are many olives stuffed with peppers or hot onions, or you can make your own just by stuffing olives with your favorite pepper.

Place gin and vermouth in a shaker with the crushed ice. Shake and pour into a cold martini glass. Serve with olives stuffed with peppers.

New Mexico Green Chile Sauce

2 tablespoons vegetable oil

2 cups finely chopped onions

1 clove garlic, minced

1 tablespoon all-purpose flour

2 to 3 cups chicken broth

1 cup chopped New Mexican
   green chiles, roasted, peeled,
   stems and seeds removed

1 small tomato, peeled and
   chopped (optional)

¼ teaspoon ground cumin

Salt and freshly ground
   black pepper to taste

MAKES 2 TO 3 CUPS
HEAT RATING: MEDIUM TO HOT

Green chile sauce is a classic, all-purpose sauce basic to New Mexican cuisine. It's at its best made with fresh green chiles, although frozen chiles can be substituted. Finely diced pork can be added, but cook the sauce for an additional half hour if you do add it. This is a lightly flavored sauce, with a pungency that ranges from medium to wild depending on the heat of the chiles. Traditionally this sauce is used over enchiladas, burritos, eggs for breakfast, or chiles rellenos, but it's also a tasty addition to nontraditional recipes. It will keep for about 5 days in the refrigerator and freezes well.

Heat a heavy skillet over medium heat, add the oil, and when the oil is hot add the onion and garlic and sauté until they are soft.

Stir in the flour and blend well. Simmer for a couple of minutes to cook the flour, being careful it does not brown. Slowly add the broth and stir until smooth.

Add the remaining ingredients, bring to a boil, reduce the heat, and simmer until the sauce has thickened, about 15 minutes. Taste and adjust the seasonings.

Texas Green Sauce for Dipping

3 pounds tomatillos, husks removed

1 bunch green onions

1 small bunch cilantro

1 tablespoon garlic in oil

2 teaspoons sugar

2 teaspoons lime juice

1 tablespoon chicken base dissolved in 2 tablespoons water

6 serrano chiles, stems removed

DIPPING SUGGESTIONS

Tortilla chips, jicama sticks, carrot sticks

MAKES 4 CUPS
HEAT RATING: MEDIUM

When you order "green sauce" in Texas, this is what you will be served. It differs from New Mexico's green sauce in that the color is derived from tomatillos rather than from green chiles. This sauce can be used with enchiladas or as a topping for grilled poultry or fish.

Roast the tomatillos in a roasting pan under the broiler until they are brown and squishy. Turn them over with a pair of tongs and repeat the process.

Combine the roasted tomatillos, including all the liquid from the roasting process, with the green onions, cilantro, garlic, sugar, lime juice, chicken base, and serrano chiles in a food processor and puree.

Simmer this mixture in a saucepan for 10 minutes before serving or incorporating into another recipe.

Fiesta Chile Cheese Fondue

1½ cups (about 6 ounces) shredded jalapeño pepper jack cheese, or substitute Monterey Jack cheese

1½ cups (about 6 ounces) shredded *queso asadero*, or substitute mozzarella cheese

2½ tablespoons cornstarch

1½ cups beer, or substitute chicken broth

4 New Mexican green chiles, roasted, peeled, stems and seeds removed, cut in thin strips

3 tablespoons minced onion

1 tablespoon lemon juice

1 teaspoon minced garlic

¼ teaspoon dried oregano, crumbled

½ pound cooked and crumbled chorizo sausage

DIPPING SUGGESTIONS

Cherry tomatoes, jicama slices, blanched broccoli florets, miniature carrots, flour tortilla wedges

SERVES 4 TO 6

HEAT RATING: MEDIUM

This fondue is based on the classic south-of-the-border fondue, Mexican queso fundido. *The addition of alcohol to fondues lowers the boiling point so that cheese proteins will not curdle, but take care not to let the cheese boil. We've added a little lemon juice, which also helps. A few tablespoons of flour or, as in this case, cornstarch with the cheese helps make for a creamy consistency and also keeps the cheese from separating. This fondue sauce, like any of the cheese fondues, should never be made far in advance of service. Note that any crust, called* la croute, *left in the bottom of the pot is considered a delicacy and should be scraped off and served.*

Arrange the vegetables and tortillas on a large serving platter.

Toss the cheese with the cornstarch in a bowl and set aside.

Heat the beer, chiles, onion, lemon juice, garlic, and oregano in a medium-size heavy saucepan over low heat until barely simmering. Add the cheese a handful at a time, stirring in a figure-8 or zigzag motion and allowing the cheese to melt before adding more. When all the cheese has been added, stir in the chorizo.

Transfer the fondue to an enamel or ceramic fondue pot and keep warm over a burner. Serve immediately with fresh vegetables for dipping.

APPETIZERS, SNACKS, AND SALADS

Garlic Cheese with Cayenne

8 ounces medium-sharp white cheddar cheese, finely shredded

8 ounces Emmentaler cheese, finely shredded

¼ cup pure sour cream (containing no additives)

¼ cup full-fat mayonnaise

8 to 10 large garlic cloves, put through a garlic press

½ teaspoon ground cayenne pepper or hot paprika (or more to taste)

¼ teaspoon salt

MAKES 3 CUPS
HEAT RATING: MEDIUM

Called pikantny syr *(spicy cheese) in Russian, this is a popular appetizer in Siberia and the Russian Far East. In restaurants it is usually served as a stuffing for ripe red tomatoes or as a spread for chewy-textured Russian bread. The combination of cheeses used in this recipe approximates the taste of the cheese used in Asian Russia. Plenty of garlic provides the kick; you can also add some cayenne pepper to make the cheese even hotter. Russians make this dish by putting all the ingredients through a meat grinder—but you can shred the cheese by hand or even use a food processor.*

Toss the shredded cheeses by hand in a large bowl. Mix together the sour cream, mayonnaise, pressed garlic, hot pepper, and salt in a small bowl, then add to the cheese, stirring to mix well.

Cover and refrigerate at least 4 hours (and preferably overnight) to let the flavors meld.

Let the cheese mixture come to room temperature before serving. Use as a stuffing for small, firm, ripe tomatoes or cherry tomatoes, as a topping for baked potatoes, or as a spread for dark bread.

Poblano Pepper Rings

1 cup flour

1 teaspoon salt

1 teaspoon freshly ground
black pepper

½ teaspoon cayenne powder

3 cups vegetable oil

3 poblano chiles, roasted,
peeled, seeds and stems
removed, cut into
¼-inch rings

1 cup buttermilk

SERVES 4 TO 6
HEAT RATING: MILD

Since poblanos make some of the tastiest chiles rellenos, it makes sense that they fry up deliciously. Why not dip these rings in guacamole?

Combine the flour, salt, pepper, and cayenne and mix well. Transfer the mixture to a plate.

Heat the oil in a large pan over medium-high heat until it just begins to smoke, then lower the heat slightly.

Four at a time, dip the poblano rings in the flour, shake off any excess, then dip them in the buttermilk and back in the flour. Drop them into the hot oil and fry until lightly browned.

Repeat with the rest of the rings and then drain on paper towels. Serve them warm.

Chipotle Tortilla Wheels

1 cup spicy cream cheese like Pikanter Philadelphia or French Cremeux Mexicano Picante

1 tomato, finely chopped

1 clove garlic, minced

1 teaspoon chipotle powder or *Pimentón de la Vera* hot

Pinch of salt

4 flour tortillas

SERVES 4
HEAT RATING: MEDIUM

Any chile-spiced cream cheese can be used to make this spicy snack.

In a bowl, combine the cream cheese, tomato, garlic, chipotle powder, and salt and mix well.

Spread the mixture on the tortillas like buttering a sandwich, leaving a ½-inch border along the edges of the tortillas.

Stack two tortillas on top of each other and roll up tight. Repeat with the other two.

To keep rolls from falling apart, wrap each one tightly in plastic wrap. Refrigerate for at least 1 hour.

Shortly before serving, unwrap rolls. Cut into slices about 1 inch thick.

Red Snapper Ceviche

1 pound red snapper filets

Juice of 8 limes

Juice of 2 lemons

1 habanero chile, stem and
   seeds removed, minced

1 large red onion, cut in strips

½ cup chopped fresh cilantro

1 tablespoon salt

1 teaspoon fresh ground black
   pepper

SERVES 4
HEAT RATING: VARIES, BUT
USUALLY HOT

More than any other dish, ceviche is the plato nacionál *of Peru. Though the recipe given here makes use of only one kind of fish, any number of seafood types including other fishes, scallops, shrimp, octopus, and crab can be used singly or in combination in preparing a ceviche. Many chefs will add some white wine to the mixture; the Ecuadorian version of ceviche calls for olive oil. Peruvians like their ceviche fiery hot, so in the interest of authenticity, don't skimp on the minced chiles.* **NOTE** *This recipe requires advance preparation.*

Cut the snapper filets into pieces about 1 inch long and ½ inch wide. Do not use pieces any larger than that, as they will not be properly "cooked" by the citrus juices.

In a large glass bowl, marinate the fish in the lime and lemon juices. Cover and let sit for 1 hour.

Soak the minced chile in a bowl of cold salted water. Soak the red onion in another bowl of cold salted water.

Add the chiles and onion to the fish along with the cilantro, salt, and pepper, mix well, and refrigerate for an hour before serving.

Yucatecan Shrimp Cocktail

2 large tomatoes, roasted, peeled, seeds removed, chopped

¼ cup bitter orange juice, or substitute ¼ cup lime juice, fresh preferred

2 tablespoons olive oil

1 teaspoon sugar

½ cup minced red onion, divided

Salt and freshly ground black pepper

1 pound cooked shrimp, shelled and deveined

¼ cup minced fresh cilantro

1 habanero chile, stem and seeds removed, minced

SERVES 4 TO 6

HEAT RATING: MEDIUM HOT

Yucatecan cooks serve seafood cocktails in tall parfait glasses with a thin sauce that is more like a juice. The chopped onions, cilantro, and habaneros are served separately so that everyone can add just as much or as little as they want.

Put the tomatoes, orange juice, and oil in a blender or food processor and puree until smooth. Stir in the sugar and half of the onion and season with salt and pepper. Simmer for 10 minutes in a saucepan and then cool.

Fill parfait glasses with the shrimp and add the juice until covered. Place the remaining onion, cilantro, and chiles on a plate and serve on the side.

Spiced Hawaiian Tuna Salad

1 pound fresh raw tuna, cut into 2-inch cubes

1 tomato, chopped

4 fresh red Hawaiian chiles, seeds and stems removed, minced, or substitute piquins or chiltepíns

2 cups chopped Maui onion, or substitute Vidalia

2 tablespoons soy sauce (shoyu)

1 teaspoon sesame oil

SERVES 4 TO 6
HEAT RATING: MEDIUM

Poke (pronounced POH-kay) is the Hawaiian version of Japanese sashimi and differs in that it is chopped, not sliced, and is highly seasoned. Serve this appetizer or salad over romaine lettuce.

In a bowl, combine all ingredients and mix well. Cover and refrigerate until serving.

Thai Chile and Artichoke Pasta Salad

1 6 ½-ounce jar marinated artichoke hearts, drained and liquid reserved

2 to 3 Thai chiles, stems removed, or substitute serranos

2 tablespoons lemon juice, fresh preferred

¾ teaspoon dried oregano

½ teaspoon dried thyme

2 cloves garlic, chopped

Freshly ground black pepper

2 tablespoons water

4 cups cooked rotini pasta

2 cups thinly sliced fresh spinach

½ cup sliced Kalamata olives

½ cup crumbled feta cheese

Chopped fresh parsley for garnish

SERVES 4 TO 6

HEAT RATING: MEDIUM HOT

This unusual combination of ingredients makes a salad that is hearty enough to be served as an entree as well as a side dish. Always prepare this salad a day before to ensure that the flavors are combined. A word of caution though: the salad seems to increase in heat the longer it sits. So make the dressing a little on the mild side or the salad may become too hot to enjoy. **NOTE** *This recipe requires advance preparation.*

To make the dressing, put two of the artichoke hearts, reserved liquid, chiles, lemon juice, oregano, thyme, garlic, black pepper, and water in a blender or food processor and puree until smooth.

Coarsely chop the remaining artichoke hearts and place in a large mixing bowl. Add the pasta, spinach, olives, and feta cheese. Pour the dressing over the salad and gently toss to combine. Cover and chill overnight.

Garnish with the parsley before serving.

Lime Soup with Tortilla Strips and Chile

3 corn tortillas, cut in strips

Vegetable oil for frying

2 chicken breasts

1 small onion, chopped

2 cloves garlic, chopped

6 whole peppercorns

1 2-inch stick cinnamon

8 whole allspice berries

1 tablespoon chopped fresh
   oregano, Mexican preferred

4 cups chicken broth

1 tomato, peeled and chopped

2 tablespoons lime juice

1 poblano or fresh New Mexican
   green chile, roasted, peeled,
   stem and seeds removed, cut
   in strips, or more to taste

Lime slices and cilantro sprigs
   for garnish

SERVES 4 TO 6
HEAT RATING: MILD

There are many variations of soup with tortillas throughout Mexico, and this is a variation that is popular on the Yucatán Peninsula. Chicken is commonly used, but you can substitute leftover turkey in this delicate soup. The Mexican limes that are used on the Yucatán Peninsula differ from the Persian limes that are common in the United States in that they are smaller, darker green, and more tart. Although they are preferred, any lime can be substituted. Be sure to add the tortillas right before serving or they will become soggy.

Fry the tortilla strips in a pan in medium-hot oil until crisp. Remove and drain.

Place the chicken, onion, garlic, peppercorns, cinnamon, allspice, oregano, and broth in a pot. Bring to a boil and remove any foam that comes to the top. Reduce the heat and simmer, covered, for 30 minutes. Allow the chicken to cool in the stock.

Remove the chicken and remove the bones. Using two forks, shred the meat. Strain the broth and add enough water to make 1 quart of liquid.

Reheat the broth with the tomato, lime juice, and chile. Add the chicken and simmer until the chicken is hot.

Place some of the tortilla strips in the bottom of a soup bowl, add the soup, garnish with a lime slice and cilantro, and serve.

Cool and Hot Tomato Soup

1 tablespoon olive oil

¼ cup chopped onion

1 stalk celery, chopped

1 clove garlic, minced

1 pound Roma tomatoes, peeled
   and seeds removed

2 chipotle or adobo chiles,
   stems removed

½ teaspoon sugar

2 tablespoons chopped fresh
   cilantro

½ teaspoon ground cumin

2 cups beef broth

1 cup red wine (optional)

Chopped fresh cilantro for garnish

SERVES 4 TO 6
HEAT RATING: MEDIUM

This refreshing, easy-to-prepare chilled soup actually needs to be made the day before to allow the flavors to blend. Make the soup a little thinner than you normally would as it will thicken some as it cools. For a creamier soup, stir in plain yogurt before serving. **NOTE** *This recipe requires advance preparation.*

Heat the oil in a saucepan over medium heat and sauté the onion, celery, and garlic until softened.

Add the tomatoes, chiles, sugar, cilantro, cumin, broth, and red wine, if desired. Raise the heat and simmer for 15 minutes.

Place the mixture in a blender or food processor and puree until smooth. Strain the soup and thin to desired consistency with wine, additional broth, or water.

Chill the soup for at least an hour or overnight. Garnish with chopped cilantro before serving.

Fiery Groundnut Chop (Chicken and Peanut Stew)

1 tablespoon ground ginger

4 to 6 pieces of chicken, such as legs or thighs

3 tablespoons peanut oil, or substitute vegetable oil

1 medium onion, chopped

3 to 4 jalapeños, stems and seeds removed, chopped

2 cloves garlic, minced

1 teaspoon minced fresh ginger

1 tablespoon hot curry powder

Pinch ground cumin

1 cup canned crushed tomatoes

3 cups chicken broth

1 cup diced yams or potatoes

1 cup frozen okra sections

1 cup smooth peanut butter

1 cup cold water

Salt and freshly ground black pepper

¼ cup chopped salted peanuts

The use of peanuts, also called groundnuts, in soups and stews is common over all of Africa but is especially popular in the western countries of that continent. "Chop" is African slang meaning food or a meal. The vegetables in this stew can be varied to suit your tastes; however, if you eliminate the okra, it will alter the consistency of the stew. The important step to remember in preparing this soup or stew is to mix some of the broth with the peanut butter before adding to the soup to keep it from curdling and breaking apart.

Rub the ground ginger over the chicken pieces.

Heat the oil in a heavy pot over medium heat until hot. Add the chicken pieces and brown, turning frequently so they don't burn. Remove and keep warm.

Pour off all but a tablespoon of the oil, add the onion, and sauté 3 to 4 minutes, scraping the browned pieces from the bottom of the pan. Add the jalapeños, garlic, and ginger and sauté a couple of minutes, until the onion is lightly browned. Add the curry powder and cumin and cook, stirring constantly, until fragrant, about 2 minutes.

Add the tomatoes and 1 cup of the broth. Raise the heat and bring to a boil, scraping any remaining bits and pieces from the bottom of the pot. Reduce the heat, add the remaining broth and the chicken pieces, and simmer uncovered 30 minutes. Add the yams and okra and continue to simmer until the vegetables are just tender and the chicken is done, about 20 to 30 minutes. Add more broth and water if needed.

MAKES 4 TO 6 SERVINGS
HEAT RATING: HOT

Mix the peanut butter with the cold water to make a smooth paste. Add ½ cup stew liquid to the paste and mix well. Stir this mixture into the stew and continue simmering until the stew is hot. Add salt and pepper to taste and garnish with the chopped salted peanuts.

Hungarian *Gulyas* (Goulash)

5 tablespoons hot paprika

1 tablespoon coarsely ground black pepper

1 cup flour

1 pound boneless beef chuck or stew meat, cut in 1½-inch cubes

2 tablespoons vegetable oil

1 medium onion, cut in thin slices

1 medium carrot, peeled and diced

1 medium potato, peeled and cubed

6 small dried red chiles such as piquin

1 teaspoon caraway seeds

1 quart beef broth

Salt and freshly ground black pepper to taste

2 cups cooked egg noodles

Sour cream and chopped fresh parsley for garnish

SERVES 4 TO 6
HEAT RATING: MEDIUM HOT

This dish probably has its roots in the roving Magyar tribes of central Europe, who cooked their meat and vegetables over campfires in large kettles. If you don't have hot paprika, increase the heat by adding small dried red chiles rather than adding too much paprika, as it can make the stew too sweet. Serve this hearty stew with a pickled beet salad and a dark rye bread.

Combine 4 tablespoons of the paprika and the black pepper with the flour and mix well. Add the beef and toss to coat the meat. Reserve 2 tablespoons of the seasoned flour.

Heat the oil in a large, heavy skillet over medium heat until medium hot, add the beef, and brown. Remove the cubes and place in a large stockpot.

Add the onion to the skillet along with a little more oil and sauté until browned. Remove and place in the stockpot.

Add the carrot, potato, chiles, caraway seeds, remaining paprika, and broth to the stockpot. Bring to just under boiling, reduce the heat, and simmer for an hour or more until the meat is very tender and the vegetables are done. Taste and season with salt and pepper and more paprika, if desired.

Divide the noodles among the bowls and ladle in the stew. Remove the chiles. Place a dollop of sour cream on top, sprinkle with the parsley, and serve.

Lady Bird Johnson's Pedernales River Chili

4   pounds coarsely ground beef

1   large onion, chopped

2   cloves garlic, chopped

1   teaspoon oregano

1   teaspoon ground cumin

6   teaspoons red chile powder
    (or more for heat)

2   16-ounce cans tomatoes

2   cups hot water

Salt to taste

Grated cheddar cheese and sliced
    green onions for garnish

SERVES 12
HEAT RATING: MILD TO MEDIUM

This recipe originally contained beef suet, but that ingredient was omitted after LBJ's severe heart attack when he was Senate majority leader. Remember to skim the fat off the chili.

Combine the beef, onion, and garlic in a skillet and sear until the meat is lightly browned.

Transfer this mixture to a large pot, add the remaining ingredients, and bring to a boil. Reduce the heat and simmer for an hour.

When done, transfer the chili to a bowl and place it in the refrigerator. When the fat has congealed on top, remove it with a spoon.

Reheat the chili and serve it as LBJ liked it—without beans and accompanied with a glass of milk and saltine crackers. Garnish with grated cheddar cheese and sliced green onions.

The Perfect Fish Tacos

1 large lime

4 white fish fillets, cut in strips about 1 inch wide

2 eggs

1 cup all-purpose flour

Salt

Vegetable oil for frying

8 corn tortillas, warmed

Minced serrano chiles to taste

Chopped lettuce or cabbage

MAKES 4 SERVINGS
HEAT RATING: VARIES

This very easy recipe is the one cooks in Baja California use. The batter used to coat the fish varies with the cook, but a wok-shaped pan is the tool of choice for frying the fish. Some cooks swear that you must use shark fillets, but any firm white fish works well.

Cut the lime in half and squeeze the juice over the fish. Allow the fish to marinate while preparing the batter.

Break the eggs into a bowl and whisk. Gradually add only enough flour to form a thin batter. Season with a sprinkle of salt.

Pour the oil to a depth of 1 to 2 inches (depending on the thickness of the fish) into a heavy skillet or wok. Heat the oil over medium-high heat to medium hot.

Dip the fish in the batter and let the excess drip off. Carefully slide the fish into the oil and fry until the fish is done and the batter is golden brown. Remove and drain on paper towels.

Place the fish in the tortillas and serve. Top with the minced serranos and chopped lettuce or cabbage.

South Texas Fajítas

2 to 4 jalapeños, canned or fresh, stems and seeds removed, minced

3 tablespoons chili powder

1 teaspoon cayenne powder

1 8-ounce bottle herb and garlic, oil-based salad dressing

1 12-ounce can beer, preferably Lone Star

1½ teaspoons garlic powder

Juice of 4 small Mexican limes

2 teaspoons cumin seeds, crushed

1 large onion, minced

2 tablespoons minced cilantro

1 tablespoon Worcestershire sauce

1 bay leaf

2 to 3 pounds beef skirt steak

SERVES 4 TO 6
HEAT RATING: MEDIUM

About the late 1970s, fajítas were "discovered." Since then, an awful lot of good meat has been wrecked, and skirt steak— once a "grinder" item—has risen sharply in price. Because skirt doesn't come from a "tender quadrant" of the carcass, some care is needed to turn it into good food. First, it needs to be marinated to tenderize and flavor it. You'll notice that we haven't said anything about chicken fajítas—that's a contradiction in terms. Serve the fajítas with flour tortillas, pico de gallo salsa, guacamole, and cold beer. **NOTE** *This recipe requires advance preparation.*

Mix all of the ingredients, except the meat, together in a bowl to make a marinade. Pour over the skirt steak in a nonreactive container, cover, and stir the marinade occasionally for 6 to 8 hours.

Fajítas can be cooked in several ways. If you have the space, smoke the fajítas for about 30 minutes with pure mesquite smoke, and then cook for 4 to 7 minutes per side over direct heat—mesquite coals being the heat of choice. Baste with the marinade throughout the cooking process. If you need to cook completely over direct heat, use a fairly slow fire, about like you should use when grilling chicken, and cook, covered if possible, for about 10 to 15 minutes per side, basting with the marinade. For medium-rare, the internal temperature should be 150°F.

Figure about a half pound of meat and 3 to 4 tortillas per person. When slicing fajítas, you'll notice that the grain of the skirt steak all runs the same way. If you slice the skirt at a 45-degree angle to the grain and hold your knife at a 45-degree angle as well, you'll find that the fajítas are much more tender!

Chiles Rellenos with Corn

2 tablespoons butter

1 medium onion, chopped

2 cloves garlic, minced

1½ cups cooked whole kernel corn

1 teaspoon dried oregano

⅓ cup sour cream

6 ounces cheddar cheese, cubed

6 New Mexican green chiles, roasted and peeled, stems left on

Flour for dredging

3 eggs, separated

1 tablespoon water

3 tablespoons flour

¼ teaspoon salt

Vegetable oil for frying

New Mexico Green Chile Sauce (see recipe earlier)

SERVES 6

HEAT RATING: MEDIUM

Chiles rellenos *literally means "stuffed chiles," and in Mexico many different chiles are used, including poblanos, jalapeños, rocotos, and even fresh pasillas. Here in the Southwest, we prefer New Mexican green chiles. Whatever type of chile you use, the preparation and fillings are the same.*

Heat the butter in a skillet over medium heat and sauté the onion and garlic until soft. Add the corn and oregano and cook for an additional 5 minutes. Remove from the heat and stir in the sour cream and cheese.

Make a slit in the side of each chile and stuff with the corn mixture. Dredge the chiles in the flour and shake off any excess.

Beat the egg whites until they form stiff peaks. Beat the yolks with the water, the 3 tablespoons flour, and the salt. Fold the yolks into the whites and stir gently.

Dip the chiles in the egg batter and fry one at a time in 1 to 2 inches of oil until they are golden brown.

Serve covered with New Mexico Green Chile Sauce.

Chicken Enchiladas with Green Chile Sauce

2 chicken breasts

2 small onions, chopped

3 cloves garlic, minced

2 whole cloves

2 cups New Mexico Green Chile Sauce (see recipe earlier)

Vegetable oil for frying

8 corn tortillas

1 cup sour cream

¼ cup black olives, chopped

2 cups grated Monterey Jack cheese

½ cup grated cheddar cheese

SERVES 4

HEAT RATING: MEDIUM

In New Mexico, after you decide to order enchiladas, there are still decisions to be made. First, blue or regular referring to the type of tortilla, rolled or stacked, red or green chile sauce, or if you can't decide and want both sauces, order "Christmas." And finally you may order them with a fried egg on top, which is true New Mexican fare.

Preheat the oven to 350°F.

Cover the chicken, half of the onions, the garlic, and the cloves with cold water in a large pot. Bring to a boil, reduce the heat, and simmer until tender, about 30 minutes. Remove the chicken. Strain and reserve the broth for use in the sauce. When the chicken is cool enough to handle, remove the skin and bones, and shred by using two forks.

Place a little of the New Mexico Green Chile Sauce in the bottom of a baking pan. To soften the tortillas, pour the oil in a pan to a depth of about ¼ inch and heat until hot enough so that a drop of water in the oil will sputter. Dip a tortilla briefly in the hot oil to soften, then remove and drain. Next dip the tortilla in the sauce and place in the baking pan.

Place some of the chicken down the center of the tortilla, top with some chopped onions, sour cream, olives, and Monterey Jack cheese, and roll, ending with the flap side down in the pan. Repeat until all the tortillas have been used.

Pour additional sauce over the enchiladas, sprinkle with cheddar cheese, and bake for 5 to 10 minutes or until thoroughly heated.

Tiger Prawns in Coconut Milk Curry

Vegetable oil

4 medium bottle gourds,
  roughly chopped in 1-inch cubes

2 medium potatoes, chopped in 1-inch squares

Sprinkling of fenugreek

Sprinkling of fennel seeds

Sprinkling of cumin seeds

Sprinkling of mustard seeds

Mustard oil

2 bay leaves

A few cloves

A few cardamom pods

1 cinnamon stick

1 onion, chopped, then processed in a blender

1 section ginger, peeled,
  then processed in a blender

1 teaspoon turmeric

1 teaspoon hot chile powder

12 shelled tiger prawns

2 cups coconut milk

Salt to taste

SERVES 4
HEAT RATING: MEDIUM

If you can't find bottle gourds, substitute pota-
toes, or potatoes and cauliflower: either two
cups chopped potatoes, or one cup each chopped
potatoes and cauliflower. If you do use these
substitutes, cook in the same way as the bottle
gourds—that is, fry separately until cooked
through.

Fry the bottle gourds in the oil in a skillet over medium heat until soft and put aside.

Add more oil and return the skillet to the heat, then fry half the potatoes in the fenugreek, fennel seeds, cumin seeds, and mustard seeds for a few minutes, until the potatoes are half cooked. Add the bottle gourds to the dish and cook another minute on medium heat.

Add some water until the vegetables are just covered, turn down the heat, and let simmer until the potatoes are cooked.

Add mustard oil to a separate skillet and when hot put in the bay leaves, cloves, cardamom, and cinnamon stick and cook 1 minute; then add the rest of the potatoes and continue frying, stirring constantly, about 3 minutes.

Add the blended onion and ginger, turmeric, and chile powder, and fry over low heat until the potatoes are cooked. Increase the heat, toss in the ingredients from the other skillet and the prawns and coconut milk, and simmer for a few minutes until the prawns are cooked.

Harissa and Seven-Vegetable Couscous

This vegetable tagine is a very popular dish served throughout Morocco. It is traditionally served on Fridays and special holidays, such as Berber weddings. The recipe has a long list of ingredients, but it's easy to prepare and can be made ahead of time. It tastes even better on the day after cooking it.

2 tablespoons extra-virgin olive oil

1 large onion, chopped

4 cloves garlic, chopped

1 cup harissa, found in ethnic markets or online

4 dried piquin chiles

1½ teaspoons ground cumin

1   teaspoon ground ginger

1   teaspoon ground cinnamon

½ teaspoon ground allspice

1   quart vegetable broth

½ teaspoon saffron, or substitute ground turmeric

1   large potato, peeled and diced

4   medium canned tomatoes, chopped

2   medium carrots, peeled and julienne-cut

1   cup canned chickpeas, drained and rinsed

2   small zucchini, julienne-cut

1   small eggplant, peeled and cubed

1   cup frozen peas

4   cups couscous

4   cups boiling water

Salt and freshly ground black pepper to taste

½ cup lemon juice, preferably fresh

Chopped Italian parsley for garnish

SERVES 6 TO 8

HEAT RATING: MILD TO MEDIUM

Heat the oil in a Dutch oven or stockpot over high heat; when hot, reduce the heat, add the onion and garlic, and sauté until soft. Add ½ cup harissa along with the chiles, cumin, ginger, cinnamon, and allspice and continue to cook for 5 minutes.

Add the broth, saffron, and potato and bring to a boil. Reduce the heat, cover, and simmer the mixture for an hour, adding water if necessary to thin if it becomes too thick.

Add the tomatoes, carrots, and chickpeas and simmer for 20 minutes. Add the zucchini, eggplant, and peas, and simmer until the vegetables are done. Taste and adjust the seasonings.

Put the couscous in a bowl and add the boiling water; cover and let stand for 5 minutes.

Stir the lemon juice into the stew, taste, and adjust the seasonings.

To serve, mound the couscous on a platter, top with the stew, and garnish with the parsley. Serve with the remaining ½ cup harissa on the side.

Enraged Pasta (Penne all'Arrabiata)

2 tablespoons olive oil

2 to 3 medium onions, chopped

2 to 3 cloves garlic, finely chopped

2 small fresh red chile pods (Thai, serrano, or birdseye), stems and seeds removed, minced

2 14-ounce cans chopped tomatoes

1 pound penne rigate pasta

3½ ounces Parmesan cheese, grated

Salt to taste

SERVES 4

HEAT RATING: MEDIUM

Of all the spicy Italian dishes, this one from Calabria is probably the best known. Feel free to increase the heat by adding more chiles.

Heat the olive oil in a pan over low heat. Add the onions, garlic, and chile and cook until the onions are golden brown. Add the tomatoes and cook, uncovered, about 15 minutes over low to medium heat.

Meanwhile, cook the pasta al dente in lightly salted water in a large pot, according to instructions on the package.

Grate the Parmesan cheese and stir half of it into the sauce. Drain the pasta well, mix thoroughly with the sauce, and sprinkle with the remaining Parmesan cheese. Serve piping hot.

Pungent Pizza on the Grill

CHILE DOUGH

1 cup warm water (100°F)

1 teaspoon sugar

1 teaspoon yeast

2 cups all-purpose flour

¾ teaspoon salt

2 teaspoons crushed red chile

Freshly ground black pepper

2 tablespoons olive oil

POWERFUL PUTANESCA TOPPING

3 cups chopped fresh tomatoes,
   such as cherry or roma

2 tablespoons chopped capers

2 tablespoons chopped nicoise
   olives

1 tablespoon chopped fresh basil

2 teaspoons crushed red chile

1 cup grated Parmigiano
   Reggiano or Pecorino Romano
   cheese

Garlic salt

Olive oil

In this recipe we attempt to recreate the wonderful thin-crust pizza from wood-fired ovens in your very own backyard. Our homemade crust has something that Pizza Doodle Express does not: chile. But if you're lazy and don't want to make your own dough, you can use a 12-inch prebaked pizza shell. You can also easily make the dough in your bread machine. It is very important to have a clean grill for this recipe, as any residue on the grill will give the crust an off flavor. Why not make both toppings and divide the pizza?

To make the pizza crust by hand, combine the water and sugar in a bowl and stir in the yeast. Let stand for 10 minutes until foamy.

In a large bowl, combine the flour, salt, chile, and pepper. Make a well in the flour and pour in the yeast water and olive oil. Stir until almost mixed, turn onto a floured board, and knead until the dough is smooth and elastic.

Place the dough in a lightly oiled bowl and cover with plastic wrap. Place in a warm, draft-free location and let rise until doubled, about an hour and a half.

Punch down the dough and divide into two balls. If preparing ahead of time, place in the refrigerator until ready to use. Bring the dough back to room temperature and then proceed with the recipe.

continued on next page

Pungent Pizza continued

MAKES 1 12-INCH PIZZA OR

2 6-INCH PIZZAS

HEAT RATING: MILD TO MEDIUM

Roll out each portion into a round or oval pizza or do it free-form. If it will fit on your grill, you can also combine the balls into one and make one large pizza.

Heat a gas grill to hot. If using charcoal, bank the coals to one side, creating a hot side and a warm side.

Brush each of the pizzas with olive oil and gently drape, oil side down, on the hot grill. Shortly, within a minute or two, the dough will start to rise and bubbles will appear. Gently lift an end to see that the underside is browned and has grill marks. Immediately invert the crust onto a pan, and turn the gas grill to low

Brush the dough with additional oil.

For the Powerful Putanesca topping, place the tomatoes on the cooked side of the pizza and sprinkle the capers, olives, basil, chile, and cheese over the top. Shake a little garlic salt over the pizza and sprinkle some olive oil over the top.

To make the Southwestern topping, lay the green chile strips over the cooked side. Top with the cheeses and a sprinkling of crushed red chiles and olive oil. Slide the pizza(s) back onto the grill. Cover and cook, rotating once or twice until the toppings are heated through and the crust is browned, about 5 minutes on the cooler part of the grill.

Jamaican Jerk Pork for the Grill

1 Scotch bonnet chile (or habanero), stem and seeds removed, minced

1 cup chopped onion

1 tablespoon fresh thyme

1 teaspoon freshly ground black pepper

1 tablespoon ground allspice

¼ cup vinegar

2 tablespoons soy sauce

2 large tomatoes, chopped

1 tablespoon freshly grated ginger

2 pounds pork tenderloin

¼ cup commercial jerk rub or seasoning

SERVES 6
HEAT RATING: MEDIUM

Escaped Jamaican slaves known as Maroons invented this dish as a way to preserve pork. Now it has become a signature dish of that island nation. **NOTE** *This recipe requires advance preparation.*

Combine the chile, onion, thyme, black pepper, allspice, vinegar, soy sauce, tomatoes, and ginger in a bowl.

Cut the pork tenderloin lengthwise, scoring the meat. Roll the pork in the mix, and then lavishly cover with jerk rub, ensuring that you stuff some inside the score marks. Put the seasoned meat in a resealable plastic container and refrigerate at least 2 hours.

Prepare a charcoal grill, adding 2 cups of soaked chips from lemon, orange, or pecan wood. Grill over low heat until the interior reaches 140 to 145°F, about 2 hours.

Grape-Grilled Quail with Goat Cheese Rounds

12 quail

2 ancho chiles, stems and seeds removed

⅔ cup olive oil

¼ cup orange juice

2 tablespoons lime juice

1 clove garlic

6 2-ounce goat cheese rounds

2 tablespoons olive oil

¼ cup dried corn bread crumbs

6 6-inch pieces of thick grape vine clippings, soaked in water

Salsa of choice

SERVES 6
HEAT RATING: MILD

Although many Southwest barbecues and grilled meats use mesquite, it is not the only aromatic wood to use—experiment with pecan, apple, peach, and grape clippings. If you use charcoal for the main fire, be sure to soak the wood for an hour in water before grilling. **NOTE** *This recipe requires advance preparation.*

Cut the wing tips off the quail, then split the birds down the back and remove the backbone. With a knife tip, remove the rib bones from each quail, and then slice open the thigh bones to remove the bones and joint, taking care to keep the skin intact. Open up each quail and press the legs together, securing them with toothpicks.

Simmer the chiles in water for 15 minutes. Place the chiles in a blender along with the olive oil, orange and lime juices, and the garlic, and puree. Pour this sauce over the quail and marinate for an hour.

While the quail are marinating, prepare a medium-hot charcoal fire and preheat the oven to 350°F. Brush each goat cheese round with olive oil, coat with corn bread crumbs, and bake for 5 minutes. If you start the baking just when the quail are being grilled, both should be done at the same time.

Add the grape clippings to the coals, arrange the quail skin side down on the rack, and grill for 2 minutes, taking care not to burn them. Turn the quail and grill for an additional 2 minutes. If the skin is not yet crisp, turn once more and grill for an additional minute.

Serve two quail on each plate with a goat cheese round and garnished with the salsa.

Grilled Green Chile-Stuffed Pepper Steaks Wrapped in Bacon

4 boneless ribeye steaks, or substitute filet mignon or sirloin steaks, 1 to 2 inches thick

4 roasted and peeled hot New Mexican green chiles, stems and seeds removed

4 strips raw bacon

2 tablespoons each red, white, and black peppercorns

2 tablespoons Caribbean habanero sauce

2 tablespoons Worcestershire sauce

2 tablespoons soy sauce

2 tablespoons rice wine vinegar

2 teaspoons garlic powder

MAKES 4 SERVINGS
HEAT RATING: MEDIUM

This is one of our favorite ways of grilling steaks, and we find ourselves using the basic recipe and altering it again and again. The combination of the different peppercorns and the chiles provides different spice and heat sensations in the mouth, and the green chile pulls all the tastes together. Serve this with roasted garlic mashed potatoes. Leftover steak can be turned into a fabulous Southwest steak sandwich by thinly slicing it and adding it to sourdough bread with Muenster cheese and more chile. **NOTE** *This recipe requires advance preparation.*

Slice the steaks horizontally to create a pocket. Do not cut all the way through the steak. Place a green chile in each of the pockets. Wrap a strip of bacon around each steak horizontally and secure with a toothpick.

Place the peppercorns in a towel and pound with a hammer or mortar until roughly crushed. Press the coarse pepper into each side of the steak.

Combine the habanero sauce, Worcestershire sauce, soy sauce, vinegar, and garlic powder. Place the steaks in a nonmetallic pan, pour the marinade over the meat, and marinate in the refrigerator for a couple of hours. Bring the steaks to room temperature before grilling.

Grill the steaks over a medium-hot fire for 8 to 10 minutes, turning often, for rare, and 12 to 16 minutes for medium rare. For medium-rare steaks, the internal temperature should be 150°F. Feel free to slice steaks to check doneness.

VARIATION For those not enamored of peppercorns, omit and wrap the steaks in peppered bacon.

Grilled Alaskan Salmon with Apricot-Chile Glaze

2 pounds of Alaska salmon fillets at least ¾-inch thick

¼ cup plus 2 teaspoons chili powder

¼ cup apricot preserves, melted

SERVES 4

HEAT RATING: MEDIUM

This easy sweet-hot glaze demonstrates a perfect marriage between fruit and Alaskan salmon. Delicious on any cut of salmon, this glaze (enough for 2 pounds of fish) can be used on either grilled or baked fish.

Rub the salmon fillets with ¼ cup chili powder, massaging the spice into the meat. Using a pastry brush, coat the salmon with the warm apricot preserves. Sprinkle the remaining chili powder evenly over the glaze.

Grill or bake the salmon, according to your preference. For a fish 1 inch thick, allow about 10 minutes total cooking time. When the fish tests done, transfer it to a warm serving platter.

Tandoori Murg with Mint Raita (Chicken Cooked Tandoori-style)

4 chicken breasts, skin removed

2 to 3 teaspoons ground cayenne pepper

1 tablespoon ground paprika

½ teaspoon freshly ground black pepper

½ cup lemon juice

3 tablespoons melted butter

Lemon slices for garnish

Mint raita *(recipe follows)*

MARINADE

1 cup plain yogurt, drained

¼ teaspoon crushed saffron threads dissolved in ¼ cup hot water

1 tablespoon grated ginger

1 tablespoon chopped garlic

1 tablespoon ground red chile, such as New Mexican

2 teaspoons garam masala, commercial

1 teaspoon ground coriander

Tandoori chicken is one of the most famous Indian dishes and also one of the tastiest. The word tandoori *refers to any food cooked in a tandoor, which is a giant unglazed clay oven. The chicken in this recipe is marinated twice, first with the lemon juice and then with the yogurt mixture. You can approximate a tandoor by using a charcoal grill or gas broiler but won't achieve the exact flavor. The taste is hard to duplicate since the tandoor reaches such high temperatures, up to 800°F, but even if the chicken is not strictly traditional, it's still tasty. Those who are watching their fat intake will like cooking in the tandoori-style. And using a low-fat yogurt in the marinade will reduce the fat content even further. This chicken is traditionally served with a cooling mint raita.* **NOTE** *This recipe requires advance preparation.*

Line a strainer with dampened cheesecloth, add the yogurt for the marinade, and place over a bowl. Put in the refrigerator and let the yogurt drain for 4 hours to thicken.

Make slashes in the chicken about 2 inches deep. Combine the cayenne, paprika, and black pepper in a bowl and stir to mix. Rub the mixture into the slashes, add the lemon juice, and marinate the chicken for 30 minutes at room temperature, then drain.

Put all the ingredients for the marinade in a blender or food processor and puree until smooth. Place the chicken in a nonreactive bowl and pour the marinade over the chicken. Using your fingers, rub the marinade into the meat. Cover and refrigerate 24 hours, turning occasionally.

continued on next page

Tandoori Murg continued

½ teaspoon ground turmeric

½ teaspoon freshly ground black pepper

½ teaspoon ground nutmeg

½ teaspoon ground cinnamon

¼ teaspoon ground cumin

¼ teaspoon ground cloves

½ teaspoon salt

Start a charcoal or hardwood fire in your barbecue. Place the grill 2 inches over the coals and grill the chicken for 10 minutes, turning once. Use the marinade to baste the chicken as it cooks. Raise the grill to 5 inches and continue cooking 5 minutes, turning once.

Remove the chicken and brush with the melted butter. Return to the grill and continue to cook for an additional 5 minutes, turning once, until the chicken is done and the juices run clear.

Serve the chicken garnished with lemon slices and the mint raita on the side.

Mint Raita

½ cup plain yogurt

2 tablespoons chopped fresh mint

1 tablespoon minced onion

½ teaspoon garam masala, commercial

½ teaspoon minced serrano chile

Pinch of sugar

Salt to taste

MAKES ½ CUP
HEAT RATING: MILD

Raitas, or raytas, *are yogurt-based salsas or salads that are served as cooling counterpoints to hot and spicy Indian foods. The vegetables used can be raw or cooked, and low-fat or whole-milk yogurt can be used. If you use whole-milk yogurt, thin it with a little water to produce a smooth texture. Because of the coolness of the yogurt, raitas are served during hot weather only. This raita can also be served with crudities or pieces of Indian bread or naan as an appetizer.*

Combine all the ingredients in a bowl, cover, and let sit at room temperature for an hour to blend the flavors. Refrigerate until ready to use.

The traditional spices of ancient India create an exotic and intense dish.

Basque Peppers Stuffed with Venison

FILLING

3 tablespoons olive oil

1 dried New Mexican red chile, crumbled with seeds

1 medium yellow onion, chopped

½ cup chopped mushrooms

1 pound venison, fat removed, and ground

½ teaspoon sage

½ teaspoon rosemary

½ teaspoon dried mint

2 tablespoons chopped pimento chile

½ cup beer

2 eggs, lightly whipped

¼ cup dry bread crumbs

½ teaspoon salt (optional)

4 large whole green (or red) bell peppers

1 cup chicken broth

When it comes to cooking game, it's hard to beat the Basques. After all, Basque herders have been living off the land for hundreds of years. The knack of blending wild game with native herbs and spices is a heritage passed on from family to family.

Heat a Dutch oven until a drop of water quickly sizzles away. Add the olive oil, red chile, onion, and mushrooms; sauté until the onion is limp. Add the venison and cook until the meat is browned.

In a bowl, blend the sage, rosemary, mint, pimento, beer, eggs, bread crumbs, and salt. Add the venison mixture to the bowl and blend to make the filling.

Cut around the pepper stems and remove the seeds; save the stems. Spoon in the filling, taking care not to break the peppers; replace the stems. Reheat the Dutch oven, add the chicken broth, and bring to a simmer. Place the stuffed peppers, stems up, in the broth, cover the oven, and steam for 30 minutes. Remove the peppers to a warm plate, keep them upright, and cover with foil to retain the heat.

To make the sauce, add the olive oil, scallions, garlic, tomatoes, parsley, and wine to the Dutch oven. Bring the sauce to a simmer and cook for 10 minutes. Discard the stems from the peppers and serve them covered with the sauce.

SAUCE

3 tablespoons olive oil

½ cup chopped scallions

1 clove garlic, minced

4 tomatoes, diced

¼ cup chopped parsley

½ cup dry red wine

SERVES 4
HEAT RATING: MILD

Chicken Basquaise with Espelette Piperade

½ cup olive oil

4 medium onions, chopped

3 cloves garlic

4 green bell peppers, stems and seeds removed, chopped

2 red bell peppers, stems and seeds removed, chopped

4 large tomatoes, peeled and chopped

3 tablespoons (or more to taste) Espelette powder, or substitute hot paprika or New Mexican red chile powder

Pinch of thyme

Salt and pepper to taste

1 chicken, cut up

SERVES 4 TO 6

HEAT RATING: MILD TO MEDIUM

Piperade is a colorful pepper sauce that is only spicy when made in the Basque region. This simple but delicious dish is often served at the Celebration of the Peppers. Serve it with boiled potatoes and green beans.

Heat ¼ cup olive oil in a large sauté pan and sauté the onions and garlic for 5 minutes, stirring occasionally. Add the bell peppers and cook over medium heat for 10 minutes. Add the tomatoes and Espelette powder and cook for 20 minutes, stirring occasionally. Add the thyme, salt, and pepper and transfer to a bowl.

Wipe out the pan and heat the remaining ¼ cup of oil. Brown the chicken in the oil until golden, turning often. Pour the piperade over the chicken, reduce the heat, cover, and simmer until tender, 30 to 40 minutes. Add salt and pepper to taste.

Spit-Roasted Chicken with Spicy Wild Rice Stuffing

1   2½-3-pound whole chicken

3   tablespoons chile BBQ rub

½ cup wild rice

1⅓ cups boiling water

½ cup white rice

2   teaspoons vegetable oil

2   cups chicken broth

2   cups chopped onions

4   sun-dried tomatoes, chopped

½ teaspoon cayenne powder

½ teaspoon dried sage, crumbled

SERVES 4

HEAT RATING: MILD

You will need a grill equipped with a turning spit for this recipe. Roasting the chicken along with the stuffing makes for an easy dinner. To complete the meal, cut zucchinis lengthwise and brush them with chile oil. Grill during the last 15 to 20 minutes of cooking, remove, and sprinkle with grated Parmesan cheese.

Rub the chicken with the barbecue rub, being sure to put some under the skin. Allow the rub to penetrate at room temperature while you prepare the stuffing.

Cover the wild rice with the boiling water in a saucepan, return to a boil, reduce the heat, and simmer 40 to 45 minutes or until tender. It is not necessary to drain the rice thoroughly, but drain off any excess water.

Sauté the white rice in the oil for 2 to 3 minutes. Bring the broth to a boil, add the white rice, and return to a boil. Reduce the heat and simmer, covered, 15 to 20 minutes. Do not drain. Add the wild rice, onions, tomatoes, cayenne, and sage to the rice and mix well.

Spoon the mixture loosely into the chicken cavities. Secure the neck skin to the back of the chicken. Insert the spit rod through the bird, tie the wings together, and tightly secure the bird to the rod. Place a drip pan under the bird on the grill, lower the cover, and grill over medium heat 2 hours or until the chicken is done.

Rosemary-Scented Lamb Chops

1 cup fresh lemon juice

1 cup dry red wine

1 cup red wine vinegar

¾ cup barbecue sauce

1 tablespoon mustard

¾ cup chile-and-herb-infused olive oil

4 cloves garlic, minced

2 tablespoons chopped fresh rosemary

2 tablespoons minced onion

2 to 3 chiltepíns or piquins, crushed

Salt and freshly ground black pepper

4 lamb chops

SERVES 4
HEAT RATING: HOT

Chiles and rosemary are a wonderful combination. Depending on your preference, the marinade can be strained before reducing. This recipe will also work well with ribs, roasts, or even cubed lamb, which can be made into kebabs. **NOTE** *This recipe requires advance preparation.*

Combine the lemon juice, wine, vinegar, barbecue sauce, and mustard in a nonreactive bowl. Whisk the mixture while slowly adding the oil in a steady stream. Add the remainder of the ingredients, except the lamb chops, and mix well.

Marinate the lamb chops in the mixture for an hour at room temperature. Remove the lamb chops and reserve the marinade.

Grill or broil the lamb chops to the desired doneness. Place the reserved marinade in a saucepan and simmer the sauce, stirring occasionally, until reduced by half, about 20 minutes.

To serve, place some of the cooked marinade on a plate and arrange the chops on top. Additional sauce can be served on the side.

Grilled Tuna Steaks with Salsa Pimentón

2 tablespoons extra-virgin olive oil

3 tablespoons hot pimentón, or substitute ground New Mexican chile and chipotle chile powder in equal proportions

2 tablespoons chopped fresh Italian parsley

Salt and freshly ground black pepper

4 tuna steaks, 1-inch thick

1 cup chopped red onion

6 cloves garlic, minced

2 medium tomatoes, chopped

2 red bell peppers, roasted, peeled, stems and seeds removed, chopped

½ cup minced green olives

Sprigs of Italian parsley for garnish

SERVES 4
HEAT RATING: MEDIUM

In this seafood specialty from Spain, the pimentón is used in the marinade and in the sauce that seasons it at serving. Salmon steaks or the steaks of any large fish can be substituted. Serve with a Caesar salad and saffron rice. **NOTE** *This recipe requires advance preparation.*

Combine 1 tablespoon of the oil, 1 tablespoon of the pimentón, and the parsley in a bowl and stir to mix. Season to taste with the salt and pepper. Rub the mixture over each side of the tuna steaks, cover, and marinate for an hour at room temperature.

Heat a saucepan over medium heat, add the remaining oil, and when hot, add the onion, garlic, and another tablespoon pimentón and sauté for about 2 minutes. Add the tomatoes and bell peppers and cook until the mixture thickens, 5 to 10 minutes.

Place the onion mixture in a blender or food processor, add the remaining pimentón and the olives, and puree to a smooth sauce. Return the sauce to the saucepan and gently simmer.

Grill the fish over a medium fire to the desired doneness, or cook under the broiler.

To serve, place the fish on individual plates, pour the sauce over the top, and garnish with the parsley.

Onion-Beer Tri-Tip Roast

2 cups finely chopped onion

2 tablespoons butter

¾ teaspoon salt

2 teaspoons New Mexican red chile powder

1 12-ounce can bock or other full-flavored beer

2 beef tri-tip (bottom sirloin) roasts, about 2 pounds each

Salt and pepper to taste

SERVES 8
HEAT RATING: MEDIUM

Try this when you don't have the time to do a brisket. It's delicious and makes great sandwiches. **NOTE** *This recipe requires advance preparation.*

Cook the onions in the butter in a small saucepan over medium-low heat until tender, about 10 minutes. Stir in the salt and chile powder. Add the beer and simmer 5 minutes. Remove from the heat and cool thoroughly.

Place the roasts in a large plastic bag and add the cooled marinade, turning to coat. Close the bag securely and marinate in the refrigerator 6 to 8 hours (or overnight), turning occasionally.

Remove the roasts from the marinade; reserve the marinade. Boil the marinade in a pot for 10 minutes. Place the roasts on the grill over medium coals. Grill 30 to 35 minutes, or until the internal temperature is 150°F, turning and brushing frequently with the marinade. Roasts will be rare to medium in doneness.

Remove the roasts from the grill, tent with aluminum foil, and allow to stand 15 to 20 minutes before carving. Carve across the grain into thin slices. Season with salt and pepper to taste.

Chicken, Chile, and Cheese Chimichangas

1 medium onion, chopped fine

1 tablespoon vegetable oil

4 New Mexican green chiles, roasted, peeled, stems and seeds removed, chopped

3 cups cooked chicken, diced

½ teaspoon ground cinnamon

¼ teaspoon ground cloves

1 small orange, peeled, seeded, and chopped

6 flour tortillas

1 cup grated Monterey Jack cheese

Vegetable oil for deep frying

Chopped lettuce and tomatoes for garnish

SERVES 4

HEAT RATING: MILD

These sweet chicken chimichangas with fruit are lighter than the more traditional beef and bean recipe popular in Arizona.

Sauté the onion in the oil in a saucepan over medium heat until soft. Add the chiles, chicken, and spices and sauté for an additional 5 minutes. Add the chopped oranges and mix well.

Wrap the tortillas in a moist towel and place them in a warm oven to soften. Place approximately ½ cup of the mixture in the center of each tortilla and top with cheese. Fold the tortilla like an envelope and secure with a toothpick.

Deep-fry the chimichangas, one at a time, in 375°F oil until well browned. Drain on paper towels and remove the toothpick.

Serve topped with shredded lettuce, chopped tomatoes, and your favorite salsa.

Jalapeño Corn Muffins with Chile Orange Butter

BUTTER

1 tablespoon New Mexican red chile powder

1 tablespoon grated orange zest

2 teaspoons orange juice

1 pound unsalted butter, at room temperature

MUFFINS

4 jalapeño chiles, stems and seeds removed, minced

2 cups milk

1 cup buttermilk

3 eggs

1 cup cornmeal

¾ cup flour

¼ cup sugar

3 tablespoons baking powder

1½ teaspoons salt

MAKES 24 MUFFINS
AND 1 POUND FLAVORED BUTTER
HEAT RATING: MILD

Take these "hot" muffins on your next picnic in place of ordinary bread or even chips. Flavored butters (or margarine) are easy to prepare and make tasty alternatives to plain butter. Any unused butter can be frozen for later use as a spread or for sautéing foods such as shrimp.

Combine all the ingredients for the chile butter in a bowl and allow to sit at room temperature for an hour to blend the flavors.

Preheat the oven to 375°F and grease a muffin tin.

To make the muffins, mix the jalapeños, milk, buttermilk, and eggs together in a bowl.

In another bowl sift together the cornmeal, flour, sugar, baking powder, and salt.

Add the dry ingredients to the liquid. Gently mix them until the dry ingredients are absorbed, being careful not to overmix.

Pour the batter into the greased muffin tins and bake 20 to 30 minutes or until done.

Potato Curry with Lima Beans

1 tablespoon vegetable or olive oil

3 large onions, chopped

4 cloves garlic, minced

1 1-inch piece ginger, peeled and minced

1 teaspoon cumin powder

1 teaspoon coriander powder

1 teaspoon cayenne powder

½ teaspoon turmeric powder

¼ teaspoon freshly ground black pepper

6 large potatoes, peeled and diced

4 large tomatoes, sliced

½ cup water

2 cups frozen lima beans

Salt to taste

½ cup cilantro leaves for garnish

SERVES 8
HEAT RATING: MILD

This simple curry from the Mangalore region in southwestern India makes a colorful, tasty addition to any meal. Use it to spice up a breakfast or accompany the main meal. For a spicier curry, double or triple the amount of cayenne powder.

Heat the oil in a skillet over medium heat for 1 minute, add the onions, and fry them for about 1 minute. Add the garlic and ginger and continuing frying for 1 minute.

Add the dry powders and the pepper, mix well, and then add the potatoes and tomatoes along with the water and cook, covered, for 12 minutes. Add the lima beans, mix well, and cook for 5 minutes.

Just before serving, add the salt and garnish with the cilantro.

Red Chile Pilaf

2 ounces butter

2 cups long-grain white rice

1 onion, chopped fine

2 cloves garlic, minced

2 New Mexican red chile pods, stems and seeds removed, soaked in hot water to hydrate them

4½ cups chicken stock

SERVES 6

HEAT RATING: MILD

Here is one of our favorite ways to cook rice. The style is from the Middle East but the chile transforms the dish into a favorite New Mexican accompaniment. Believe it or not, some people serve salsa over this rice!

Preheat the oven to 350°F.

Melt the butter over medium heat in a saucepan and sauté the rice until golden brown, stirring often.

Add the onion and sauté until soft, about 3 minutes, taking care that the rice does not burn.

In a blender, puree the garlic, chile, and ½ cup stock. Add this to the rice and stir. Add the remaining stock to the rice, bring to a boil, and transfer to a deep glass baking dish.

Cover and bake 45 minutes, removing the lid during the final 10 minutes. Fluff with a fork and serve.

Pasta with Green Chile Pesto

1 cup chopped New Mexican green chile

1 cup chopped fresh cilantro

⅓ cup piñon nuts

½ cup grated Parmesan or Pecorino Romano cheese

½ cup virgin olive oil

1 pound pasta of choice, cooked al dente and kept hot

SERVES 4 TO 6

HEAT RATING: MEDIUM

Of course we have our own version of pesto! It's a topping for pasta but can also be added to soups, stews, and rice. Although we have specified cilantro in this recipe, you can use the traditional basil or even Italian parsley. Pecans, another New Mexican crop, can be substituted for the piñon nuts.

Place the chile, cilantro, nuts, and cheese in a food processor and, while processing, slowly drizzle in the oil to form a pesto. Mix the pasta with the pesto to taste.

Argentinean Empanadas

Empanadas, or meat-filled turnovers, are very popular throughout Latin America, where they are most often eaten as a snack. **NOTE** *This recipe requires advance preparation.*

CRUST

1⅔ cups all-purpose flour

⅛ teaspoon salt

1   4-ounce stick butter
    or margarine

⅓ cup milk

FILLING

1   pound ground beef

2   tablespoons vegetable oil, olive preferred

1   large onion, finely chopped

1   red bell pepper, stem and seeds removed, finely chopped

2   jalapeño chiles, stems and seeds removed, minced

10 to 12 green olives, finely chopped

1   medium potato, peeled, boiled, finely chopped

2   hard-boiled eggs, finely chopped

2   tablespoons raisins

1   tablespoon ground mild paprika

1   tablespoon chopped fresh parsley, or substitute dried

Salt and freshly ground black pepper to taste

GLAZE

1   egg, beaten

1   tablespoon milk

MAKES 10 EMPANADAS
HEAT RATING: MEDIUM

Preheat the oven to 400°F.

To make the crust, sift the flour and salt into a bowl. Work the butter or margarine into the flour using your fingers or two forks. Add the milk and mix just until the dough comes together and can be formed easily into a ball. Refrigerate for at least an hour.

Sauté the beef in a skillet over medium heat until well done, stirring frequently with a fork to keep the meat broken up. Sauté the onion, bell pepper, and jalapeños in a separate skillet over medium heat until the onions are golden brown. Combine all the ingredients for the filling and mix well.

Divide the dough in two, roll out to a thickness of $\frac{1}{8}$ inch, and cut into circles 7 inches in diameter. Spoon the filling onto one half of each, leaving room to fold in half and seal. Press the edges with the tip of a fork and cut a 1-inch slit in the top. Place on an ungreased baking sheet.

Bake 10 minutes, then reduce the heat to 350°F and continue baking until the crust turns light brown.

Combine the ingredients for the glaze in a bowl. Brush the tops of the crusts with the glaze and bake an additional 5 minutes.

German Potato Salad with a Twist

2 pounds new potatoes

2 hard-boiled eggs, chopped

2 chipotle chiles in adobo sauce, drained and chopped, reserving the adobo sauce

1 medium onion, chopped

2 small sweet pickles, chopped

DRESSING

2 cups high-quality mayonnaise

1 cup low-fat yogurt

1 tablespoon Dijon mustard

1 tablespoon of the adobo sauce

1 teaspoon cayenne powder

Sprinkle of sugar

Salt and pepper to taste

Chopped chives for garnish

SERVES 4 TO 6

HEAT RATING: MEDIUM

Few recipes are more typically German than potato salad. Our friends and fellow chileheads Harald and Renate Zoschke of Kressbronn in southwestern Germany gave this national dish a spicy twist. It makes a great complement for bratwurst on the grill! **NOTE** *This recipe requires advance preparation.*

Brush the potatoes thoroughly under running water. Boil the potatoes in their skins in salted water until tender (about 25 minutes). Slice hot into a large bowl.

Add the hard-boiled eggs, chipotle pods, onion, and pickles to the sliced potatoes.

Blend together the mayonnaise, yogurt, mustard, adobo sauce, cayenne powder, and sugar very well in another bowl.

Fold the dressing gently into the potatoes and add salt and freshly ground pepper to taste.

Refrigerate at least 1 hour, so flavors blend well.

Sprinkle with chives and serve at room temperature.

Peperonata

5 tablespoons olive oil

2 onions, chopped

4 red and yellow bell peppers, quartered, seeds and ribs removed, thinly sliced

1 clove garlic, minced

Salt to taste

1 pound ripe tomatoes, peeled and chopped

2 teaspoons crushed red chile, or more to taste

Freshly ground black pepper

1 tablespoon chopped Italian parsley

SERVES 4
HEAT RATING: MEDIUM

Peperonata is a vegetable side dish that doubles as a pasta sauce. It is made all over Italy, but in the south the cooks add crushed hot peperoncini, or chile peppers.

Heat the olive oil in a large pan over medium heat and sauté the onions for 5 minutes, stirring well.

Add the pepper slices, garlic, and salt and sauté for 10 minutes, stirring well.

Add the tomatoes and the crushed red chile, cover, and cook over low heat for about 30 minutes, stirring occasionally and making sure the mixture doesn't burn.

When done, add pepper to taste and stir in the parsley.

Cascabel Caramel Turtles

24 soft caramels

2 tablespoons frozen whipped topping

Butter-flavored vegetable cooking oil spray

72 pecan halves

4 ounces semisweet chocolate chips

8 dried cascabel chiles, stems and seeds removed, finely crushed

MAKES 2 DOZEN
HEAT RATING: MEDIUM

The word cascabel *means "rattle" in Spanish, and this full-flavored dried chile probably received its name thanks to its shape and the fact that its seeds rattle around when you shake it. These turtles are like no others you've tasted before, hot as well as sweet.*

In a microwave-safe mixing bowl, combine the caramels and whipped topping and cook on 50 percent power for 45 seconds. Remove the bowl, stir, and place back in the microwave. Continue this process in 10-second increments until the mixture has melted and is smooth and well blended. Let the mixture cool slightly.

Spray a cookie sheet lightly with the cooking oil. Place the pecan halves on the sheet in groups of five, arranged so that each pecan group forms a shape like a turtle's body with four legs. Carefully spoon the caramel mixture over each, leaving the ends of the pecans showing. Set aside until the caramel has hardened.

Place the chocolate chips in a microwave-safe bowl. Cook in the microwave on 50 percent power for 45 seconds, remove and stir, and repeat the process in 10-second increments until the chocolate is melted and smooth. Stir in the cascabels and let the chocolate mixture cool slightly.

Spoon the melted chocolate over the caramel, being careful not to cover the exposed ends of the pecans.

Set aside until hard, then store in a covered container in a cool place.

Double Trouble Chocolate Truffles

8 ounces baking chocolate

4 ounces white chocolate chips

2 tablespoons sugar (or more, to taste)

1 tablespoon ground New Mexican red chile (or more, to taste)

½ teaspoon ground cinnamon

1 14-ounce can light sweetened condensed milk

Finely chopped piñon nuts, or substitute pecans

MAKES ABOUT 4 DOZEN
HEAT RATING: MEDIUM

New Mexican red chile is the heat source in this tremendous treat. With the combination of baking chocolate and white chocolate, it's exceptionally wonderful to munch on. Try substituting 2 teaspoons of cayenne powder for the New Mexican chile to heat the truffles up even more.

Use a double boiler, or fill a 3-quart saucepan three-quarters full of water, and heat until the water is almost boiling.

Place both kinds of chocolate in a smaller saucepan and melt over the hot water, stirring until smooth.

Add the sugar, red chile, cinnamon, and milk, mixing until very smooth. Remove the mixture from the heat and let it cool until it is shapeable.

Shape the chocolate mixture into 1-inch balls, then roll them in the nuts. Chill the candy in the refrigerator in an airtight tin.

White Chocolate Ancho Chile Ice Cream

3 ancho chiles, stems removed

½ teaspoon ground cinnamon

¼ teaspoon ground cloves

6 ounces (2 bars) good quality white chocolate such as Tobler or Lindt

2 cups heavy cream

2 cups milk

¾ cup sugar

1 vanilla bean

6 egg yolks

Cinnamon stick and shaved dark semisweet chocolate for garnish

MAKES 1 QUART
HEAT RATING: MILD

This stunning ice cream is from Suzy Dayton, former pastry chef at the Coyote Cafe, who served it at the Santa Fe Wine and Chile Festival, where we collected the recipe.

Cover the chiles with hot water and let them soak until pliable, about 30 minutes. Remove the chiles and discard the seeds. Place the chiles in a blender or food processor and puree finely with a little of the soaking water. Stir in the cinnamon and cloves.

Melt the chocolate in a double boiler over hot water.

Combine the cream, milk, and sugar in a medium saucepan. Split the vanilla bean and scrape some of the seeds into the mixture. Bring the mixture to a boil.

Whisk the egg yolks in a bowl while pouring in about a third of the hot milk mixture. Reheat the remaining milk mixture and add the egg yolks. Heat for 1 minute, whisking constantly.

Strain the mixture into a bowl. Stir in the chile mixture and the chocolate, and chill 15 minutes in the freezer.

Freeze in an ice cream maker according to the manufacturer's instructions. Serve garnished with a cinnamon stick and the shaved chocolate.

Cranberry and Chipotle Tiramisu

CRANBERRY CHUTNEY

2 Granny Smith apples, chopped

2¼ cups cranberries, picked through and rinsed

2 chipotle chiles, rehydrated and minced very finely

1 cup brown sugar

½ cup raisins

½ cup apple cider vinegar

½ teaspoon cinnamon

½ teaspoon salt

½ teaspoon ground ginger

½ teaspoon ground cloves

TIRAMISU

24 ladyfingers, either purchased or homemade

4 cups vanilla pudding, preferably homemade

3 cups cranberry chutney

1 cup whipped cream

2 cups toasted almonds

SERVES 8
HEAT RATING: MILD

This is a holiday version of the popular Italian dessert. It can be served in a large glass bowl or in individual dessert bowls or large wine goblets. The cranberry chutney can be made in advance, and then the dessert can be put together the morning of the party. The red and white color is beautiful and very dramatic.

To make the chutney, place all ingredients in a medium saucepan and bring to a boil over medium heat. Reduce heat to low and simmer for about 25 minutes, or until the cranberries have begun to cook down and the chutney has thickened. Cool the chutney to room temperature.

In a large bowl or in individual glasses, layer first the ladyfingers, then the vanilla pudding. Add a layer of the cranberry chutney. Sprinkle a few almonds over the layer. Repeat the layering again until either bowl or glasses are filled.

Refrigerate until ready to serve. Garnish with whipped cream and toasted almonds.

Caribbean Fresh Fruit Compote with Habanero-Spiked Syrup

3 tablespoons cider vinegar

2 tablespoons sugar

½ teaspoon ground habanero chile

1 cup cubed fresh mango

1 cup cubed fresh papaya

½ cup sliced strawberries

Fresh mint leaves for garnish

SERVES 4

HEAT RATING: HOT

Use this "hot" fruit compote to accent any breakfast or brunch. Since the habanero syrup complements a wide variety of fruits, vary the ones you use depending on what's in season.

Combine the vinegar, sugar, and chile in a small saucepan and stir to mix. Heat the mixture over high heat until just below the boiling point, reduce the heat, and simmer for 5 minutes. Allow the syrup to cool to room temperature.

Combine the fruit in a large mixing bowl. Pour the sauce over the fruit and toss to coat.

Ladle the fruit into individual bowls, garnish with the mint leaves, and serve.

Kahlua, Ancho, and Chocolate Fondue

1   8-ounce milk chocolate bar

½ cup heavy cream

3   tablespoons Kahlua or other
    coffee-flavored liqueur

1½ teaspoons ground ancho chile

24 to 30 bite-size cubes
    angel food or pound cake

SERVES 4
HEAT RATING: MILD

Chocolate dessert fondues don't have to be bland! Add chile powder for a pungent punch as evidenced by this recipe. Substitute other liqueurs such as kirsch, cognac, Cointreau, brandy, or raspberry schnapps for the Kahlua. Fruits such as slightly underripe bananas, pineapple chunks, or strawberries are also great dipped in this fondue.

Break up the chocolate into small pieces and melt it in the top of a double boiler or in a saucepan over a pot of simmering water, over a very low heat. Be sure that none of the water gets into the chocolate.

Add the cream, stir well, and cook for 5 minutes or until thickened.

Remove the pan from the heat, add the Kahlua and chile, and stir well.

To serve, place the sauce in a ceramic fondue pot over low heat and place the pot on a large serving plate. Surround the fondue with the cake cubes and serve with long forks or bamboo skewers. Guests spear the cubes, swirl in the chocolate to coat, and enjoy.

Red Chile Pumpkin Chiffon Pie

CRUST

1 cup all-purpose flour

1 teaspoon sugar

½ teaspoon kosher salt

3 tablespoons unsalted butter

3 tablespoons lard or vegetable shortening

3 to 6 tablespoons ice water

FILLING

¼ cup very hot water

1 envelope (2 teaspoons) unflavored gelatin

3 large eggs

⅔ cup sugar

½ teaspoon kosher salt

½ teaspoon cinnamon

½ teaspoon nutmeg

½ teaspoon ground ginger

3 tablespoons (more or less) mild New Mexican red chile powder

1¼ cups canned pumpkin

½ cup heavy cream

SERVES 8

HEAT RATING: MILD

New Mexico food editor Gwyneth Doland shares her recipe for this spicy dessert. This fluffy pie is a lighter alternative to the dense, rich pumpkin pie most of us are used to. It's served chilled, so the red chile kick comes as a pleasant contrast. **NOTE** *This recipe requires advance preparation.*

Combine the flour, sugar, and salt in a bowl and stir to mix.

Using a pastry blender, your hands, or two butter knives, quickly work the butter and lard into the flour mixture until it resembles coarse meal with some big, pea-sized chunks.

Sprinkle the ice water 1 tablespoon at a time over the flour and mix with a fork or your hands, adding just enough water so that the mixture comes together and can be gathered into a ball. Press the ball into a thick disc, wrap the disc in plastic, and refrigerate 20 minutes.

Remove the chilled dough and allow it to rest at room temperature 5 minutes. Roll it out into an ⅛-inch-thick round, transfer it to a pie pan, and flute the edges.

Preheat the oven to 425°F and refrigerate the crust another 20 minutes.

Remove the crust and prick it all over with a fork. Place a piece of aluminum foil over the bottom of the crust and weigh it down with dry beans.

Bake the crust 10 minutes. Remove the foil and beans, lower the temperature to 350°F, and bake until the crust is golden, about 10 to 15 minutes. Cool the crust on a wire rack.

Place a mixing bowl and beaters in the freezer to chill.

Pour the hot water into a small bowl and sprinkle the gelatin over

continued on next page

Red Chile Pumpkin Chiffon Pie continued

it, stirring vigorously until the gelatin is completely dissolved.

Separate the eggs, putting the yolks into the top of a double boiler (or, if you don't have one, a large stainless steel bowl that you place over a pot of boiling water) and the whites into a mixing bowl.

Add ⅓ cup sugar to the yolks and whisk until the mixture is thick, creamy, and pale yellow. Add the salt, cinnamon, nutmeg, ginger, chile powder, and dissolved gelatin. (Don't worry about clumps in the gelatin—they'll dissolve when the mixture is heated.) Start heating the water in the double boiler, or if you're using a large bowl instead, set the bowl over a pan of boiling water, making sure the bowl doesn't actually touch the water.

Stir constantly until the mixture thickens considerably and thickly coats the back of a spoon.

Remove the yolk mixture from the heat and whisk in the pumpkin until combined. Set the bowl over another, larger bowl of ice water. Whisk the mixture about 5 minutes or longer, if you can. Remove the bowl from the ice water and chill in the refrigerator.

In a standing mixer or with a hand mixer, beat the egg whites until they form soft peaks. Slowly add the remaining ⅓ cup sugar and continue beating until the soft peaks become satiny and stiff. Scrape the whites out into a small bowl.

Using the chilled mixing bowl and beaters, whip the cream until medium peaks form.

Gently fold the pumpkin mixture into the whipped cream, then into the egg whites. Scoop the mixture into the prepared crust and chill, covered, 4 hours or overnight.

Serve the pie garnished with additional whipped cream.

Resources

Articles and Further Information

Chileman.org, www.thechileman.org. Mark McMillan, publisher and editor. This U.K. site contains the best glossary of chile pepper varieties, with about four thousand listed.

The Chile Pepper Institute, www.chilepepperinstitute.org. Paul W. Bosland, publisher; Danise Coon, editor. The shop at this site contains books, chile information, and seeds of many of the varieties featured in this book.

Fatalii.net, www.fatalii.net, is a Finnish site, in English, with extensive information about chile growing and bonsai chiles.

The Fiery Foods and Barbecue SuperSite, www.fiery-foods.com. Dave DeWitt, publisher and editor. This site has more than four hundred articles on varieties, gardening, history, and cooking.

Pepperworld, www.pepperworld.com (German language). Harald Zoschke, publisher and editor. This site has many articles and the best products available in the European Union.

Seeds and Plants

UNITED STATES

All of the varieties described earlier in "Top Hundred (or So) Chile Peppers for the Garden" are available from just two sources in the United States:

- For seeds, go to The Chile Pepper Institute, www.chilepepperinstitute. org.
- For five hundred varieties of chile pepper bedding plants in season and fresh chile pods in the late summer and early fall, go to Cross Country Nurseries, www.chileplants.com.

CANADA

Many U.S. seed companies will ship to Canada. You will have to do an Internet search to find them.

EUROPEAN UNION

The shop at Pepperworld, www.pepperworld.com (German language), carries seed for fifty to a hundred varieties.

UNITED KINGDOM

The Chilli Pepper Company, www.chileseeds.co.uk

Nickys Nursery Ltd., www.nickys-nursery.co.uk

Roguelands Seed Co., www.seedfest.co.uk

Suttons Seeds, www.suttons.co.uk

U.K. Chile Farm, www.chilefarm.co.uk

AUSTRALIA AND NEW ZEALAND

Eden Seeds, www.edenseeds.com.au

Fireworks Foods, www.fireworksfoods.com.au

SOUTH AFRICA

The Great Chilli Farm, www.chillifarm.com

Food Products

Peppers.com, www.peppers.com, has a huge selection of fiery foods products of all kinds.

Library Collections

The Chile Pepper Institute Library, 265 Gerald Thomas Hall, New Mexico State University, Las Cruces, New Mexico, has more than six hundred books plus its own archive of papers and photographs. Email: hotchile@nmsu.edu.

New Mexico State University Library, Las Cruces, New Mexico, has the Dave DeWitt-Chile Pepper Institute Collection, containing thousands of books, papers, and photographs. Email: shussman@lib.nmsu.edu.

Glossary of Specialized Chile Pepper Terms

This glossary is a compilation of mostly unfamiliar worldwide chile pepper terms, many in Spanish. Not included here are the names of the U.S. cultivars, which, after more than a century of breeding, number in the thousands.

achocolatado   "Chocolatety"; in Mexico, another name for pasilla, a reference to its dark brown color.

acorchado   "Corky"; in Mexico, cultivated variety of jalapeño. The name is a reference to the "corking" or brown streaks on the pod.

ahumado   "Smoked-cured"; in Mexico, referring to chipotle chiles.

ají   Common name for chiles in South America and some parts of the Caribbean; usually *Capsicum baccatum*.

ají amarillo   "Yellow chile"; in Peru, the most common chile grown and eaten. This member of *Capsicum baccatum* var. *pendulum* is 3 to 5 inches long and matures to a deep orange color. It has a medium-hot pungency and is grown in all regions of the country. Also called ají escabeche.

ají ayucllo   In Peru, semi-cultivated hot variety of *Capsicum baccatum*. The small, thick-fleshed, oval-shaped pod matures to a bright orange color.

ají cereza   "Cherry chile"; cultivated in backyards in Peru, this semi-domesticated chile bears pods that are round and about 1½ inches in diameter. They are extremely hot and mature to a deep red color. The plant belongs to either *Capsicum chinense* or *C. baccatum*.

ají charapa   In Peru, wild chile harvested near the city of Iquitos. The pods are spherical, about ¼ inch in diameter, and very hot. They mature to a red or yellow color. The species is either *Capsicum chinense* or *C. baccatum*.

ají chombo   *Capsicum chinense* varieties or cultivars in Panama.

ají escurre-huéspedes   In Cuba, chile that makes the guests sneak away.

ají lengua de pájaro   "Bird's tongue chile"; in Cuba, variety of piquín.

ají limo   Popular on the northern coast of Peru, this member of *Capsicum chinense* bears very hot pods that are 2 to 3 inches long and mature to a yellow, orange, or red color. The word *limo* has no known meaning.

ají mono   "Monkey chile"; grown in the Peruvian jungles, this chile has pods that mature to bright red and measure 4 to 5 inches long. It has high pungency and is thought to be a member of *Capsicum baccatum*.

ají norteño   "Northern chile"; in Peru, this chile is grown in northern coastal valleys. The ripe pods mature to yellow, orange, and red and measure 3 to 4 inches long. They have moderate pungency and are commonly eaten fresh with seafood. Thought to be a member of *Capsicum baccatum*.

ají panca   Thought to be a member of *Capsicum frutescens*, this Peruvian chile has pods that grow from 3 to 5 inches long and have a mild pungency. They are deep red to purple when ripe and dry to a dark purple color.

ají pinguita de mono   "Little monkey penis chile"; found in Peru's central valley of Chanchamayo, these are wild or semi-cultivated chiles of unknown species with pods that are ½ to 1 inch long, very elongated, and bright red when mature. The species is *Capsicum chinense* or *C. baccatum*.

ají yaquitania   *Capsicum chinense* varieties or cultivars in Brazil.

aleppo   Syrian chile powder.

'Altamira'   In Mexico, cultivated variety of serrano.

amarillo   In Mexico, any yellow chile, but specifically chilcoxle.

amash   Very hot piquín chile that grows wild in the Mexican states of Tabasco, Chiapas, and Yucatán and is consumed in the green form. This chile is thought to be the progenitor of the pods transferred to Louisiana and called tobasco or tabasco; if true, then amash belongs to *Capsicum frutescens*.

amatista   South American purple ornamental chile, probably a member of *Capsicum annuum*.

amomo   Variety of piquín chile in Mexico. This is a botanical name referring to the resemblance to grains of paradise, or melegueta pepper.

Anaheim   The California produce industry's name for the New Mexican pod type. Typically a long, mild chile primarily used in the green form, 'Anaheim' is now considered to be a cultivated variety of the New Mexican pod type.

ancho   "Wide" or "broad"; dried poblano chile. In Mexico and the United States, it is a large, broad, mild chile with a raisiny aroma and flavor. Confusingly, ancho is called pasilla in Morelia, Michoacán, and chile joto in Aguascalientes, Mexico. It is also mistakenly called pasilla in some northern U. S. states and in California.

'Apaseo'   In Mexico, cultivated variety of pasilla.

'Ardida Do Chile'   Commercial variety of *Capsicum baccatum* grown in Brazil.

ata   Generic term for chile pepper among the Yoruba of Nigeria. *Ata funfun* resembles the jalapeño, while *ata wewe* is a tabasco-like chile. *Ata rodo* is a member of *Capsicum chinense*, the habanero relative.

'Bakolocal'   Cultivated variety of chile in Ethiopia.

'Balín'   "Bullet"; in Mexico, cultivated variety of serrano chile.

bandeño   In the state of Guerrero, Mexico, name for the green costeño; refers to the bank of a river.

barkono   Term for chile in northern Nigeria.

berbere   Amharic word for chile; in Ethiopia the term refers generically to both the pod and a paste made from the pods.

bhere khorsani   In Nepal, wolf chile.

bola   "Ball" or "marble"; see *cascabel*. Also, in Jalisco, Mexico, a spherical piquín.

bolita   "Little ball"; see *cascabel*.

boludo   "Bumpy"; see *cascabel*.

bonda man Jacques   *Capsicum chinense* varieties or cultivars in Martinique and Guadeloupe.

bonney pepper   *Capsicum chinense* varieties or cultivars in Barbados; considered to be the Red Caribbean pod type.

bravo   "Brave, wild, savage"; in Mexico, local name for chile de árbol.

byadgi   Variety of *Capsicum annuum* in India that resembles a wrinkled, dried cayenne.

caballo   "Horse"; another name for rocoto in Mexico.

cabe (also cabai)   General term for chile peppers in Indonesia and Malaysia. *Cabe hijau* are green chiles; *cabe merah*, red chiles; *cabe rawit*, bird chiles (*Capsicum frutescens*).

cachucha   "Cap" chile; rocotillo in Cuba.

cambray   Long, narrow chile grown in San Luis Potosí, Mexico, and marketed in Monterrey.

canario   "Canary"; in Mexico, yellow variety of the rocoto.

capones   Deseeded (or "castrated") chipotles.

capsaicinoids   Seven related compounds that cause the sensation of heat (pungency) in chile peppers.

Capsicum   Chile genus. In Southeast Asia, this means bell pepper. From the Greek *kapto*, "to bite."

Capsicum annuum   Species of capsicum most commonly grown around the world, including bell peppers and New Mexican varieties. *Annuum* means "annual," a misnomer because chile peppers are perennial.

Capsicum baccatum   *Baccatum* means "berrylike"; species of capsicum consisting of South American peppers.

Capsicum frutescens   *Frutescens* means "shrubby"; capsicum species including the Tabasco chile.

Capsicum pubescens   Species of capsicums that includes the Mexican manzanos and the Peruvian rocotos. *Pubescens* means "hairy," referring to the leaves, and this species has black seeds.

caribe   Variety of yellow chile grown in Aguascalientes, Mexico. Usually found fresh, the pod has a conical shape and is about 1½ inches long.

carrocillo   In central Mexico, the yellow chile.

cascabel   "Jingle bell" or "rattle," an allusion to the seeds rattling in the oval pods of this chile, about 1½ inches in diameter and dark red in the dried form. In the fresh form this chile is called bola, bolita, and boludo. Dried, cascabels are also known as coras and guajones. Grown in Jalisco and Guerrero, Mexico.

casero   "Homemade"; in the state of Guerrero, Mexico, the green costeño.

catarina   Dried chile from the state of Aguascalientes, Mexico, possibly a variety of de árbol. The pod is 1 to 2 inches long and ½ inch wide, with seeds that rattle.

charapilla   *Capsicum chinense* in Peru.

chawa   Mexican term for a variety of the wax pod type.

cherry pepper   Originally thought to be *Capsicum cerasiforme*, this pod type of *Capsicum annuum*, introduced into England from the West Indies in 1759, resembles a large cherry. The cherry type is familiar because the pods are commonly pickled and served as an accompaniment to sandwiches. Varieties include 'Cherry Sweet' and 'Red Cherry Hot'.

Chiapas   Chiltepín in Chiapas, Mexico.

chilaca   Fresh form of the pasilla chile. This term also refers to fresh New Mexican pod types grown in Durango and Chihuahua, Mexico.

chilacate   Chile eaten both fresh and dry in Jalisco, Mexico, that resembles a small New Mexican type. Also called tierra.

chilaile   See *mora*.

chilcoxle   Dried yellow chile used in the mole amarillo of Oaxaca, Mexico. Also spelled *chilcostle* and *chilcoxtle*.

chile caribe   Coarsely ground chile powder; a red chile paste made from crushed or ground red chiles of any type, garlic, and water.

chile colorado   Generally, any red chile; usually a guajíllo.

chile con queso   Cheese and chile dip.

chile pasado   Literally "chile of the past," in New Mexico it is roasted, peeled, and sun-dried green chile. The dried chile is later rehydrated for use in cooking.

chile seco   Any dried chile; in various states of Mexico this term refers to different chiles. For example, in the state of Colima, the term most often refers to guajíllos. In other parts of Mexico, it refers to chipotles.

chiles rellenos   Roasted, peeled New Mexican or poblano chiles that are stuffed, usually with cheese, then battered and deep-fried.

chilhuacle   In Mexico, Oaxacan chile primarily used in moles. Some sources say it is a regional variety of the guajíllo, but to our eyes it more closely resembles a small poblano. There are three forms: amarillo, rojo, and negro.

chilillo   "Little chile"; variety of piquín in Yucatán, Mexico.

chilpaya   Variety of chiltepín in Veracruz, Mexico.

chilipiquín   Term in Texas for chiltepíns.

chiltepín   Spherical, extremely hot, wild chile pepper varying from ¼ inch to ½ inch in diameter. Also spelled *tepín*, *chiltepe*, and *chiltipín*. These peppers are pickled when fresh or added to soups and stews. Dried, they are a year-round spice.

chiltepínero   Person who collects or sells chiltepíns.

chinchi-uchu   Indigenous name for *Capsicum chinense* in Peru.

chino   Dried poblano chile, especially in central Mexico and San Luis Potosí.

chipotle   Any smoked chile, but most often a jalapeño smoked until it is very dark and stiff. Also spelled *chilpotle* and *chipocle*. A typical chipotle sold in North American markets is a jalapeño that is smoked while green, rather than red, and thus has a whitish, tan color.

chombo   Local name for *Capsicum chinense* in Panama.

cili   Alternate Malaysian term for chiles. *Cili padi* are apparently the same as *cabe rawit*, the small bird chiles, while dried red chiles are *cili kering*. Chile powder is *serbuk cili*. Compare with *sili*. In the Czech Republic, *cili* is chile powder, usually hot paprika, used in many dishes.

cobán   Smoked Guatemalan piquín chile.

coffee pepper   Local Trindadian name for a wild *Capsicum annuum* variety that resembles a coffee bean.

cola de rata   "Rat's tail"; long, thin variety of chile de árbol in Nayarit, Mexico.

colombo   Type of hot curry introduced into the French Caribbean in the 1800s by migrant Indian workers mostly from Bengal.

colorado   Dried New Mexican red chile.

comapeño   Small orange chile consumed both fresh and dry in Veracruz, Mexico. Also called ozulyamero.

congo   Local name for the Trinidad pod type of *Capsicum chinense*; the term is said to mean "large" or "powerful."

'Cora'   Cultivated variety of cascabel grown in Nayarit, Mexico, where it is also called acaponeta and cuerudo. It is eaten both fresh and dry.

corazón   Spicy, heart-shaped poblano grown in Durango, Mexico.

corriente   In the state of Guerrero, Mexico, green costeño.

costeño   Small dried red chile about 1 inch long that is a variety of chile de árbol. Commonly found in the states of Veracruz, Oaxaca, and Guerrero, Mexico. Also spelled *costeña*. Other regional terms for this chile are *bandeño*, *casero*, *criollo*, and *corriente*.

'Cotaxtla'   Cultivated variety of serrano in Mexico.

coui   In the Caribbean, an ancient Carib Indian sauce of hot peppers and cassava juice.

covincho   Local name for the wild *Capsicum chacoense* in northern Argentina.

cuaresmeño   See *jalapeño*. Refers to Lent, probably an allusion to the agriculture of the chile at that time of year.

cuauhchilli   In Jalisco, Nayarit, and Aguascalientes, Mexico, a variety of de árbol.

Cuban   Pod type of *Capsicum annuum*. These mild pods are much loved when fried. There are two basic types: the long-fruited ones like 'Key Largo' and 'Biscayne' and the short-fruited types like 'Cubanelle'. Recommended varieties include 'Aconagua', 'Biscayne', and 'Cubanelle'.

cuerno de oro   "Horn of gold"; Costa Rican name for *Capsicum baccatum*.

cuicatleco   Variety of chile consumed by the indigenous people of the district of Cuicatlán, Oaxaca, Mexico.

'Dandicut Cherry'   Cultivated chile in Pakistan.

dar feller   Yemeni word for chile pepper.

datil   Local name for *Capsicum chinense* in St. Augustine, Florida.

de agua   "Water chile"; in Oaxaca, Mexico, fairly long (to 4 inches) conical chile that grows erect on plants. It is used both in its green and dried red forms in sauces and stews. Some sources say it is a variety of poblano, but that is doubtful. When red and smoke-dried, it is called pasilla oaxaqueño.

de árbol   "Tree chile"; in Mexico, where it is grown primarily in Jalisco and Nayarit, the bush resembles a small tree. Also goes by the names *pulla*, *puya*, *cuauhchilli*, *alfilerillo*, *pico de pájaro*, and *cola de rata*. In the United States, pod type of *Capsicum annuum*. The hot pods are red and about ¼ inch wide by 1½ to 3 inches long. Varieties include 'NuMex Sunburst', with bright orange, 3-inch, medium-hot pods; 'NuMex Sunflare', with bright red, 3-inch, medium-hot pods; and 'NuMex Sunglo', with bright yellow, 3-inch, medium-hot pods.

de chorro   "Irrigated chile"; in Mexico, where it is grown only in Guanajuato and Durango, variety of poblano so named because each plant is irrigated separately. Pods are used only in the green form.

de color   "Of color"; refers in Mexico to both chile pasera, a dried poblano that is left on the plant until the pods turn red and then are removed and dried in the sun, and chilessecadora, which is a green poblano that is removed from the bush and dried in a dehydrator.

de la tierra   In Mexico, another term for a dried New Mexican red chile.

de monte   "Hilly chile"; in Mexico, general term for wild chiles, the chiltepíns.

de onza   "By the ounce"; in Mexico, small, dried, brick-red Oaxacan chile about 3 inches long and ½ inch wide used in moles.

de siete caldos   Chile from Chiapas, Mexico, that is supposedly so hot that one is enough to spice up seven pots of soup.

derriere de Madame Jacques   *Capsicum chinense* in Guadeloupe.

diente de tlacuache   "Oppossum tooth"; in Tamaulipas, Mexico, name for chiltepín.

dominica pepper   *Capsicum chinense* in the U.S. Virgin Islands.

dulce   "Sweet"; in Mexico, term for bell peppers and pimiento.

'Dutch'   Hot variety of *Capsicum annuum* from The Netherlands that was developed from Indonesian varieties.

'Esmeralda'   "Emerald"; in Mexico, cultivated variety of poblano.

'Espinateco'   "Spiny"; in Mexico, cultivated variety of jalapeño.

'Fatalii'   Variety of *Capsicum chinense* grown in the Central African Republic.

felfel al har   Arabic term for chile pepper in North Africa.

filfil   General Arabic term for chile pepper.

'Flor de Pabellón'   "Flower of the Pavillion"; in Mexico, cultivated variety of poblano.

foronto   Term for chile pepper in Senegal.

'Fukien Rice'   Extremely hot variety of chile pepper grown in China.

'Funtua'   Principal chile pepper variety grown in Nigeria.

furtu   Peppers in French Guiana.

gachupin   Piquín chile in Veracruz, Mexico.

goan   Variety of *Capsicum annuum* grown in Goa, India, that resembles a pointed cascabel.

goat pepper   Local name for *Capsicum chinense* varieties in the Bahamas and some parts of Africa.

gril koreni   In the Czech Republic, dry rub composed of mild paprika, salt, and spices.

guaguao   Piquín chiles in Cuba.

guajillo   Common chile in northern and central Mexico, grown primarily in Zacatecas, Durango, and Aguascalientes. It resembles a small dried New Mexican red chile and is used primarily in sauces.

güero   "Blonde"; see *xcatic*.

Guinea pepper   Thought to be of *Capsicum chinense*, pepper grown in Nigeria, Liberia, and the Ivory Coast. Introduced into England in 1548.

gulasove koreni   In the Czech Republic, a spice mixture for goulashes composed of hot paprika, salt, carraway seeds, and other spices.

'Guntur Red'   Variety of *Capsicum annuum* named for Guntur, reputedly the chile capital of India. It resembles a dried red jalapeño.

habanero   "From Havana"; hottest chile in the world, belonging to the species *Capsicum chinense*. The fresh pods, usually orange, are about 1 inch wide and 1½ inches long, with a distinct aroma reminiscent of apricots. Grown in the Yucatán Peninsula of Mexico and in the United States.

harissa   North African chile paste.

huachinango   Term for a large jalapeño; term for chipotle in Oaxaca, Mexico.

huayca   Amara (Peruvian) term for chile pepper.

'Inia'   A cultivated variety of habanero in Mexico.

jalapeño   Familiar small green chile of medium heat, about ¾ inch wide and 1½ to 2 inches long. Called chipotle in its dried, smoked form. Also spelled *xalapeño* and called cuaresmeño.

Japón   "Japan"; small, pointed chile grown in Veracruz and San Luis Potosí, Mexico.

joto   Term for ancho peppers in Aguascalientes, Mexico.

Kashmiri   Originally a variety of *Capsicum annuum* grown in Kashmir, India, but now the generic term for any medium-long dried red chile. An appropriate substitute would be guajillo.

kayensky peper   In Hungary, cayenne pepper.

kochikai   Tamil (southern India) word for chile pepper.

kochu   In Korea, cayenne-like chiles. Also *gochu*.

kulai   Cayenne-like chile grown in Malaysia.

'La Blanca'   "The white one"; a cultivated variety of mirasol in Mexico.

la-jiao   Chile peppers in China. Also *hung fan jiao*.

'Largo'   "Long," "large"; cultivated variety of serrano in Mexico.

loco   "Crazy"; in Mexico, term for mutants, especially those chiles hotter than normal.

locoto   See *rocoto*.

lombok   Indonesian term for chile peppers.

'Loreto 74'   Cultivated variety of mirasol in Mexico.

macho   "Manly"; another name for piquín in Mexico.

mak phet   Chile peppers in Laotian. *Mak phet dip* are fresh green chiles; *mak phet deng*, fresh red chiles; *mak phet nyai*, large chiles; *mak phet kuntsi*, small chiles; *mak phet kinou*, tiny, "rat-dropping" chiles; *mak phet haeng*, dried red chiles; *mak phet pung*, ground red chiles.

malagueta or **melagueta**   *Capsicum frutescens*; a Brazilian chile related to tabascos. It grows both wild and cultivated.

mango   Local term for bell peppers in Indiana and Illinois.

mano   Term for chile in Liberia.

manzano or **manzana**   "Apple"; pepper of the species *Capsicum* *pubescens*. Grown in the states of Michoacán, Chiapas, and Guerrero, México, these chiles resemble small apples and are usually used in the red form. They have thick flesh and black seeds. The variety is also called *cirhuelo* (in Queretaro), *cera, malinalco*, and *rocoto*.

'Marekofana'   Cultivated variety of chile in Ethiopia.

mata-frade   In Brazil, "friar-killer" chile.

max   Another name for piquín in Yucatán, Mexico.

meco   Blackish-red smoked jalapeño in Mexico.

'Miahuateco'   Large variety of poblano grown only in the states of Puebla and Oaxaca, Mexico, and used only in its green form.

mirasol   "Looking at the sun"; chile pepper primarily grown in Zacatecas, Mexico, with erect (sometimes pendant) pods 2 to 4 inches long, quite hot, used both fresh and dry. Also called miracielo, "looking at the sky." In the United States, a pod type of *Capsicum annuum*. Varieties include 'De Comida', 'Guajíllo', and 'Costeño'.

mirch   Hindi term for hot capsicums in northern India. Red chile is *lal mirch*; green chile is *hari mirch*; cayenne is *pisi hui lal mirch*; dried red chiles are *sabut lal mirch*; Kashmiri chiles are *degi mirch*.

miri   Sinhalese word for chile.

mole sauce   Thick, spicy sauce made with chiles and spices in Puebla and Oaxaca, Mexico. It sometimes contains unsweetened chocolate as an ingredient.

molido   Finely ground chile pepper powder.

'Mombasa'   Principal chile variety cultivated in Uganda.

mora   "Mulberry" or "blackberry"; a smoked red serrano or jalapeño that is pliable. Also called morita in many parts of Mexico and chilaile in Quintana Roo, Mexico.

'Morelia'   Variety of poblano grown only in Queréndaro, Michoacán, Mexico. The pods dry to a black color, so it is also known as chile negro. Named for the capital of Michoacán.

'Morita'   Cultivated variety of jalapeño. This variety is also smoked.

morrón   Generally, in Mexico, a bell pepper, but also another name for pimiento.

mosquito   In Mexico, another name for the piquín.

mukuru   Local name for the wild *Capsicum tovarii* of Peru.

mulagay   Sri Lankan (Tamil) term for peppers.

mulato   Variety of dried poblano chile in Mexico that has very dark brown—almost black—pods. Grown primarily in Jalisco, Guanajuato, and Puebla.

murici   *Capsicum chinense* in Brazil

mutton pepper   Local name for *Capsicum chinense* in Belize.

negro   "Black"; see *'Morelia'*. Also sometimes refers to a dark pasilla chile in Mexico.

'Nellore'   Variety of *Capsicum annuum* grown in India that resembles the Mexican de árbol pepper.

New Mexican   Formerly called Anaheim, this pod type is grown in Chihuahua and other northern states of Mexico and then imported into the United States. It is also grown extensively in New Mexico, Arizona, and California. It is a long (to 8 inches), fairly mild pod used in both green and red forms.

nga yut thee   Burmese term for chiles.

ornamental   Type of pepper that is showy and colorful and used primarily for display rather than eating (although they are edible).

ot   General Vietnamese term for chile peppers. Dried chiles are *ot kho* and chile sauces are *tuong ot*.

'Pabellón 1'   Cultivated variety of pasilla in Mexico.

panameño   *Capsicum chinense* in Costa Rica.

panco   *Capsicum chinense* in Peru.

'Pánuco'   Cultivated variety of serrano in Mexico. Named for a river in northern Veracruz.

'Papaloápan'   Cultivated variety of jalapeño in Mexico.

paprika paliva   In Slovakia, very hot mix of hot paprika and salt.

paprika sladka   Mild, bright red paprika from Slovakia.

parado   Piquín in Oaxaca, Mexico.

pasado   In Mexico, another name for chilaca; in New Mexico, roasted and peeled New Mexican chiles that are sun-dried.

pasilla   "Little raisin"; a long, thin, mild, dark Mexican chile grown primarily in Guanajuato, Aguascalientes, Zacatecas, and Jalisco, Mexico, and used in mole sauces. It has overtones of chocolate and raisin in its flavor. Fresh, it is called chilaca.

pasilla oaxaqueño   Smoke-dried chile de agua in Oaxaca, Mexico.

'Pátzcuaro'   Dark variety of pasilla grown in Michoacán, Mexico, named for the famous lake.

'Peludo'   "Hairy"; cultivated variety of jalapeño in Mexico.

peperoncino   Italian term for chile pepper.

pequín   See *piquín*.

peri-peri   See *pili-pili*.

perón   "Pear-shaped"; regional name for rocoto chile in Mexico.

petit malice   In Haiti, "little prank" chile.

pichichi   Piquín in Puebla, Mexico.

pico de pájaro   "Bird's beak"; in Mexico, another name for chile de árbol; also called *pico de paloma*, "dove's beak."

pili-pili   Swahili term for the chiltepín, or bird's-eye pepper in tropical Africa. Generically, all hot chile peppers in Africa.

pilipili hoho   In East Africa, a chile that makes you say "ho-ho" after you eat it.

piment   French term for peppers.

piment bouc   *Capsicum chinense* in Haiti.

pimenta-de-bode   *Capsicum chinense* in Brazil.

pimenta do chiero   "Chile of aroma"; small-podded *Capsicum chinense* variety in Brazil.

pimento   Portuguese term for peppers.

pimiento   Familiar mild olive-stuffing pepper, a pod type of *Capsicum annuum*, sometimes spelled *pimento*. They are also used fresh in salads and are pickled. Some varieties are grown and dried for their powder, which is marketed in the United States as paprika. Varieties include 'Pimento Select', 'Pimiento Sweet', and 'Red Heart Pimiento'.

piquin   *Capsicum annuum* pod type, with a name that probably comes from the Spanish *pequeño*, meaning "small." The piquins are also known by common names such as bird pepper and chile mosquito. Most are unnamed varieties, both wild and domesticated, varying in pod size and shape from BBs to de árbol-like fruits. Generally speaking, the wild varieties (spherical "tepins") are called chiltepíns and the domesticated varieties (oblong "piquins") are called piquins or pequins, but in Texas the wild varieties are called chilipiquíns. Usually used in dry form.

piperiès   Greek term for peppers.

piri-piri   See *pili-pili*. Also describes dishes made with this hot pepper in Mozambique and Kenya. In the Caribbean, a spicy hot Portuguese pepper oil.

poblano   "From Puebla"; one of the most common Mexican chiles, it is heart-shaped and dark green, about 3 inches wide and 4 inches long. Called miahuateco in southern Mexico and the Yucatán Peninsula. The dried form is called ancho.

pochilli   In Mexico, Náhuatl name for smoked chiles.

prik   Thai word for chile peppers. *Prik kee noo* (mouse-dropping chiles, sometimes spelled *prik khee noo suan*) are the tiny, slender chiles often labeled as Thai chiles or bird peppers. *Prik khee nu kaset* is the term for serrano type chiles. *Prik leuang* is a yellow, medium-length, slender chile used in southern Thailand. *Prik khee fah* (sometimes *prik chee far*) is a term used to refer to cayenne chiles, while *prik yuak* is the yellow wax hot variety. The long, green, New Mexican types are *prik num*. Dried red chiles are *prik haeng*, while *prik pon* is red chile powder. *Prik bod* is chile paste; *nam prik* is chile sauce, while *nam prik pao* is chile tamarind paste.

pujei   Term for chile in Sierra Leone.

pulga   "Flea chile"; another name for pequín chiles in Mexico.

pulla   See *de árbol*.

'Pusa Jwala'   Cultivated chile in Liberia.

puya   See *de árbol*. Also, form of mirasol or guajíllo pepper.

'Ramos'   Cultivated variety of poblano in Coahuila, Mexico.

'Real Mirasol'   Cultivated variety of mirasol in Mexico.

reshampatti   Variety of *Capsicum annuum* grown in India. The single reshampatti resembles a straight dried cayenne, while the double reshampatti resembles the ancho.

rocotillo   Mild member of *Capsicum chinense* grown on various Caribbean islands including Cuba and the Cayman Islands.

rocoto   Peruvian name for members of *Capsicum pubescens* grown in mountainous regions of Mexico.

'Roque'   Cultivated variety of mulato pepper grown in Mexico.

sakaipilo   Term for chile in Madagascar.

sambal   Malaysian and Indonesian chile paste.

Scotch bonnet   Variety of *Capsicum chinense* grown in Jamaica. Also, the generic name for the species in other Caribbean islands.

seasoning pepper   In the Caribbean, mild, elongated *Capsicum chinense* varieties.

serrano   "From the highlands"; a common, small, bullet-shaped chile about 1½ inches long and ½ to ¾ inch wide used in salsas. Also called *balín* and *serranito*. It is the chile most commonly canned in Mexico. Grown all over Mexico, but primarily in Nayarit, San Luis Potosí, Sinaloa, and Tamaulipas.

shatta   Arabic term for hot chile pepper.

sili, siling   Filipino (Tagalog) word for capsicums in general. *Siling bilog* is bell pepper; *siling haba* is the long green or red chile; *siling labuyo* is the bird pepper, very small and very hot (*Capsicum frutescens*).

sinteh   *Capsicum chinense* in Cameroon.

spanischcher oderkercher pheffer   German term for peppers.

spansk peppar   Swedish term for peppers.

squash pepper   In the United States, a pod type of *Capsicum annuum* best known for the flattened shape of the pods. Also called cheese or tomato peppers. Varieties include 'Red Squash Hot' and 'Yellow Squash Hot'.

struchkovy pyerets   Russian term for peppers.

taa' ts'itsin its   "Chile excreted by birds"; term for chiltepín in Huastec Mayan language of Mexico.

tabia   Balinese word for chile peppers. *Tabia lombok* (sometimes called *tabia jawa*) is finger-length and resembles cayenne; *tabia Bali* is about an inch long and is the most popular chile in Bali; *tabia kerinyi* are the bird's-eye chiles, or piquíns; *tabia gede* is bell pepper.

tabiche   Chile in Oaxaca, Mexico, similar to a jalapeño, consumed both fresh and dry.

'Tampiqueño-74'   Cultivated variety of serrano in Mexico.

tiger tooth   Common name for variety of *Capsicum chinense* grown in Guyana.

tinnevelly   Common name for variety of *Capsicum annuum* grown in India that resembles a cascabel.

'Típico'   Cultivated variety of jalapeño in Mexico and the United States.

togarishi   Japanese word for chile peppers.

travieso   "Naughty," another Mexican term for guajíllo.

trompo   "Child's top"; another Mexican term for cascabel.

tuong   Chile paste in Vietnam. Also *tuoi*. *Tuong ot* is sriracha hot sauce.

tuxtla   Piquín from southern Mexico.

uchu   Quecha word for chiles in Peru.

ulupica   Local name for the wild chiles *Capsicum eximium* and *C. cardensaii* in Bolivia.

umbigo-de-tainha   In Brazil, "mullet's navel" chile.

'Uxmal'   Cultivated variety of habanero in Mexico.

'Veracruz S-69'   Cultivated variety of serrano in Mexico.

verde   "Green" or "unripe"; in Mexico, any green chile, but typically serrano.

verdeño   Pale green, cultivated Mexican variety of poblano.

wax   In the United States, a pod type of *Capsicum annuum*, so called because of the shiny appearance of the pods. Wax pods vary greatly in size, shape, and pungency. Varieties include 'Banana Supreme', 'Caloro', 'Hungarian Yellow Wax Hot', and 'Santa Fe Grande'.

xcatic   Fairly mild chile grown on the Yucatán Peninsula that is related to yellow wax and banana chiles. Sometimes called *güero* (blonde), it usually is yellow in color. Other terms are *carricillo*, *cristal*, and *cristalino*.

Selected Bibliography

Identification and Varieties

Baral, J. B., and P. W. Bosland. 2004. Unraveling the species dilemma *Capsicum frutescens* and *C. chinense* (Solanaceae): A multiple evidence approach using morphological, molecular analysis, and sexual compatibility. *Journal of the American Society for Horticultural Science* 129: 826.

Bosland, P. W. 2002. Vegetable cultivar descriptions for North America, List 26, Peppers. *HortScience* 37: 46.

DeWitt, D., and P. W. Bosland. 1996. *Peppers of the World: An Identification Guide*. Berkeley, CA: Ten Speed Press.

Garcia, F. 1908. Chile culture. New Mexico College of Agriculture and Mechanic Arts Bulletin No. 67.

Heiser, C. B. 1976. Peppers: *Capsicum* (Solanaceae). In *Evolution of Crop Plants*, ed. N. W. Simmonds. London: Longman.

Heiser, C. B., and P. G. Smith. 1953. The cultivated capsicum peppers. *Economic Botany* 7: 214.

IPGRI, AVRDC, and CATIE. 1995. Descriptors for capsicum (*Capsicum* spp.). Rome: International Plant Genetic Resources Institute; Taipei, Taiwan: Asian Vegetable Research Development Center; Turrialba, Costa Rica: Centro Agronómico Tropical de Investigación y Enseñanza.

Miller, M. 1991. *The Great Chile Book*. Berkeley, CA: Ten Speed Press.

Purseglove, J. W., E. G. Brown, C. L. Green, and S.R.J. Robbins. 1981. Chillies: *Capsicum* spp. In *Spices*. London: Longman.

Ruiz, H., and J. Pavon. 1790. Flora Peruviana, et Chilensis. Cited in Heiser, C. B., and P. G. Smith. 1958. New species of capsicum from South America. *Brittonia* 10: 194–201.

Saccardo, F., and La Gioia, N. 1982. Translocation studies in *Capsicum annuum* L. *Capsicum Newsletter* 1: 14–16.

Smith, P. G., et. al. 1987. Horticultural classification of peppers grown in the United States. *HortScience* 22: 11.

Stommel, J. R., and P. W. Bosland. 2005. Ornamental pepper, *Capsicum annuum*. In *Flower Breeding and Genetics: Issues, Challenges, and Opportunities for the Twenty-first Century*, ed. N. O. Anderson. The Netherlands: Kluwer Academic Publishers.

Votava, E. J., J. B. Baral, and P. W. Bosland. 2005. Genetic diversity of chile (*Capsicum annuum* var. *annuum* L.) land races from northern New Mexico, Colorado, and Mexico. *Economic Botany* 59: 8.

Votava, E. J., and P. W. Bosland. 2002. A cultivar by any other name: Genetic variability in heirloom bell pepper 'California Wonder'. *HortScience* 37: 1100.

Wang, D., and P. W. Bosland. 2006. The genes of *Capsicum*. *HortScience* 41: 1169.

Zoschke, H. 2007. Bhut/Bih/Morich: The Jolokia comparison. Fiery Foods and Barbecue SuperSite (www.fiery-foods.com).

———. 2006. Pepper profile: 'Naga Jolokia'. Fiery Foods and Barbecue SuperSite (www.fiery-foods.com).

Horticulture, Gardening, and Post-Harvest Preservation

Allard, R. W. 1960. *Principles of Plant Breeding*. New York: Wiley.

Bailey, L. H., ed. 1930. *The Standard Cyclopedia of Horticulture*. New York: Macmillan.

Bessey, P. 1990. Southern Arizonans hot on the trail of chiles find crop is good. *Arizona Daily Star*, September 28, 1E.

Birkeland, C. J. 1987. Plant breeding as a hobby. University of Illinois Circular 817.

Black, L., et al. 1991. *Pepper Diseases: A Field Guide*. Taipei, Taiwan: Asian Vegetable Research and Development Center.

Black, L. L., and Rolston, L. H. 1972. Aphids repelled and virus diseases reduced in peppers planted on aluminum foil mulch. *Phytopathology* 62: 747.

Bosland, P. W. 2001. *Capsicum: A Comprehensive Bibliography*. Las Cruces, NM: The Chile Pepper Institute.

———. 1992. The chipotle mystery—Solved at last!" *Chile Pepper* (Issue 6): 46.

Bosland, P. W., et al. 1992. Capsicum pepper varieties and classification. New Mexico State University Cooperative Extension Service Circular 530.

Bosland, P. W., A. L. Bailey, and D. J. Cotter. 1991. Growing chiles in New Mexico. New Mexico State University Cooperative Extension Service Guide H-230.

Briggs, F. N., and P. F. Knowles. 1967. *Introduction to Plant Breeding*. New York: Reinhold.

Brucher, H. 1989. *Useful Plants of Neotropical Origin*. New York: Springer-Verlag.

Carr, A. 1980. *Rodale's Color Handbook of Garden Insects*. Emmaus, PA: Rodale Press.

Cheng, S. S. 1989. The use of *Capsicum chinense* as sweet pepper cultivars and sources for gene transfer. In *Tomato and Pepper Production in the Tropics*, ed. S. K. Green. Taipei: Asian Vegetable Research and Development Center.

Chioffi, N., and G. Mead. 1991. *Keeping the Harvest*. Pownal, VT: Storey Communications.

Cihacek, L. 1985. Managing saline soils. New Mexico State University Cooperative Extension Service Guide A-107.

Clapham, W. M., and H. V. March. 1987. Relationships of vegetative growth and pepper yield. *Canadian Journal of Plant Science* 67: 521–30.

Cochran, H. L. 1935. Some factors which influence the germination of pepper seeds. *American Society of Horticultural Science* 33: 477–80.

Composting yard waste. 1991. Iowa State University Cooperative Extension Service PM-683.

Conway, K. E., and L. S. Pickett. No date. Solar heating (solarization) of soil in garden plots for control of soilborne plant diseases. Oklahoma State University Extension Facts No. 7640.

Cook, Jim. 1986. Practices to speed vegetable growth in Wyoming's climate. University of Wyoming Cooperative Extension Bulletin B-684.6.

Cotter, D. J. 1980. A review of studies on chile. New Mexico Agricultural Experiment Station Bulletin 673.

Courter, J. W., et al. 1984. Growing vegetable transplants. University of Illinois at Urbana-Champaign Cooperative Extension Service Circular 884.

Cox, J. 1979. Climate control—The key to pepper production. *Organic Gardening* (December): 30.

Creasy, R. 1990. Chiles for flavor. *Organic Gardening* (March): 32.

Dainello, F., and R. R. Heineman. 1982. Antitranspirant effects on chile pepper production. Texas Agricultural Experiment Station Bulletin PR-4021.

———. 1986. Plant arrangements and seedling establishment techniques for long green chile pepper production. Texas Agricultural Experiment Station Bulletin PR-4369.

Dana, M. N. 1986. Soil sampling for homeowners. Purdue University Cooperative Extension Service Pamphlet HO-71.

Davidson, R. H., and W. F. Lyon. 1987. *Insect Pests of Farm, Garden, and Orchard*. New York: Wiley.

Decoteau, D. R, M. J. Kasperbauer, and P. G. Hunt. 1990. Bell pepper plant development over mulches of diverse colors. *HortScience* 25: 460–62.

DeWitt, D. 1990. So you want to be a chile farmer, eh? *The Whole Chile Pepper* (March/April): 17.

———. 1991. The ultimate chile patch, Part III: Capsicums in containers. *Chile Pepper* (March/April): 20.

———. 1991. Chili con brio. *Countryside* (December): 70.

———. 1992. *Chile Peppers: A Selected Bibliography of the Capsicums*. Las Cruces, NM: The Chile Pepper Institute.

————. 1992. The ultimate chile patch, Part IV: Mystery pods. *Chile Pepper* (March/April): 28.

DeWitt, D., and P. Bosland. 1993. *The Pepper Garden*. Berkeley, CA: Ten Speed Press.

DeWitt, D., and J. Gerlach. 1989. The ultimate chile patch. *The Whole Chile Pepper* (Spring): 14.

————. 1989. If you can't stand the heat . . . don't bring these chiles into your kitchen. *Harrowsmith* (November/December): 44.

————. 1990. Chile peppers: Growing fire in the garden. *Fine Gardening* (January/February): 54.

————. 1990. The ultimate chile patch update. *The Whole Chile Pepper* (March/April): 13.

DeWitt, D., and N. Gerlach. 2001. *Too Many Chiles*. Phoenix: Golden West.

Dufault, R. J., and S. C. Wiggins. 1981. Response of sweet peppers to solar reflectors and reflective mulches. *HortScience* 16: 65–67.

Edwards, R. L., and F. J. Sundstrom. 1987. After-ripening and harvesting effects on tabasco pepper seed germination performance. *HortScience* 22: 473.

Ellis, R. H., et al. 1985. *Handbook of Seed Technology for Genebanks*. Rome: International Board for Plant Genetic Resources.

Erwin, A. T. 1937. Anthesis and pollination of the capsicum. *American Society for Horticultural Science Proceedings* 28: 309.

Eshbaugh, W. H. 1983. *Genetic Resources of Capsicum*. Rome: International Board for Plant Genetic Resources.

Everett, T. H., ed. 1964. *The New Illustrated Encyclopedia of Gardening*. New York: Greystone Press.

Facciola, S. 1990. *Cornucopia: A Sourcebook of Edible Plants*. Vista, CA: Kampong Publications.

Farmer, C. 1991. Blinded by the light . . . indoors. *Chile Pepper* (March/April): 25.

Fehr, W. R., and H. H. Hadley. 1980. *Hybridization of Crop Plants*. Madison, WI: American Society of Agronomy.

Garcia, F. 1908. Chile culture. New Mexico Agricultural Experiment Station Bulletin 67.

Gent, P.N.M. 1989. Row covers to produce red or yellow peppers. Connecticut Agricultural Experiment Station Bulletin 870.

Gerlach, N. 1989. Too many peppers. *The Whole Chile Pepper* (Spring): 26.

Gerson, R., and S. Honman. 1978. Emergence response of the pepper at low soil temperature. *Euphytica* 27: 151.

Ghate, S. R., and M. Chinnan. 1987. Storage of germinated tomato and pepper seeds. *Journal of the American Society of Horticultural Science* 112: 645.

Goodspeed, J., and L. Sagers. No date. Composting. Utah State University Cooperative Extension Service Horticulture Fact Sheet FS-H10.

Greenleaf, W. H. 1986. Pepper breeding. In *Breeding Vegetable Crops*, ed. M. J. Basset. Westport, CT: AVI Publishing.

Growing peppers in California. 1976. UC Davis Division of Agricultural Sciences Leaflet 2676.

Heiser, C. B. 1987. *The Fascinating World of the Nightshades*. New York: Dover Publications.

Johnson, M. M. 1991. Canning green chile. New Mexico State University Cooperative Extension Service Guide E-308.

————. 1991. Freezing green chile. New Mexico State University Cooperative Extension Service Guide E-311.

Kaiser, S. 1935. The factors governing shape and size in capsicum fruits; a genetic and developmental analysis. *Bulletin of the Torrey Botanical Club* 62: 433.

Lafavore, M. 1983. A pepper talk. *Organic Gardening* (March): 34.

Lagoe, R. 1992. Chilly chiles. *Chile Pepper* (March/April): 34.

Lantz, E. M. 1943. Home dehydration of chili. *Journal of Home Economics* 35: 222.

Lyon, D. 1990. Cool nights and chile days. *National Gardening* (February): 26.

Making and using compost. No date. U.S. Department of Agriculture Fact Sheet 4-5-1.

Master chile gardeners. 1990. *The Whole Chile Pepper* (March/April): 15.

McReady, J. J., and D. J. Cotter. 1987. Preplant seed treatment effects on growth and yield of chile pepper. *HortScience* 22: 435.

Mitchell, I. 1983. A chile for every taste. *Organic Gardening* (June): 64.

Monette, S., and K. A. Stewart. 1987. The effect of a windbreak and mulch on the growth and yield of pepper. *Canadian Journal of Plant Science* 67: 315.

Moore, F. D., and J. C. Hansen. 1974. Suggestions for high altitude home vegetable gardens in Colorado. Colorado State University Cooperative Extension Service Pamphlet 158.

Nickel, J. 1987. Hot fun in the sun, or how to make chile ristras. *Albuquerque Tribune*, October 19, B-1.

Odland, M. L., and A. M. Porter. 1941. A study of the natural crossing in peppers. *Proceedings of the American Society of Horticultural Science* 38: 585.

Perry, L. No date. Organic mulches. University of Vermont Extension

Service Bulletin GL-6.

Pestle, R. No date. Plastic mulch facts. University of Vermont Extension Service Bulletin GL-7.

Pety, E., and D. J. Cotter. 1984. Growth of long green chile pepper fruit. New Mexico State University Agricultural Experiment Station Research Report 556.

Porter, W. C., and W. W. Etzel. 1982. Effects of aluminum-painted and black polyethylene mulches on bell pepper. *HortScience* 17: 942.

Proulx, E. A. 1985. Some like them hot. *Horticulture* (January): 46.

Rast, A. B., and C.C.M.M. Stijger. 1987. Disinfection of pepper seed with different strains of capsicum mosaic virus by trisodium phospate and dry heat treatment. *Plant Pathology* 36: 583.

Rivas, M., et al. 1984. Germination and crop development of hot pepper after seed priming. *HortScience* 19: 279.

Ruttle, J. 1992. Rubbish! *National Gardening* (May/June): 38.

Sais, J. R. 1991. Make your own compost. New Mexico State University Cooperative Extension Service Guide H-110.

Schoch, P. G. 1972. Effects of shading on structural characteristics of the leaf and yield of fruit in *Capsicum annuum* L. *American Society for Horticultural Science* 97: 461.

Shannon, E. 1984. Identifying chile diseases. New Mexico State University Coopoerative Extension Service Circular 511.

———. 1989. Chile disease control. New Mexico State University Cooperative Extension Service Guide H-219.

Sherf, A. F., and A. A. MacNab. 1986. Pepper. In *Vegetable Diseases and Their Control*. New York: Wiley.

Sundstrom, F. J., et al. 1987. Effect of seed treatment and planting method on tabasco pepper. *Journal of the American Society of Horticultural Science* 112: 641.

Tanksley, S. D. 1984. High rates of cross-pollination in chile pepper. *HortScience* 19: 580.

Tozer, E. 1992. Quest for fire. *National Gardening* (May): 36.

Watson, H. 1988. Power peppers. *National Gardening* (April): 60.

Wilson, J. 1991. Pepper partners. *National Gardening* (November/December): 30.

Yepson, R. B., ed. 1976. *Organic Plant Protection*. Emmaus, PA: Rodale Press.

Your compost pile. 1991. Louisiana State University Cooperative Extension Service Publication 2414.

Zoschke, H. 2006. Candied capsicums: Preserving peppers the sweet way." Fiery Foods and Barbecue SuperSite (www.fiery-foods.com).

History, Nutrition, and Cookery

Andrews, J. 1995. *Peppers: The Domesticated Capsicums, New Edition*. Austin, TX: University of Texas Press.

Bosland, P. W., and E. J. Votava. 1999. Peppers: Vegetable and Spice Capsicums. Oxfordshire, U.K.: CABI.

DeWitt, D. 1999. *The Chile Pepper Encyclopedia*. New York: William Morrow.

DeWitt, D., and N. Gerlach. 1990. *The Whole Chile Pepper Book*. Boston: Little, Brown.

Krajewska, A. M., and J. J. Powers. 1988. Sensory properties of naturally occurring capsaicinoids. Journal of Food Science 53: 902–05.

Mathur, R., R. S. Dangi, S. C. Dass, and R. C. Malhortra. 2000. The hottest chilli variety in India. *Current Science* 79: 287–88.

Moscone, E. A., et al. 2007. The evolution of chili peppers (Capsicum-Solanaceae): A cytogenetic perspective. *Acta Horticulture* 745: 137.

Naj, A. 1992. *Peppers: A Story of Hot Pursuits*. New York: Knopf.

Pickersgill, B. 1969. The domestication of chili peppers. In *The Domestication and Exploitation of Plants and Animals*, ed. P. J. Ucko and G. W. Dimbleby. London: Gerald Duckworth.

———. 1984. Migration of chili peppers, *Capsicum* spp. in the Americas. In *Pre-Columbian Plant Migration*. Cambridge, MA: Peabody Museum of Harvard.

Plotnikoff, D. 1991. The little shop of peppers. *San Jose Mercury News*, October 10, 1D.

Rupp, R. 1987. *Blue Corn and Square Tomatoes*. Pownal, VT: Garden Way Publishing.

Schweid, R. 1987. *Hot Peppers*. Berkeley, CA: Ten Speed Press.

Somos, A. 1984. *The Paprika*. Budapest: Akadmiai Kiadó.

Story, G. M., and L. Cruz-Orengo. 2007. Feel the burn. *American Scientist* 97: 326.

Tang, W., and G. Eisenbrand. 1992. *Chinese Drugs of Plant Origin: Chemistry, Pharmacology, and Use in Traditional and Modern Medicine*. New York: Springer.

Vietmeyer, N., ed. 1989. *Lost Crops of the Incas*. Washington, DC: National Academies Press.

Wall, M. M., and P. W. Bosland. 1998. Analytical methods for color and pungency of chiles (capsicum). In *Instrumental Methods in Food and Beverage Analysis*, ed. G. Charalambous. Amsterdam: Elsevier Science Publishers.

Zoschke, H. 2006. Saga Jolokia: Searching for the new "world's hottest chile." Fiery Foods and Barbecue SuperSite (www.fiery-foods.com).

Index

Published in 2009 by Timber Press, Inc.
New paperback edition published in 2014 by Timber Press, Inc.

The Haseltine Building
133 S.W. Second Avenue, Suite 450
Portland, Oregon 97204-3527
timberpress.com

6a Lonsdale Road
London NW6 6RD
timberpress.co.uk

Paperback ISBN: 978-1-60469-580-9

Printed in China
Hardcover edition fifth printing 2014

The Library of Congress has cataloged the hardcover edition as follows:

DeWitt, Dave.
    The complete chile pepper book : a gardener's guide to choosing,
growing, preserving, and cooking / by Dave DeWitt and Paul W. Bosland.
—1st ed.
        p. cm.
    Includes bibliographical references and index.
    ISBN 978-0-88192-920-1
 1. Hot peppers. 2. Cookery (Hot peppers) I. Bosland, Paul W. II. Title.
    SB307.P4D49 2009
    633.8'4—dc22
                        2009006032

A catalog record for this book is also available from the British Library.

Also by Dave DeWitt
The Chile Pepper Encyclopedia
Da Vinci's Kitchen: A Secret History of Italian Cuisine
Cuisines of the Southwest

With Nancy Gerlach
The Whole Chile Pepper Book

With Chuck Evans
The Hot Sauce Bible

Also by Paul W. Bosland
Capsicum: A Comprehensive Bibliography
Descriptors for Capsicum (Capsicum spp.)

With Dave DeWitt
The Pepper Garden
Peppers of the World

With Eric J. Votava
Peppers: Vegetable and Spice Capsicums

Half title: *Capsicum annuum* 'Chilly Chili'. Photo by Paul W. Bosland.
Frontis: Jack & Jill fruit crate label. Photo courtesy of Dover Publications.
Photographs by the authors except:
Chel Beeson, 82, 87, 115 (top), 188, 214
Edward S. Curtis, courtesy of the Palace of Governors Photo Archives
    (NMHM/DCA), #144664, 75 (top)
Courtesy of Dover Publications, frontis, 40
Jim Duffy, 128, 129
Jeff Gerlach, 36 (left), 39 (left), 43 (bottom right), 84, 116, 191
Norman Johnson, 197, 198, 200, 220—319 (food styling by Denice
    Skrepcinski)
Jukka Kilpinen, 130, 131, 132, 149 (top)
Courtesy of Rio Grande Historical Collections, New Mexico State
    University Library, 22, 25, 33
Harald Zoschke, 27 (right), 32 (top left), 39 (bottom right), 46 (bottom), 55
    (top), 60 (bottom), 62 (right), 68, 70, 71 (top), 72 (top), 74 (bottom), 79,
    93, 104, 105 (top left, bottom left, bottom right), 106 (right), 144, 145,
    146, 151 (left), 166, 167, 189, 190, 202, 203, 204, 205

Snow
Country